# AND NOT TO YIELD

## Other books by Ella Winter

# AND NOT TO YIELD

AN AUTOBIOGRAPHY

by ELLA WINTER

Harcourt, Brace &
World, Inc. /New York

THIS BOOK IS FOR PETE

Come, my friends,
'Tis not too late to seek a newer world.
Push off, and sitting well in order smite
The sounding furrows; for my purpose holds
To sail beyond the sunset, and the baths
Of all the western stars, until I die.
It may be that the gulfs will wash us down;
It may be we shall touch the Happy Isles,
And see the great Achilles, whom we knew.
Tho' much is taken, much abides; and tho'
We are not now that strength which in old days
Moved earth and heaven, that which we are, we are,—
One equal temper of heroic hearts,
Made weak by time and fate, but strong in will
To strive, to seek, to find, and not to yield.

—Tennyson, "Ulysses"

# CONTENTS

# LIST OF ILLUSTRATIONS

*(Between pages 148 and 149)*

# PART I

# UNDUTIFUL DAUGHTER

# 1

# THE CHEEKY ONE

My name at home was Fidgety Philip, from the children's story *Struwwelpeter*. How often was his fate pointed out to me—but quite in vain. I was impatient, bored, and irritated if I had to sit still or wait, doing nothing. I fainted when I had to stand for a dressmaker. A succession of white-faced women, their hair untidy, their mouths full of pins, adjured me to "for goodness sake keep still, stop hopping," but I couldn't; even at that age I could not bear being bored.

I was an avid tomboy, full of energy, climbing the highest branches, dreaming wild adventures to share with my gentle brother, who was just a year older. Friends commiserated with my mother. "The Cheeky One should have been the boy," and she agreed, and kept my hair short like a boy's until I was six. Rudi was docile, obedient, almost submissive, and Mother adored him. Not that I felt left out; I adored him, too, he was my other self. My sister, Rosa, nearly three years older, was unadventurous and did not share in Rudi's and my games.

My parents had come to Melbourne from Germany in 1894. After my father and his brother had lost their father's Nuremberg business, my father was persuaded to try his luck as an import agent in Australia. He married my mother at Brighton, England, she being just eighteen and he thirty, and they traveled in a P. and O. liner to Melbourne. I came to consciousness four years later in a house called "Noris" in the suburb of Elsternwick; all our homes were called by this old poetical name for Nuremberg, my father's birthplace, to which he was very sentimentally attached.

Our third Noris, in Balaclava, another suburb of Melbourne, had a grassy paddock where we kept geese, chickens, and a goat.

*3*

Every night Rudi and I waited with the buckets of bran, maize, and water for Father to feed them when he came home; then we looked for the eggs all over the paddock. It was like an Easter egg hunt every day.

The goat was bought for me when I became very ill at three months with summer dysentery. The doctor thought I could not live, but he did not know my mother. With all the trouble of putting a child into the world, give up? Not my mother. The doctor's final despairing advice had been to try goat's milk, so Father led the animal on foot across Melbourne. The milk saved my life, and as her reward, the goat stayed with us for years, despite her habit of chewing the leaves of the mulberry trees, which we needed for our silkworms.

I remember a beloved black spaniel, Carlo, with long silken ears, who accompanied us on daily walks with our governess, Miss Bagnall. The walks were boring and made tolerable only by playing hopscotch in secret competitions, making challenging commitments to cross or not cross the lines between the paving blocks. Miss Bagnall scolded and threatened us interminably with the police—"they'll put you in jail if you don't behave." It was years before I could see a policeman without feeling guilty, looking on the ground, and walking sedately. Only "our" organ-grinder, with a monkey in a red coat who ran on a long chain and gazed at us sadly as he waited for peanuts, interrupted the dullness of the strictly disciplined daily walk.

Rudi and I shared everything. Having learned to read at four, I could read aloud to him as we lay on our stomachs on the nursery floor. He liked it better than reading for himself, and I loved it. My parents had thought me too young, and forbade me the schoolroom, but I sneaked in and surreptitiously followed Rudi and Rosa's reading from the other side of the table. One day they found I could read—but upside down. Thinking I suffered some appalling eye deformation, Mother rushed me to an oculist, but after that they let me read, and I did so—Grimm, Bechstein, Hans Andersen, Kipling, German stories like *Struwwelpeter* and *Max and Moritz;* Australian books such as *Seven Little Australians* and *The Family at Misrule;* legends and myths; *Gulliver, Crusoe, Alice in Wonderland* and *Water Babies* and, of course, *Fauntleroy;* and moral tales of the time like *Eric or Little by Little.* Our imaginative life was lived in books; no movies, radio, or television. I

remember many of them so vividly, from the alliterative alpha-
bet poem *Awkward Ada* to our favorite, a "torture" book called
*John O'Strathbourne,* which gave us delicious shivers of horror
and which we read over and over. I can still visualize the gray-
green binding of that book, with its chained figure on the cover.

My parents believed in discipline and good manners, and
Mother was the stricter of the two. She would frown and scold
and disapprove and reprimand but not punish physically save
for a box on the ears, with the exception of one hiding, which,
strangely enough, Rudi, the beloved little son, got. He could not
resist playing with the forbidden garden hose, and one day when
we were freshly dressed for a party, he fell into his usual temptation.

"Mind now," Mother had warned, *"don't touch the hose,"* but
Rudi could not resist and of course got wet and muddy. I saw
him dragged indoors in parental fury, and presently I was called in
to see the reward of disobedience. There sat that beloved little
figure, pants down, face red and puckered with sobbing, picking
piteously at his trousers. It broke my heart; I squatted next to
him and sobbed with him and hated my mother till I was dragged
away.

In addition to the three R's, we were taught to recite. I had a
dramatic gift and recited with so much natural expression that
Mr. Phillips, our lawyer neighbor, said I should become an actress.
I loved learning the little poems, then telling an audience of the
woeful or happy dramas, the shocking experiences or downfall of
kitten, elephant, or frog.

> Five little pussy cats invited out to tea.
> Cried "Mother let us go, for good we'll surely be!
> We'll always say 'Yes, if you please' and 'Only half of that!' "
> "Then go, my darling children!" cried the happy Mother Cat.

Rudi and Rosa had a more advanced Reader, but I soon knew
their poems as well, and to Rosa's dismay, recited them with more
feeling. Rudi's

> Twenty froggies went to school
> Down beside a rushy pool,
> Twenty little coats of green
> Twenty vests all white and clean.

"We must be in time," said they,
First we study, then we play.
That is how we keep the rule
When we froggies go to school.

or Rosa's moral tales:

I knew a man and his name was Horner,
He used to live at Grumble Corner,
Grumble Corner in Crosspatch Town,
And he never was seen without a frown.

Secretly I thought my older sister, who corrected me often, had some resemblance to Mr. Horner.

Learning to write was much harder than reading, and with my tongue out, I laboriously traced the pothooks and hangers, and got furiously impatient.

"Keep your tongue in, it isn't your tongue that makes the *t*. Another blot! Can't you be more careful? Write that out again six times."

"Why can't I write in pencil? It makes the letters just the same."

"One writes in ink."

"But the pen makes blots."

"Don't always put the blame on something else."

That was the end to so many arguments in which I couldn't see where I was wrong—a failing that has accompanied me through life. I despaired as I gazed at the perfection of the model lines that I could never approach, any more than I could achieve the moral rectitude of the proverbs:

PRACTICE MAKES PERFECT.   A STITCH IN TIME SAVES NINE.   WELL
BEGUN IS HALF DONE.   WASTE NOT, WANT NOT.

When we learned to write German I had other troubles—I spelled *ich,* the German "I," with a capital, and was told by our then German governess that it could only be gross egotism that prompted this.

We were not, despite governess and maid, well-to-do. Mother even took in a boarder for a time, a Mr. Snewin. She did the housework and cooking, and looked after the children, washing and ironing all our clothes at home—drawers, lace petticoats, white frocks and sashes, and Rudi's tunics to starch and iron and pleat. Even the brims of our large white linen hats were "goffered"— starched into waves with a curling iron. Both the children and the house were kept spotlessly clean and neat; Mother was thorough, punctilious, and house-proud. She also helped Father in his business; shrewd, practical, and persistent—while he was easygoing, trusting, and uncompetitive, with an artist's temperament—Mother "managed" better than he. Father had wanted to be an architect if not a musician.

Mother kept household accounts with ruled, detailed columns to be added up and checked every night. In addition to Food, Clothes, Fares, Haircuts, there were Acquisitions, Dentist, Outings, Kerosene, and so forth, each item to be tortured into its proper column, added, checked, and studied, so one could see where to cut down. One had always spent too much, never too little. A halo surrounded the virtue of saving; spending was a vice always to be curbed, like filching jam or lying or disobedience.

Prudent as well as saving, Mother kept everything locked. We had to embark on endless searches for two objects that she carried around with her—her purse and her small key basket. No one was allowed into linen closet, pantry, or glass cupboard; Mother doled out sheets, glass and silver, the good china and lace tablecloths. Inset drawers in her bedroom contained her jewelry, a fur stole, or feather boa; the glass cupboard with ivories and Dresden figurines was never opened. "Where can my key basket be?" became a household refrain.

We had to save our pocket money, first a penny, then threepence, then sixpence a week, dropping it through a slot in a cocoa-tin lid (we never had piggy banks). Since spending was unthinkable, I never got over a feeling of wrongdoing if I spent money I had not myself earned. But earning money was proper and we could add to our savings by heroic behavior, for instance, when my birthmark was removed. The doctor said the mole in my cheek would grow and should be taken out, and removing the stitches is vivid in my mind.

"A penny, a penny, if you don't cry!" Rudi and Rosa and Father pleaded, holding up the copper coins as Mother busied herself with hot water, lint, and scissors. I was terrified, and it was all I could do to hold back the tears; but the coins sliding into the slot of my cocoa tin proved a powerful incentive, and when they were mine, I felt virtuous indeed, though I did sympathize with Rudi's sacrifice.

Despite all the morals and the practical safeguards against evil, theft entered our lives. We never opened our cocoa tins, but shook them and gloated over their increasing weight till one day, when Rudi and I shook our tins, there was no sound. Unbelievable! So we summoned up courage and for the first time pulled off the lids. The tins were empty. What could have happened? A bad joke? No one would dare—our savings banks were holy ground. We could not imagine what had occurred, and the grownups had no solution either.

The mystery was never solved, but my sense of a secure, unthreatening world had begun to be undermined; the more so when, shortly afterward, Mother's two diamond rings disappeared. She always wore them, her engagement ring and another, a present from Father. The rings were never out of her sight; at night she hung them on an ivory-branched ring holder by her bedside. Though the house was ransacked, every corner and closet, hall, cellar, garden, yard, carpets pulled up, linoleum and floor boards —even sticks poked down waste pipes—they were never found. But presently we lost Miss Bagnall and were not told why; I thought we were given Miss French, our new governess, to learn French. When, much later, I suspected that it must have been Miss Bagnall who stole both rings and cocoa-tin savings, my main feeling, I think, was a sense of justice. Miss Bagnall had so terrorized Rudi and me with the threat of policemen and jail that she had received her deserts. All the same, Miss Bagnall a thief? It was scarcely imaginable. Life was indeed mysterious.

Mother took pains to be scrupulously fair to us three, not to play favorites, and we felt equally loved. All the more grisly the "joke" played on me when one day they informed me I was not really their child but a foundling. My whole world collapsed.

"And Rudi and Rosa are your real children?"

"Of course."

I took this information to bed with me, and never did anything seem so dreadful. I was not the same as the others—Rudi was not my brother, nor Rosa my sister. I began to harbor the fear "Will they keep me?" This was before the days of Freud, and Mother must have assumed that the very impossibility of the whole thing would have amused me as it did them. When she saw how it affected me, she thought she could "make it better," like a scratch or bump, but she never healed that wound, even after I accepted it as teasing. I was left with the feeling: how could one ever be sure of anything?

We had a "Mother's help" called Hilda, whom I loved, but once she turned into an enemy. Mother had to go to hospital, left Hilda in charge, and made us promise to "behave"; we must not give Hilda trouble. Mother was never ill, had rarely gone away, and no one would say what was wrong, so I was upset and behaved badly. When Mother returned, she came into the schoolroom with her scolding frown and her eyes hard.

"You were disobedient and rude to Hilda while I was away," she accused. "So I can't trust you when I'm gone?" I felt betrayed. Hilda had told!

"You will apologize," Mother said, ending her reprimand. But I could not apologize; Hilda had tattled and one did not do that. I remained mute and we ate dinner in silence.

"Before you get down you will apologize," Mother repeated. Everyone waited, but words would not come. I felt myself harden; I knew I was forfeiting everyone's good opinion, Rudi's too, but I could not speak. I don't know how long we sat, but finally Hilda murmured something to Mother.

"You didn't mean to behave badly, did you?" She tried to comfort me, and I shook my head because I could not speak, and we all suddenly got up and I ran away. I was exasperated at my own obstinacy, I could not understand why it had been so impossible for me to give in, and still did not as I cried myself to sleep that night.

I adored Father, the God-being of my life. He had dark wavy hair brushed back, a mustache, and warm friendly brown eyes, and he smelled in a special way. He played the piano beautifully and sang Schumann and Schubert lieder in the evenings, so that I often listened to him at night as I went to sleep. He played all the songs, Heine's lyrics, *Tom der Rhymer,* or *Erlkönig;* and we shivered at that terrifying ghostly night ride that Father did make easier occasionally by quoting the joke *"Er hält in den Armen das sechzehnte Kind"* ("sixteenth" instead of *ächzende*—"moaning" child).

But I was aware of some indefinable sadness about him. Was it because he missed his homeland or because his work was uncongenial? The stories he told about his family were often unhappy as well as nostalgic: about his hot-tempered but well-loved father, who became suddenly blind late in life; his unhappily married, musical elder sister in Berlin, who had entertained Wagner and who had a son who had done something unmentionable in Africa (much later I discovered that it was a liaison with a native woman); the dear but "unsuccessful" brother, Sigmund; the mother he adored, and the equally beloved housekeeper, Fritzi, both now dead. The blind father was strong-willed, quick, and impatient, and my father told a terrible story of a night the brothers forgot to leave their hotel bedroom door open for their father to feel his way back from the bathroom, and how he had spent the night tapping up and down the corridor.

When their father died, the brothers—Sigmund and my father— had to take over the family hop concern. They traveled in Russia on business, and Father told about aristocratic Russian barons "arrogantly lighting cigars with one-hundred-ruble notes." Neither of the brothers was a very good businessman, and when these same Russian buyers did not pay, the business collapsed.

Yet, there were also gay stories of his early life that Father loved to tell. There was the year at the international Swiss school where his companions were princes and courtiers' sons from every corner of the globe—Turkey, Siam, Greece, Persia—and a laundry basket full of apples and chocolate was brought for afternoon tea.

At eighteen he went to Scotland to learn English and was adored by a dour Scots landlady who called him "the Ger-r-r-rman" and teased him about his "cur-r-r-ly pow." He recounted his lighthearted trips to Vienna, where he took part in a famous men's choir and waited outside the opera house with a bouquet for some great singer. He would warn us: "Never try to know a great performer off stage."

I turned to Father in all my tribulations, which included early-morning practice at the piano. We had to get up very early for this, indeed in the dark. (The difference between my finger exercises in the cold room and the glorious sounds when Father played Wagner or Schumann!) One very cold morning, when I was hammering away, a frightful crash came out of the eerie silence. My heart stopped, I screamed and ran straight into Father's room —Mother was away—leaped into the bed, pulled the blankets over our heads, and could only scream in terror, "It isn't burglars! It isn't burglars!" so that Father would not be afraid. He tried to soothe me, patted and caressed me, and when I dared go back into the drawing room, we found a picture had crashed from its frame. But what I remembered were Father's strong, loving, reassuring arms. I was certain I could never marry anyone but my father.

Melbourne is a sketchy memory to me now, almost a place of the imagination, but the flowers and trees are vivid, and I see the bridge over the river Yarra, the open dummies of the trams clanging their way into Collins Street; the dunes at Mentone and Mordialloc where we picnicked and where Rudi and I paddled and went in too far and got our knickers wet; the giant fern trees of the Bush when we went on holiday, and my terror of the snakes that they said crawled under its thick vegetation.

We lived a great deal out of doors. In summer around Christmas time, when the north wind blew from Queensland across the desert, it could grow distressingly hot. Mother suffered, and drank innumerable cups of tea; but we children enjoyed it, especially when Father watered the lawn and showered us as we ran naked under the hose, or paddled our feet in the ice water dripping into the zinc-lined drawer under the wooden ice chest.

I loved the flowers. There was always some heavenly smell, wattle or the white catalpa or magnolia or the miraculous scent of the tiny black boronia, and everywhere the acrid smell of eucalyptus trees—with their blue young leaves that give the tree its name of "blue gum" and to Australians the name of "gum suckers." We had a mulberry in the yard and a magnolia in the front garden, with the black hooks on their fruit like crooked dwarfs. At the back of Noris, St. Kilda Road, we had a passion vine, but were not allowed to eat the astonishing, egg-shaped, purple fruit, because some little boys were known to have died of appendicitis from eating their pips.

The St. Kilda Road garden was big. I used to dig the beds and collect the dahlia bugs in pots filled with hay. I remember the blood-red canna, the shiny dark leaves of the calla, and its extraordinary blooms with yellow bananas in the middle that so intrigued us. We also kept silkworms. I don't know that we ever got much silk, but Rudi and I watched for hours the worm spin

its cocoon, and waited for the cocoons to grow fatter, until finally
the drab gray moth broke through.

The Botanical Gardens, with a zoo, were within walking distance.
We felt patriotic about our special Australian animals: wallaby
and platypus, kangaroo and possum, wombat and dingo. When I
learned the long Latin name of the webbed platypus, *ornitherin-
cus paradoxus,* I paraded it on all occasions. One must be quite
an animal to be called that, I thought. The Laughing Jackass—
which they sometimes called me, though my father's name for
me was "Monkey Tail"—had a more dignified title, kookooburra,
a name that looked and sounded as unlikely as the bird itself. The
lyrebird and panda, and a variety of monkeys and orangutans,
with their brilliant purple, orange, and red behinds, always enchanted us.

When I was seven we were taken by Mother—Father had to stay
home for his business—on a trip to Germany for eight months.
We visited Munich, Berlin, and Nuremberg and met all the cousins,
uncles, and aunts. I remember running into my father's arms on
our return and deciding for myself that he must never, never be
left alone again. It was on this trip that I came to know Father's
home town, with its fearsome iron maiden with spikes that put
out the eyes of wrongdoers, and the twelve dancing apostles in the
clock tower who marched around chiming the hour; but I was
also led through museums and galleries and made to behave, so
I knew that nothing was duller than walls and walls of old pictures
you had to admire because they were in the *Alte Pinakothek* or
because Rubens or Tintoretto had painted them.

When the time came to go to school, Rosa and I went to the
Church of England Girls' Grammar School, Rudi to the Boys'.
Melbourne schools were denominational; there were a Presbyterian
and a Methodist Ladies' College besides our CEGGS. Workers' children went to elementary schools, beyond the pale, although I didn't
know anything about that.

I started in the lowest form and moved up rapidly. I enjoyed
everything but written arithmetic. In contrast, I was good at
mental arithmetic—I had a good memory and enjoyed the cerebral
gymnastics—but the subjects that held my interest were History and
English. I was quickly promoted to the Middle School, to my
sister's annoyance and embarrassment, because we were then in
the same class.

The first day in Middle School I was introduced to Algebra by Miss Grey, a small, sharp-featured, black-haired woman, who explained or thought she explained simple equations and then gave a written test: "$4x = 16$; what is $x$?" I had not the slightest clue. I had not understood any of it. I sat as long as I could, my mind a blank, but more and more in a panic. I tried to look busy, then felt I must get out of that room, away from those scribbling pens; so I raised my hand, and Miss Grey said, "You may go, but don't be long." I fled to the stone lavatory downstairs and cried. If only time would pass and it would all be over. When I got back, the lesson had ended. I handed in my blank page. Miss Grey glanced over the papers, calling out the marks, "Ten, ten, nine, ten . . ." Then she came to mine.

"Why, you didn't do any, not one sum! No marks." My humiliation was intense. Apparently my otherwise active mind was not yet ready for abstract conceptions.

In school they laid stress on clear handwriting, spelling, and the power to express yourself. You wrote imaginary letters or compositions and stories, which I loved. Miss Hardy read aloud one story of mine that began "A single, solitary crow sat all alone on a tree."

"Maybe it's a little much," she grinned, "but one gets the idea."

I wrote stories for the Children's Corner of the Sydney *Herald,* and achieved an ambition when a paragraph was published in Pet's Corner with my name attached—my first by-line. I knew then I was born to be a journalist.

We first went to the theater when I was about ten; Oscar Asche and Lily Brayton came to Melbourne with a Shakespeare repertory. We saw *The Merchant of Venice, King Lear, The Taming of the Shrew.* It was a dazzling treat that few of our school friends shared. We read the plays aloud at home first. To read a play or study the score of an opera before you saw it was a family law. I admired extravagantly Portia's cleverness; it may have been this early contact with her that helped lay the roots of my feminism. To Mother's dismay Portia justified my own argumentative tendencies, for when Mother ended some interminable hithering-and-thithering with the conclusion "All right, you win," I now had the perfect reply: "Portia did, didn't she?"

Educational ideas have changed, and children, with their questions about sex, politics, racial discrimination, and other social problems, are now usually treated with the dignity of adults. But we were still a minority, to be treated like any minority, according to the ideas of the adult majority—which meant children could be lied to "for their own good"—and when we were not supposed to know something, Mother and Father would talk French. Sex was never mentioned; I knew babies were brought by the stork because my parents said so—and parents do not lie.

My earliest political recollections are connected with the murder of President McKinley in 1901. A friend believed that if they collected his bones in a sack and prayed over them, he would knit together again and live. Rudi and I wondered a long time, sitting up in the mulberry tree: how would the man get out of the sack once his bones were knit together?

The "race" problem came into our lives through a strange event in our street. A few doors down lived a doctor's family named Cherry, with whose two little boys we often played; but when another baby was born, a mysterious silence descended, and looks were exchanged between the grownups, who were obviously trying to keep something from us. We were shushed out of the room when talk turned to the Cherry baby; presently everyone spoke in the same peculiar tones about it, and soon the Cherrys moved away. One day Mother said the new baby had been born with black spots. "Somewhere in that family there was a black man," our governess said, though we didn't know why that was so awful. "She should have told her husband," Mother said, but what they should have told each other we couldn't find out.

We didn't understand what the affair with John meant, either. Fruit and vegetables were brought to the door by Chinese greengrocers in horse-drawn carts. These men were lonely, for Oriental wives were not permitted into Australia, which with its population of four million whites feared for the balance of "color." The Chinese Orientals were all called John (for "John Chinaman"). We loved our John and he had a great affection for us, especially me, whom he called "The Leedle One" and to whom he always brought some special present—a jar of ginger or a jack-in-the-box or an embroidered frock, and once for Christmas, a whole bolt of Chinese silk. When John's cart appeared, we would rush to the gate and clamber among its apples and cauliflower and watermelons, and he never objected. But one hot afternoon I was playing alone with my dolls on the back verandah, everyone was out, and John stopped to talk to me. He stayed awhile and then suddenly picked me up and kissed me. He had never done it before, and its suddenness startled me so that I dropped and broke my doll, which started me crying, and just then Mother came home. There were questions and sharp talk for John, and Mother sent him angrily away. He never came again.

Class lines, like moral rules and race barriers, were strict, but I learned about them obliquely, as well as the fact that one could step over them upward without disapproval. In our street lived a girl, Mollie Fink, whose family my mother called "common." But one day Mollie married a maharajah, and everyone's attitude changed. We children puzzled over the fact that it was all right to marry an Indian but not to have a baby with black spots, that John Chinaman could play with us but not kiss us like all our other friends, that if you married a prince your "commonness" didn't matter.

We crossed class lines again when we went to Government House to present a kitten to the Governor's children, the Honorable Dudley Ward and his sister, Lady Penelope Ward. Our French governess taught them, too, and had told them about our kittens. We found the five-year-old lordship more tongue-tied than we, until the kitten broke the ice and we all played with it. But this did not lead to further friendship, which we regretted because the little brother and sister seemed so lonely in those vast rooms. We used to look up at their windows from the Botanical Gardens and think of them as the little prisoners in the Tower. "At least they have Fluffy now to make things more human," Rudi and I said, silently comforting the Honorable Wards.

Then the pettiness of school class lines reared its head. A pair of gloves was stolen from a locker, and investigation pointed to a pasty-faced little girl with pimply skin whom no one liked very much. Cissie's mother washed clothes for some of our mothers, and Cissie was the one "working-class" girl in school. When she was suspected, we "good" little girls sent her to Coventry; but when I saw her in the playground, so pale and isolated, I felt stricken. She tried to hide behind the big oak tree, but some girls came by just then and I dared not speak to her—they would send me to Coventry, too. Cissie left school, but Mother attacked the unfairness: "Her mother is poor and perhaps couldn't afford gloves," she said. I wondered why the school did not explain that, and stop our meanness.

I wondered most of all about the differences I often felt between us and the other girls. Was it that our parents cared for things like books and plays and about our marks in school, which most others didn't? Or that Mother and Father were foreigners? I had learned with humiliation about that when our history teacher asked, "If there were a war between England and Germany, which side should win?" Everyone answered "England," but I felt I had to be loyal to my parents and said "Germany." The girls hooted and the teacher looked shocked; I had obviously said something wrong, but surely one must be on the side of one's parents? The teacher explained that we were Australian and that meant British, but I was aware only of the jeering of my schoolfellows.

Or were we "different" because we didn't visit at school friends' houses after school? We had to come straight home, and Mother centered our activity there; family seemed to mean more to her than to other mothers. We were not allowed to visit at Irene's, the bookmaker's daughter, either, as other girls did, though I couldn't see what was wrong with making books when they were so respected in our house.

Was it, perhaps, because we had less money? Mother wouldn't let us buy buns or candy at the Tuck Shop, nor were we ever allowed to spend in shops: "You are given all you need at home." Or was it the fact that we didn't believe in God? Mother knew that God didn't exist; Father said he didn't know, but Mother argued fiercely: "How could a just God permit all the injustice and poverty and cruelty in the world?"

And then I found out an astonishing thing. One day after school a girl, for no apparent reason, chased Rosa and me violently around the school. Most girls had gone home and the buildings were empty. At first I thought it was fun, but she shouted something, called some name, till I realized she was quite furious. I saw Rosa's tormented petticoats fly as she tore up some stone stairs, and the girl called to a friend, "Go after her, Dot." We were both out of breath, almost sobbing, and I kept crying, "What's the matter? What have we done?" But they wouldn't answer.

Next day I found scrawled next to my name on my ruler ". . . is a little Jewess." I thought I recognized the handwriting as that of the girl who had chased us. It was a new experience for me to feel unpopular and I was utterly puzzled.

"But why," I asked Mother when we got home, "why would they say something untrue?"

To my astonishment Mother was not indignant; she had a whispered consultation with Father and then said, "It's time for us to tell you, it wasn't untrue, we were Jewish but we had you baptized when you were born, and Father and I were, too. So we are not Jewish now."

"Why didn't you tell us before?" we all wanted to know; it was so surprising.

"It wasn't important," Mother said. "We did it because there was so much hatred of Jews in Germany. We thought, in a new country one should make a fresh start. Why should one suffer disabilities needlessly?" Jews could not be officers, she said, in the Army or Navy, or judges, or other high officials. She kept explaining: "Since neither Father nor I have any religion, why should you children suffer possible disadvantages and discrimination, especially in another country where no one knows us or our background?"

"But here those drawbacks don't exist?" I asked. It was all so strange.

"One never knows. Those girls did chase you, didn't they?" That was true, and it was such a peculiar thing, I didn't know what to feel.

"If anyone says it again, you must deny it," Mother was saying, "We've had you baptized, we are not Jews any more."

"What are we then?"

There was a pause. "Lutherans, I suppose," Mother said, "that's the German branch of Protestantism."

It was rather dramatic having a secret from the world. Mother was quite emphatic: it was an advantage, why not take it, and no harm to anyone; and her feelings carried over to us. Jews were "they," not "we," and once one got over the first surprise, it didn't matter one way or the other. What I remembered was the peculiar way I learned this, and my sense once more of a world that I so unquestioningly accepted, and which could yet hold such quite undiscerned, unknown mysteries.

# 2

# MISS BUSS AND MISS BEALE,
# GOD AND PAN

Soon after this we were called into solemn family conclave once more.

"We have something important to tell you," Mother started, very gravely. "We have decided you're old enough to benefit from a good education, and we think you will get a better one in England. You're the right age, later you won't want to change schools. So, after sixteen years in Australia"—she took a deep breath—"we're going back to Europe."

Astounding news—almost impossible to digest. A whole new life would start, in another world!

And as this world-shaking event came closer to realization, I began, in bed at night, to look back "over my Australian years," as my Victorian-novelist imagination put it. I recalled ruefully the little school gardens we had created every year and for which I never gained first prize; the spelling bee when, at ten, I almost beat the school, but was edged out by a big girl of eighteen, the daughter of the Prime Minister, because I had pronounced Socrates to rhyme with "plates" and Themistocles with "cockles." I thought with triumph of the early-morning bicycle rides with Rudi to the violet farm, to gather violets for Mother's birthday. With Rudi, who had been growing away from me into his own boy's world—"no girls wanted." I was just learning to ride, and fell sprawling off my new bike, spilling the flowers and wrecking the machine, but not minding so much because Rudi showed such old-time tenderness and concern. I recollected, slightly shamefacedly, how, when Miss Morris came to see Mother about my turned ankle, I hid the *John O'Strathbourne* I was engrossed in and pretended to be reading *David Copperfield* because that was a classic; and then, not having quite the courage to carry through the deception, how I had uncomfortably disclosed the hidden book, and how I had appreciated her forgiving, indulgent laughter.

Rudi and I rode off to bid farewell to all our old haunts: the Botanical Gardens, Government House, St. Kilda Beach, the Yarra, the kookooburras and kangaroos. We rode to Elsternwick a last time to wrinkled old Mrs. Stubbs, who had brought us into the world, and now ran a sweet shop. We said good-by to mulberry and magnolia, wattle and gum tree, the earwigs in the hay, the dummy trams, his boys and my girls at school. Then the day came when everything was packed; the house stood empty, friends had given their final kisses and gone. It was really good-by, for we were never coming back. The last handkerchief waved, the steamer gave one last, long, drawn-out hoot; ahead lay six weeks of ocean and then—England and a new life.

The voyage by steamer to London was enchantment for a lively little girl of eleven filled with curiosity and exuberance. The steamer stopped at Adelaide and Perth, Colombo, Aden, Port Said, Suez, Naples. There was the long stretch between Western Australia and Ceylon, with only sea and sky, when for ten days we played hide-and-seek around the lifeboats on the top deck or investigated the hold, both strictly forbidden.

Everything was delightful. There was evening coffee on deck, which I was allowed to pour for the officers. I fell in love with all of them in their beautiful white uniforms and kept a diary detailing every blush, advance, or repulse. Among the passengers was Hackenschmidt, a world-champion wrestler, who walked ten miles a day, even when we crossed the Equator, dressed to his chin in sweaters and coats, perspiring in the hot sun. He set me on his knee and told extravagant stories while I marveled at his rope-like muscles and elephantine arms, yet he always handled me gently.

In Ceylon, monkeys shinnied up the palm trees like the little black boys, shied coconuts at us and tore away. The Ceylon trees had such wonderful names—ebony, satinwood, calamander, tamarind, and something they called a "sack-yielding tree." We drove past white sand beaches with storks and herons picking their way, and kingfishers flying high. A file of pink flamingoes lined the sea edge, treading delicately on the wet sand.

Between Colombo and Aden, Rudi and I got caught. We had

met secretly in his cabin after supper to find out how girls and boys differed, but Rudi was disappointed. "Haven't you anything else?" he asked, dissatisfied. I was ashamed at cheating him; he had more to show than I, and I was wondering how I could make it up to him when a terrifying white face pressed against the dark porthole window. We rushed into our clothes as William, our room steward, broke in. He had been our friend, but now he was furious. He boxed Rudi's ears and slapped his face. "I was just passing and expected to say 'hullo' to you," he cried. "Now I shall tell your parents and you'll be put off the boat at the next port."

We lived in torment for three days. William's manner changed completely. He either ignored us or wagged a castigating finger. "Your parents trusted you!" he kept repeating. It spoiled our pleasure in the Red Sea and the Suez Canal. Our one question to each other, expressed only by agonized eyes, was "Has he told yet?" Had Mother or Father given any indication they knew? We stole about, and every time we ran into William he seemed to threaten us. The uncertainty was torture.

Port Said came. The *Bremen* lowered her anchor, ropes were thrown to the pier and passengers called to the dining room to be checked before landing. We did not even know if we were to be put ashore alone. All the time in Port Said we waited, scared. When the ship finally raised anchor and steamed slowly into the Mediterranean and neither Mother nor Father had said anything, we realized William had meant the uncertainty, fear, and anxiety to be our punishment. They were.

Mother's first duty in London, after we had settled in a rather ugly boardinghouse near Swiss Cottage, was to look for schools, which she did in her usual conscientious way, canvassing the field, consulting everyone. Finally she chose the North London Collegiate School for Rosa and me, and University College School for Rudi. Mother still felt the cohesion of the family more important than yielding to the English custom of sending a boy away to boarding school.

Our girls' school was in Camden Town and we went by yellow horsebus, sitting on the open top behind the driver. He came to know us so well that he stopped at our house for Rosa and me. One half-holiday I was dismayed to see the bus outside, patiently waiting. As I rushed out to apologize, a buzz of irritated exclamations came from the other passengers and I was sure he would never stop for us again, but all he said, rather good-naturedly, was "Next time yer might let me know." The bus dropped us at Camden Town for a ten-minute walk up gray, noisy, clattering Camden Road, so different from our bright, tree-lined, clean Melbourne streets. Brick buildings with sooty basements, tenements with clothes hanging out, traffic and a smoky railroad replaced our flowered gardens and lush greenery.

What I found peculiar in this staid British girls' school was that it had been originally established with funds from commercial companies with names like Worshipful Company of Fishmongers, Haberdashers, Merchant Taylors. In my young life I thought culture and commerce were at opposite poles—part of Father's tragedy, I thought, was that he loved the first but had to devote so much time to the second. Another irony was that, because "the Worshipful Company of Brewers" had contributed the largest sums, our school coat of arms bore a sheaf of hops—symbol of my mother's abomination, drink.

The founder of our school, Frances Mary Buss, had been, with Dorothea Beale, a pioneer English educator who championed female emancipation. Nicely behaved girls as we were, we still had irreverent moments when we chanted surreptitiously a celebrated couplet about our founders:

> Miss Buss and Miss Beale
> Cupid's darts do not feel.
> Oh, they are not like us
> Miss Beale and Miss Buss.

Our Head, Mrs. Bryant, was a soft-voiced Irishwoman with a lively face and gray hair worn in a topknot. She had married at nineteen; when her husband died a year later, leaving her childless, she devoted the rest of her life to girls' education, believing that a good education was as much needed by girls as by boys—at that time still an original idea. Once a week she gave us a little sermon on world events that contained some "moral" or improving lesson, or the recital of a heroic act, to develop our admiration for courage, responsibility, duty to others—in a word, high English ideals, the "playing fields of Eton." I decided I would get onto those playing fields.

During a jolly summer holiday in France, at Le Touquet-Paris-Plage with our French relatives, the well-to-do branch of the family, came a new experience. I fell madly in love. Jerome Meyer, a twenty-four-year-old medical student, seemed to me wonderful beyond compare. I said his name to myself over and over, watched his every move jealously and possessively. When he went to the beach, I thought up some excuse to be with him on the sand, though for some reason this was frowned upon. I knew absolutely nothing of sex, but I did know about romantic love, and I knew that every moment with Jerome, even looking at him across the dining room or watching him stroll down the road, was bliss.

One day on the beach Jerome let me comb his hair, which filled me with passionate joy, but that evening Mother was angry. She had watched from our balcony and seen it, she said, and I was never to touch him again, never. She would give no reason.

"But I only combed his hair!" I flamed. Why must I give up such pleasure? But Mother repeated the prohibition, and added, "What else do you do?"

"What do you mean?" I shot back. "We talk."

"And he hasn't touched you?" I could not understand and asked Jerome what the questions meant, but he only smiled. "I understand your mother," he said, "I know why she's worried."

"I don't," I fumed, but, press as I might, he would not say any more.

When we were to leave, I was so desolate, I could not keep the tears back. There was the usual confusion at the station, losing and finding tickets, luggage, the compartment. I had not had the chance to say good-by to Jerome and could not find him. I strained my eyes toward the gates as the last minutes ticked away. I was suffocating, I would never see him again; and then, striding rapidly toward us, in dazzling white flannels that made him look handsomer than ever, there he was. I was blissful, wretched, terrified, tongue-tied; my heart pounded, my throat was parched. The train whistle blew. I heard Jerome ask Mother, "May I kiss your daughter good-by?"

What could she say in that rush? So he kissed me—Jerome kissed me. For the first time. I kissed him back and clung to him, and then the train started and they bundled me back into the carriage, but I leaned out and waved and cried, tears and rapture, ecstasy and misery, all mixed up in one big heaving lump in my stomach.

That summer I had to lie to Rudi on the days I could not go swimming; Mother said, "Tell him you have a headache."

"But I never have headaches, only grownups have headaches, he'll think I'm a sissy. Why can't I tell him the truth?" I did not want to seem just another useless female to Rudi, and I had never lied to him, but Mother wouldn't let me tell him the truth.

It had happened a few months before. I had run to Mother, very scared, and Mother had put on her "wise" air, Rosa her superior elder sister's, while Mother explained the physiology of women. I only half understood.

"You've kept all this from me," I said, the world again reeling away from me with all those concealed and baffling mysteries. "Tell me now, will you, all of what is going to happen, tell me everything now. Am I going to have a baby?"

They laughed and said not to be absurd—but what was absurd? What else would I be discovering that I had no inkling of, that was still undivulged, that they had hidden from me? I wondered many nights about the things they didn't tell you—how babies really came, what happened when you were married. I had observed for myself the fact that you didn't get a baby till you were married, and you got married in church, so something happened in church that made you have a baby. Simple logic, but when I tentatively broached this, they ridiculed me again. "Then what does happen?" I countered defiantly. "Wait till you're married" was all Mother said.

Mother's authority was so firm and I so blindly accepted it that even these successive discoveries of lies, prevarications, or withheld truths did not, strangely enough, weaken it or create distrust in me. Rather, they undermined my own self-assurance. If I could so wrongly believe things that were not so, there must be something wrong with me. Why did I not catch on sooner? When I found that my school friends knew about menstruation, I distrusted myself even more, felt even more incapable, incompetent, inept. I did not know either the world or people. Possibly I never would. How did one learn?

After eighteen months in our Finchley Road boardinghouse, Mother found and furnished rather handsomely, in the bourgeois style of the period, a house in Hendon Lane, Finchley, at that time still quite countrified. It was a short tram ride from Golders Green, then the northern end of the underground line. There was a big garden, a tennis court, and we called the house, as usual, "Noris." It was to be our home for ten years, and so much of our growing-up took place there that I thought it a pity houses cannot write biographies.

At the North London Collegiate School I made firm friendships with several girls, two especially, Kitty and Mollie. Mollie's mother was a schoolteacher, and despite Mollie's straight silky brown hair and her fresh milky complexion, she sometimes displayed her mother's tart manner. Kitty was quite different; she had huge, gray-blue eyes, brilliant teeth, and bright red cheeks. For years we shared our thoughts, ideas, and all our new experiences. We were "best friends," and though Mollie ran a close second, she never shared fully in Kitty's and my intimacy. We maintained almost tribal-like laws in the "sets" of friends at school, and there could be strong feelings of jealousy. I disliked Mondays, for example, when Kitty and Mollie had something between them that I was not in on—the discussion of the Sunday sermon. Both were churchgoers, while I had never been inside any place of worship, and had to go through the mortification of having Kitty and Mollie titter about my ignorance. I did not even know what the "offertory" was, and Mollie pushed her advantage with Kitty in common ridicule of me. On the other hand, Mollie and I shared a passionate love of the theater and went to plays in the top gallery at the Old Vic, while Kitty went suburbanly home to Palmers Green.

Kitty and I shared our reading and loved the same poems: "Paolo and Francesca," "La Belle Dame," and especially, from *Hassan:*

What would you, ladies, it was ever thus.
Men are unwise and curiously planned.
They have their dreams and do not think of us.
*Chorus of Pilgrims:* We take the Golden Road to Samarkand.

We read the prose poems of Tagore's *Gitanjali;* I found Dowson and Rosetti, she Keats and *A Kentucky Cardinal.* For a time we disagreed. I went for Robert Louis Stevenson, Kitty for the Brontës and Jane Austen, though *Jane Eyre* was my romantic love. But our likes met again when Francis Thompson "fled him, down the nights and down the days"; in Mrs. Browning's "Pheidippides," "joy in his veins, bursting his heart, he died—the bliss"; but especially in "A Musical Instrument," which we never ceased to quote to one another.

Sweet, sweet, sweet, O Pan!
Piercing sweet by the river!
Blinding sweet, O great god Pan!
The sun on the hill forgot to die,
And the lilies revived, and the dragon-fly
Came back to dream on the river.

I didn't think Pan was treated quite fairly, especially after his music had been so highly praised, but authors weren't always just, I had learned. I didn't understand how one made "a poet out of a man" either, as the next verse claimed, and I thought the "true gods" might have done better than merely "sigh for the cost and pain." But then, if it had been I, I wouldn't have let Orpheus look back, either, or Icarus fly so near the sun—I'd have managed things more practically and perhaps avoided quite a number of the world's tragedies.

Every term a motto printed on large cards was tacked up in the classrooms. The texts were taken from maxims, proverbs, or some classic essay like Bacon's on talk being just a tinkling cymbal, and were to act as guideposts for us through life. I remember a few that particularly impressed me.

OPPORTUNITIES ARE VERY SENSITIVE THINGS. IF YOU SLIGHT THEM ON THEIR FIRST VISIT, YOU SELDOM SEE THEM AGAIN.

KEEP THE FACULTY OF EFFORT ALIVE IN YOU BY A LITTLE GRATUITOUS EFFORT EVERY DAY. EVERY DAY DO SOMETHING FOR NO OTHER REASON THAN ITS DIFFICULTY, SO THAT WHEN THE DAY COMES, IT WILL FIND YOU READY TRAINED TO STAND THE TEST.

One term came a motto that led to an amusing occurrence: CHOOSE WELL: YOUR CHOICE IS BRIEF AND YET ENDLESS. Its author was given as Goethe and I thrilled to the fact that they had a German author I knew, and triumphantly I brought it home to Father. But what was it from? Father looked through his eighteen Goethe volumes in vain, he could not find it, until some friend suggested, half in fun, why not ask our War Minister, Lord Haldane, who was known as a great Goethe expert?

I immediately decided I would, and surprise Father. Haldane would be too busy, of course, nor would he think of answering a schoolgirl's letter, but still, what could I lose? One must dare.

My name of "The Cheeky One" must be lived up to. After a long interval, a handwritten note arrived.

If Miss Ella Winter will look up Carlyle's translation of Goethe's *Mason Lodge* she will find what she is looking for. *Haldane.*

It had worked. The audacity or "cheek" they always seemed so to disapprove of did pay off. I showed the letter to everyone and Father had it framed, and with Johnston Forbes-Robertson's reply to a fan letter Mollie had once dared me to write, it hung over my bed till we gave up the house.

Teachers played an important role in our school lives. We had "crushes"—you had to have one or be out of the running. I developed a really serious crush that lasted the rest of school, when I venerated Miss Eleanor Doorly, a very tall, slender, blond-haired woman, with large features and limpid gray eyes. She had long slender hands, which she used as she read aloud verse or parts of plays; it was she who discovered for me the Brownings, Shelley, Coleridge, Addison.

What was the enchantment of a "crush"—the unattainability of its object? Someone has called it "undifferentiated sex impulse." Whatever its nature, it made you tremble, fearful, and pumped the blood to your heart at unexpected encounters. When it was my turn to sit next to Miss Doorly at lunch, I suffocated and afterward suffered tortures because I hadn't known what to say. When I had scarlet fever and she wrote me a letter, I insisted, against Mother's orders, that it be fumigated, along with the bedclothes and Jerome's postcards, so that I could keep it "forever."

My other crush in these adolescent years was on a tall, hearty, black-haired Australian musician, an expansive professor from the Melbourne Music Conservatoire whose name was G. W. L. Marshall-Hall. He had been let go from his post because of his controversial "bohemianism" and atheism, which he took no pains to hide, had in fact expressed in a celebrated epic poem. He had come to Europe to put on two of his own operas, and my very first encounter bound me to him "with hoops of steel." It was a hot day when he came booming up our garden path, and Father sent me quickly into the cellar for cold beer. I brought up a bottle that he stretched out for with a bellow of happy anticipation and drained at a gulp. Then he made a frightful grimace and roared at me: "Lucrezia Borgia! She who would poison her father's guests—what have you given me?"

We discovered it was vinegar. My mother had bottled it in old beer bottles and forgotten to change the labels: the enormous man exploded into Gargantuan laughter, and ever after his only name for me was Lucrezia Borgia.

He was romance, the attic, the poet in the garret, the true bohemian to me. I would hurry home from school to sit and listen avidly to his and Father's talk of music, art, and life. Among other things, the professor told us how he sent his students into the world. " 'I've taught you all the technique I can,' I tell them, 'now go out and fall in love.' " That seemed to me such daring, I sat open-mouthed.

Father tried to get Marshall-Hall's opera *Stella* produced, but in vain. Finally the London Palladium agreed to present a version cut to one hour "if the Professor conducted it himself in white gloves."

"White gloves!" the composer exploded. "I haven't worn white gloves to conduct in my whole life." He accepted the humiliating terms, but on opening night we heard, dismayed, the gallery whistle and boo, and for two weeks our friend had to listen to jeers and catcalls. The music-hall audience did not understand this semi-classical work. At the end of two weeks we received a card in bad German: *"Die Reste der heiligen Stella wird heute abend abgeräumt."* Marshall-Hall returned to Melbourne at the outbreak of war, but died a few weeks after from an undiagnosed appendicitis. It was the first time I had known and loved someone who had died. I kept every scrap about him for years, in a cretonne box Father gave me—letters, postcards, his poems, opera programs, and photographs—and often dreamed over them, wishing this marvelous man could still come booming up our garden path, roaring his welcome from that other, artistic world.

It was indeed the "romantic" era. We lived sex and "the broken heart" in books and poetry, were faithful to Cynara in our fashion. Dowson and Beardsley, Swinburne and Rossetti and the *Yellow Book* partly filled the yearning in our lives, and we suffered their faithlessness, heartbreak, and agonies as if they were our own.

When I discovered Oscar Wilde, I took him to my innermost heart. He became a passion; I read everything he wrote and all I could lay hands on that was written about him. Perhaps because he symbolized liberation from the bonds I chafed at, or because he was so long forbidden me, I thought him badly treated, his downfall unmerited, though I did not understand its cause. I shared his contempt of conventions and of the threats of "What will people say?" that were so constantly thrown at me. Wilde's paradoxical wit was so satisfying to me and expressed my own needs so well that I felt him to be a personal friend. My own defiance grew with his. "I must kiss thy lips, Jokanaan"—that was as forbidden to me as whatever "it" was that had been forbidden to Wilde.

I approved of every argument in *The Soul of Man Under Socialism* and recited all of *The Ballad of Reading Gaol*. How dreadfully they treated him! I treasured my volumes in their pale-blue bindings and asked only for Wilde as presents. I stood up for him against all comers; my friend had gone to jail, unfairly, I thought, and I was on his side.

Mother called it my *Sturm und Drang*. I argued interminably and aggravatingly, no doubt, about sex and free love, marriage and platonic friendship, conventions and the need to break them. What was wrong with free love? Why shouldn't a girl? Wasn't it better to live together in love without marriage than cling to a bad marriage? I fought fiercely even while I was being unconsciously riddled with Mother's unrelenting *"Nur mit dem Ring am Finger."* I wanted freedom, a room of my own, to feel myself me; Rudi had his own room, why not I? Couldn't I have the spare room? "The sewing woman uses it," "We have to store things there," didn't satisfy me. Rosa didn't seem to have my needs, but she hadn't intimate friends like Kitty to spend the night with, talking. It wasn't only that I wanted to talk to Kitty through the night, either; I felt an overwhelming need to be alone with my self-ness.

"It's only an idea" was Mother's familiar, reiterated, contemptuous response.

Although I was a good scholar, I never could quite get to top place, but I did win two Special Prizes; one for Civics and, rather ironically, one for Scripture. Our teacher was the Reverend Septimus Buss—the seventh brother of our founder—a spare, ascetic old man dressed in black, with thin white hair and sparse white beard. He taught Jesus as a historical character and set us the task of making a book of the natural history, plants, archaeology, and geography of Palestine from the Bible. I threw myself into this with passionate interest. It was new to me, I enjoyed the research and liked the Bible as history. When the Reverend Buss announced the award of the prize to me, there was some eyebrow-raising, as the girls knew of my atheism. I felt I owed the gentle, bent old man a confession of my lack of a state of grace, and after class stuttered something about my unreligious upbringing; but he cupped his hand to his ear and beamed: "Yes, yes, your zeal comes from your regular attendance at church, you have shown your deep attachment to the Holy Word." I could not shatter the old man's happy ignorance.

In much the same way I felt I was not quite playing the game when I stayed the weekend with Kitty and her strictly Presbyterian family. She had many older brothers and sisters, and on Sunday everyone went to church. I watched and imitated during the service; at lunch Kitty's father, a deacon, talked about church politics. I was accepted as a regular churchgoer like the rest. But one Sunday Kitty's tall, stoop-shouldered mother, serving the Brussels sprouts, asked, "Your family attends Presbyterian service, too?"

"Er—really—we don't usually—that is—" I stuttered, fumbling with my knife and fork.

"You mean, you don't go to church?" The fateful words were out. Conversation stopped as they all stared at me in silence. The subject was never mentioned again in Kitty's house.

Kitty's religious devotion made me try desperately to share her beliefs. Best friends should surely agree on important matters; there was so much for her to tell me, so much to discuss. Afterward I would have person-to-person talks with God: "If I'm good, and behave as I ought, You can't be angry just because I don't believe in You? After all, I'm obeying Mother when I don't." Or "If You do exist, it can't make any real difference if just I don't happen to believe it?" This argument seemed to me foolproof. But to clinch the matter, I made a secret pact with God: "If You will let me believe in You, I will." It was really up to Him now, wasn't it?

# 3

# THE BELLS OF HELL

It was July 1914. In Basel, on a long walk in the hills, I felt a peculiar new sensation.

"I think I've begun to think!" I said to Father.

There was a brooding restlessness in the air; our second day in Basel we saw scrawled on a wall WAR IS COMING. Ridiculous, of course. One did not have wars—they belonged to history, like the dinosaur. When a Serbian student assassinated the heir to the Austrian throne in Sarajevo, it could have no relation to our lives. And I had more important things on my mind. I had passed my matric and must now decide what to do. What was going to be my profession, my life work? I kept quoting that old school motto, "Choose well: your choice is brief and yet endless," but nothing pointed to an answer. There still weren't many professions open to women; what fascinated me was public life, foreign affairs—but what profession plunged you into public life?

There was the Law. I argued so much that Mother frequently burst out with "You should be a lawyer," but it wasn't my first love. I hugged my secret ambition to be a journalist, which I thought would combine my wanting to be in the middle of things, to know what went on behind the scenes, with my desire to write, but I had no idea how you set about it. I supposed one day, when I knew enough, I would write an article. But I kept this to the last, like the cherry in the lemonade.

Father was upset. I had never seen him so depressed. We packed and left for the Rhone Valley. The Adelboden Hotel was filled with people of a dozen countries, Germans, Italians, Dutch, Americans, arguing and debating; and the newspapers were full of threats,

counterthreats, and "veiled warnings." Then one morning we read
with unbelief that the Germans had presented Belgium with an
ultimatum. And now everything went helter-skelter. Our hotel shattered into camps of raging, hostile abuse. Poles, Austrians, Belgians,
Serbs hurriedly said good-by, and the place emptied. A few Swiss
and British remained. We could not get home because there was
no transportation.

Events were occurring that would change all our lives. But our
summer holiday went on; I flirted with an American writer with
long untidy golden hair and a bit of a stutter, Lawrence Vail. He
lisped in a slightly foreign voice, was on the prowl, and pursued
both Rosa and me, which made us both jealous but also drew us
together, especially when Mother's familiar admonitions descended.

"Walk with me as far as the white gate," Vail tempted each of us
in turn.

"You are not to go out alone," Mother prohibited.

When I asked if we couldn't go just to the gate, Vail mocked
our subservience. After dinner we sat in the lounge, knees touching.
If we moved, he moved nearer, talking all the while about writing,
life in Paris or New York's Greenwich Village. He quoted from the
*Rubaiyat,* "one of the great hymns to love, you must let me read
it to you. It's too noisy down here, come to my room where it's
quiet." Since he invited us both, we went, the first time either of
us had "been in a man's room," and my heart beat as I listened
to Vail declaim:

> Come fill the cup, and in the fire of Spring
> Your winter garments of Repentance fling.
> The Bird of Time hath but a little way
> To flutter, and the bird is on the wing.

I listened avidly; Rosa sat silent. "You understand, don't you?"
Vail exhorted. "Pleasure, enjoyment are more important than con-
vention." He read the whole poem and left me in a trance. When
Rosa got up, I reluctantly trailed after her.

When Mother found out, she was furious, particularly that Rosa
had been disobedient, too. "But we were there together," I argued.
"What could happen? Nothing did happen, he just read us a poem."
Rosa was silent. She never discussed Lawrence Vail with me, and I
was puzzled whether to go ahead myself or leave him to her. I did
both by turns, and by turns felt mean or self-sacrificing.

Finally, at an hour's notice, three trains were put on for stranded British tourists, and there was a wild scramble for seats. We said good-by to Vail, who remained behind without any "Bird" at all; and we got on one, fourteen to a compartment, spending five days on the journey. There were no restaurant cars and we were not allowed out. Some people handed bread around; at Lyons there was rancid butter. The train loitered, stopped, jerked, started again; it shunted onto sidings and stayed for hours. But the worst were the scenes at stations as soldiers said good-by to scared and weeping families. At one station we had to march through two lines of bayonets into booths where we and our luggage were thoroughly searched. Soldiers stood stiffly at attention, eying us, making one feel guilty. I was guilty. I didn't want poilus killed, or German young men, or Austrians. I didn't want anyone to have a bullet in his stomach or hang on barbed wire, whatever country he was born in.

I had looked forward to getting back to England, to a known, familiar country; instead, everything was strange. Victoria Station in London was seething with blue and khaki; somber men hunting for someone, clinging or being clung to. Fathers stood about looking lost, and tried to carry some object, a duffel bag, a thermos. A booth was marked RED CROSS, another RECRUITING. Instead of HAVE YOU USED PEARS SOAP or MAZZAWATTEE TEA, posters advertised: KITCHENER WANTS YOU  *  FOR KING AND COUNTRY  *  BRAVE LITTLE BELGIUM. A Tommy was trying to strike a match and saying with a grin, 'ARF A MO', KAISER.

Outside we didn't find the London we knew, either. Queues stood before the shops—in front of Sainsbury's for rationed sugar and butter! The whole aspect of the city had changed. But, "The war can't last, it'll be over by Christmas," everyone said. We comforted ourselves with that.

Instead, war became a way of life; daily living fell into a routine pattern. But the central war dilemma for me—how you justified killing more men every day—remained unsolved. I could not justify it. No one became a "Hun," "vulture," "the enemy" just because he was born on a different side of a boundary. The papers screamed hate and atrocity stories, spilled over with sickening talk of "ideals" and "patriotism" I knew was false. Some might think the "boys" were defending homes, protecting sisters, ending German militarism forever, defeating the Prussian vulture, but I could not. I felt alone and alien, and at night I quoted to myself a poem of Newbolt's that moved me intensely:

> What of the chamber dark where she was lying
> For whom all life was done?
> Within her heart she rocks a dead child, crying
> "My son, my little son."

At school we had Red Cross drives and made bandages, knitted socks, and arranged concerts for the wounded, but no one asked my questions. The big girls compared notes on the white feathers they had handed to boys who "ought to be in khaki." I saw one boy in the street burst into tears. "Why don't you ask first whether they're medically fit, or conscientious objectors, or under eighteen?" I argued. The girls scoffed. We were worried about Rudi, though he was still under eighteen; he was at school but was restless and wanted to get into it. At Christmas he left school and went into a war factory.

The Belgian Van Drutens, our closest friends, argued with us about the war. Mr. Van Druten had been my particular friend, had egged me on to become a doctor and called me "Doctor Ella." Jackie, their younger son (later John Van Druten the playwright), played tennis with us; but now the Van Drutens came less and less.

Father could not find work, and had no income. The capital he had brought from Australia and invested in England did not yield enough for his growing family, so he had borrowed. When war was declared and stocks plummeted, the bank demanded immediate payment. "That day?" I couldn't believe it. "They couldn't wait?" To repay the debt, Father had to sell every stock at rock-bottom prices and was left with nothing. He looked for work, any work, in vain; he was a "friendly alien," but German. Our old friend J. A. Amschel, a metallurgist from Melbourne, came to our assistance— all through the war.

I could not decide what to do with my life. Medicine and Law were now out of the question because of the long and costly study, and so, too, were Oxford and Cambridge. I must go to a London college and live at home. Marion Phillips, the brilliant daughter of our lawyer neighbor in Melbourne who had so admired my reciting, had come to London to study and kept saying how important Economics was; one "could not understand the war

without it." The London School of Economics, where Marion had
gone, held out chances for different professions and it was coedu-
cational—in my view definitely an advantage. My visions of Oxford
died hard, of those "dreaming spires" of Compton Mackenzie's
*Sinister Street,* which I so loved. The School of Economics was a
dull, red-brick building right on the street, with no fields or river,
not a flower, not a spire. But what else was there?

During my last school summer vacation, sixteen of us went
farming as war work. The Misses Debenham (of the large British
department store) owned farms in Dorsetshire, and we were to
replace farmers who could then go to war. We were promised
newly built stables to live in, and would be paid fourpence a day.
We felt fine, patriotic, adventurous, got ourselves farm smocks
and boots, picked out our Hardy novels (the farms were in Hardy
country), and crowded into a jolly train "off for the land."

It wasn't quite as pictured. Our lodgings were stables, but cold,
bare, with stone floors and walls, tiny bunks jammed together, no
electric light, no furniture, and no privacy. We were also underfed.
Ravenous from the unaccustomed physical labor, we had to write
home for food parcels, like the boys at the front. Most of the work
was hoeing mangel-wurzels, but we also scrubbed pigs for market,
followed the harrow, picking up the potatoes by hand, gathered
fruit. It was backbreaking work, but we were romantic and glad to
be doing something to make it up to the boys who had to fight.
We formed ourselves into platoons and battalions with commanders
in chief and officers, and wrote ribald verses, especially about the
beastly harvest bug, a biting insect that got under the skin and
itched ferociously. We took turns at scratching backs till they bled.

But we did have Sundays to ride our bicycles all over Egdon
Heath and trace the travels of Tess and Jude and other Hardy
characters. The actual place names of our villages were better than
Hardy's—Affpuddle, Bryantspuddle. It was also the locale of the
Tolpuddle Martyrs, the farm laborers transported to Australia for
trying to form a union. Our last Sunday the Misses Debenham
invited us, their "hands," for tea. We dressed neatly (at last),
brushed our hair, had a last scratch (hoping it would carry
through the visit), and cycled to the big house set in smooth wide
lawns surrounded by shrubs, great oaks, and beeches. We sat on the
grass expecting, at last, one Gargantuan feast. But what we were
handed were plates with one peeled peach and a teaspoon, neither

knife nor fork—and how could you eat a ripe, juicy peach with
a teaspoon? We were too well behaved to take them in our hands;
one just had to try to bring the rolling thing to a standstill. A few
succeeded and were gobbling; I couldn't catch mine and almost
burst into tears from hungry frustration. Then I caught it, and
was about to bite when Miss Debenham rose to signal that tea was
over. We got up and filed by our gray-haired, aloof employer,
putting our rough, calloused hands in her delicate manicured one.
I could think only of the untasted joy of that peach. Later we
heard that the owner of these acres had fired real farm workers
and their families; schoolgirl labor was much more economical.

That summer our band of school friends broke up. Kitty went
to Cambridge, Mollie to Bedford College, London. Mrs. Bryant
worried about me. "You're too young for so serious a study as
Economics," she said. "In fact, you're too young at sixteen for
college at all. Why not put in a year at something else first; would
you like to teach? I'm adviser to a little school that happens to be
looking for a young teacher for a year." Anxious to help financially
at home, even more anxious to feel useful, I agreed. It put off the
decision I still had to make about my life.

In my year as a teacher I was given one piece of good advice:
"If you don't know something, don't pretend you do; the children
will respect you more for it." Despite my youth, which made me
too strict, I made friends with the children, but I always feared
I would not be able to keep order. The children liked me, but the
person who didn't—not at all—was Miss Baker, the Head of this
little school. Long-nosed, cold, and angular, with rolls of hair piled
high on her head, she resented me and enjoyed humiliating me. I
was inexperienced, but must have communicated some of my joy
of life to the children; that was not Miss Baker's idea of a teacher's
function.

I taught all subjects, including Astronomy and Nature Study, of
which I knew nothing. I took the ten-year-olds on long walks,
pointing out fruits and wild flowers I had just looked up in the
encyclopedia. History, my own favorite subject, I soon made theirs
by letting them draw pictures of historical scenes—common in
teaching now, but not practiced then—and the children loved it.
When, at the end of the school year, a special exhibition was held of
these pictures made in my lessons, I was congratulated fulsomely,

while parents told me gratefully how much their children had learned.

Once I had a funny scare; for a few days I was avoided and could not fathom why. Miss Baker came to me, very solemn.

"I have had complaints from parents," she said. "They tell me you are Austrian."

Austrian! What had been said? I could not imagine. A pupil came to commiserate. "I like you even if you are Austrian!" "But I'm not, Jennifer." "Yes, you said you came from Melbourne, Austria." In the war atmosphere of the time it was dynamite.

"I'm glad," Miss Baker said, coldly resentful as ever. "Had you been Austrian, I'm afraid I should have had to let you go."

When the year was over, I was sorry to say good-by to the school and the children, but college beckoned. I must know more about my world, about this incredible, savage, tortured, fascinating earth.

My first day at the School of Economics was ecstatic. When the black-haired professor spoke of Knowledge, Ethics, Logic, of Aristotle and Plato, he opened doors that made my mind reel. The cold barrenness of the classroom vanished; I thought there could never have been ideas so exciting, or a lecturer as clear as Doctor Wolf. He tied bits and pieces of experience into a scientific whole.

Dr. Edwin Cannan (Economics) was a short man with a short gray beard, a monotonous voice, but a biting ironic wit. He exploded all economic theories with the same mumbled phrase, "Nothing much in that." His comments on our essays were sardonic and cutting. When I wrote "The penny post is exorbitant," I found in the margin the query "How much would you like to pay for a penny stamp?"

Theodore Gregory taught Economics also; he was short, slender, and pale, with great sad blue eyes in a pleading face. He had a sharp analytic mind and a beautiful voice. Morris Ginsberg, small and scared-looking, with enormous soft brown eyes that expressed age-old Judaism's sorrows ("noncarnivorous eyes," as Hemingway later said of another Jewish writer), introduced us to Sociology. Both these men were intellectual giants to me.

Every subject opened new fields: psychology, economic theory (not at all a "dismal science"), the history of political ideas, the "infant science" of sociology. Edward Westermarck, a stout blond Finnish sociologist, expounded on his book, *The History of Human*

*Marriage,* and had never married. Goldsworthy Lowes Dickinson nervously twisted and untwisted his hands, squeezing long bony fingers as he clarified political ideas from the Greeks on. R. H. Tawney analyzed the acquisitive society and the economic role of religion in our world; short, stubby Sidney Webb, with squat brown beard and a lisp, delved into his enormous array of facts and the panorama of colonial history; while frizzy-haired, no-nonsense Doctor Lilian Knowles, a stout woman lecturer who looked like a provincial housewife, revealed to me the economic underpinnings of history. I knew little about Russia, not much more than that it was a Czarist tryanny with boyars, wars, assassinations, and pogroms. Doctor Knowles's picture of the Russian "mir" or early communal village was vivid: "The centers of Russian rural life were small holdings, strip farming is so backward that cucumbers, the staple peasant food, are growing smaller year by year so that soon the peasants will be almost starving: something has to happen." When the first Russian Revolution came, I told everyone about the diminishing size of cucumbers in order to explain it.

Huge, lionlike L. T. Hobhouse, great hands folded over one another (quite different from Lowes Dickinson's nerve-wracked, trembling timidity), examined mind and morals evolving, somewhat counteracting Mother's absolutes. A rather unimpressive lecturer called Clement Attlee explained the usefulness of charity and took us to see the slums, "which most certainly must be reformed."

What picture of the world did I get from these "best minds" of my time? A reasonable, coherent universe that committed errors but showed a general upward trend called Progress, where man learned from experience, mind and morals evolved, and we all grew better and better, perhaps not every day in every way but at least in some ways and part of the time. Reasoned, intelligent action could abolish social evils—poverty, ignorance, disease, inequality, slums. Eugenics would breed a better race.

We were very social-minded, went to meetings, lectures, debates, political gatherings of every kind, and discussed these problems endlessly. I joined the 1917 Club, the meeting ground for liberals and radicals, reformers, journalists, politicians. I read one book that, clinching much of what I had been learning, was a great influence—H. N. Brailsford's *War of Steel and Gold*. It showed the underpinnings of exploitation, its hypocrisy and cruelty, and de-

termined me more than ever to help do something about the evils
of my world. I didn't like John Morley's *On Compromise,* though
our teachers did; I preferred all or nothing. "Why give in?" I
argued. "How can one compromise between right and wrong?"

My second year at college I became secretary of the Student
Union and arranged our lectures and debates. Indian, African,
and other colonial students enlarged on the indignities of their
colonial status, and in one bitter debate an Egyptian student called
Bakry was particularly violent.

"You British came as guests for a weekend," he stormed, "but
what do you think of a guest who comes for a weekend and stays
thirty-four years?"

At the lunch table one was in the center of affairs, too, always
with some government official or foreign visitor to discuss problems
or analyze events. Lecturers and students sat together and argued.
Harold Laski beamed as he recounted, with childlike relish, what
Bevin or Churchill "told me about their next move as they came
out of the Cabinet." Laski tutored me my last year; always invigo-
rating and original, his acute mind could penetrate all one's de-
fenses and make one feel small. As students left his house one after
another at the end of a discussion session, Laski would comment
with a shrug: "Second-class mind." I tried to outstay the rest so he
couldn't thus finish me off.

On one of my Student Union evenings I invited Doctor Ernest
Jones, one of the early British psychoanalysts, to speak. I had met
him through a medical-student friend who had been reading "that
Viennese doctor, Freud," and who had suggested I interview this
English disciple. Doctor Jones invited me for tea and we struck
up a friendship. He was small, white-faced, and intense, with a
warm engaging voice. I was intrigued by this new science, which
Graham Wallas had considered worthy only of a footnote in his
classic *Human Nature in Politics.* Anxious to spread the new ideas,
Jones gave an intense talk at our Union, but the students, like
Wallas, were unimpressed. Jones walked home with me after, quite
disappointed, and sighed that he supposed it would take a long time
to be understood and accepted, especially by people who thought
as politically as our students. When he explained the Russian
Revolution to me as "a curse on the Russian people for killing
their father [the Czar]" I was inclined to agree with the students.

The war made all the problems that were examined at the school
or argued by the Fabians much more actual. Theory and practice

were for once united. The great Fabian lecturers, Sidney and Beatrice Webb, Bernard Shaw, H. G. Wells, Emil Davies, and my own
professor, Graham Wallas, also taught at LSE, and their lectures
dealt with a newspaper's everyday items—as the plays of the time
dealt with the problems dramatically. We did not have to make
the distinction between "art" and "propaganda." When Graham
Wallas lectured at the Fabian Society, he quoted (to the audience's
delight) the Tommy's war verse:

> The bells of hell go ting-a-ling-a-ling
> For you but not for me.
> For me the angels sing-a-ling-a-ling,
> They've got the goods for me.
>
> O death, where is thy sting-a-ling-a-ling?
> O grave, thy victor-ee?
> The bells of hell go ting-a-ling-a-ling
> For you, but not for me.

My developing interest in politics was vastly stimulated by our
friend Marion Phillips. She was deep in Labour politics, soon to be
Chief Woman Officer of the Labour party, and we all admired her
extravagantly—her brilliant mind and effectiveness as a speaker, her
activities as suffragist, pacifist, labor organizer. It was a red-letter
day for us all when Marion came. She was striking-looking, with
black hair, small hands and feet, intense brown eyes—and a stout,
uncorseted, ungainly body, which one forgot in the acute discussions
she always brought into being. I sat on a hassock, ears and eyes
glued to her, drinking in what she said about events, political personalities—she knew everyone—and policies. She made public questions so alive and fascinating that I was sure politics must fill my
world; Marion lived as I wanted to live, I would pattern my career
on hers. I would not need to marry, any more than she had. My
life, like hers, would be in my work.

When Mother's friends discussed servant problems, children,
illnesses, clothes—"the four D's" we called them, domestics, descend-
ants, diseases, dress—I grew bored and sidled over to the men, who
of course were talking about what was happening in the great world.
I dreaded that a similar boredom might come with marriage, as it
so often seemed to. Love was quite another thing.

The intellectual ferment of the times reached into every sphere,
into race and class, prostitution and poverty, slums and solitary

confinement, eugenics, war, and sex of course. We went to sex problem plays as well as social problem dramas, Eugène Brieux's *Damaged Goods, Ghosts, Widowers' Houses,* as well as *The Dynasts, Pygmalion, Man and Superman, Milestones,* and John Galsworthy's social dramas. The writers and artists we admired were politically minded. Wells, Galsworthy, Bennett, Shaw, Granville Barker and Lillah McCarthy were explosive off stage or on. Catholic conservative writers like Belloc and the Chestertons were as political as the socialists, and many of the best journalists—H. J. Massingham, H. W. Nevinson, Brailsford, Alfred G. Gardiner (A. G. G.), and A. R. Orage—held socialist or near-socialist views; hardly an intelligent person did not, it seemed.

The Fabian arguments seemed self-evident to me: people, all people, must have food, shelter, clothing; inequalities of any kind were indefensible. How could one justify a system under which some were well off, warm, and well fed, while others lived cold, shabby, and crowded in slums? Shaw said it paradoxically: "I hate the poor, that's why I want to get rid of them," or, "The workers need air, some air, not too much, but some, just enough to work"; and when it came to discussion of better distribution, of nationalization, he asked, "Would a conductor punch much less ticket on a municipal tramway than on a private line?" I listened to arguments between Father and his business acquaintances, who maintained that "the poor use their bathtubs only for coal," or that "socialism gives no incentive to work." Mrs. Sidney Webb gave a delicious reply to that one, I thought:

"They'll work if the alternative is to starve," she maintained.

"But if the man still refuses to work?"

"When he gets hungry enough, he'll work."

"Yet if, despite hunger and discomfort, a worker persists, stubbornly declines, to work?" the interlocutor persisted. "What would you do then?"

Beatrice Webb gave her answer serenely. "We'd look at him," she said, "just look at him." I treasured that response.

One result of all this exciting, fermenting mass of ideas on me was to make me sure of one small task I was definitely going to undertake: reform the world.

Rudi could not bear his Welsh war factory any longer; he wanted to be like everyone else, to "do his bit." He joined the

Royal Artillery, was commissioned second lieutenant, and in 1917 was sent to the Western Front. From then on, like millions of other families, we knew no peace—any day could bring the fatal telegram.

He wrote often, but censorship was strict and we never knew what actual danger he was in, or where. Father pored over his little flags on the big maps, and with every "push," we lived a lifetime of fear.

He came on leave once, badly tear-gassed, and was in hospital several months. He talked little about the war, and it was not for a year that we heard of the time he had found himself in the midst of a German shelling as he was bathing in a tub in a field, and how frightened he felt until he had dressed again—"as if clothes were a protection against bullets," he marveled to me.

I would lie awake and try to imagine the trenches. Why should I, just because I was a girl, be able to lie in my own bed, warm, comfortable, sheltered, out of danger? I felt I owed it to those boys, not much older than I, to try and imagine myself in their place, in those fields and trenches, cold, wet, muddy, and terrified. I could not bear to think of being blind, but I forced myself to imagine that, too. We saw the blinded soldiers at St. Dunstan's, when they had stopped being people like us and were something alien, out of life. I tried to imagine having to die when all life lay before you, and I certainly did not feel with Rupert Brooke that it was turning "like swimmers into cleanness leaping."

For a while Rudi was forward observation officer for his regiment, and we could not get through the days. The worst scare was in the last war year. Five officers were playing cards in a field when a bomb burst in the middle of their circle and killed four of them outright, all but Rudi. Long afterward he told me how he had run for cover, sobbing, unable to grasp what had happened, except that "as I ran I saw Watts' brains running out on the ground."

The war and our common fear for Rudi drew Rosa and me closer. She adored Rudi, but in our childhood had probably, in some way, had to cede him to me. She did not share Rudi's and my close, tree-climbing intimacy and she did not, later, make the close friendships at school that I did; but though we quarreled bitterly and incessantly at home, with Rudi in this daily danger we did weep together about our common fears for him.

Mother was so anxious to center all life in our home that I

brought professors and student friends to the house, though I longed
to go with them to their bohemian meals in hidden little Soho
restaurants, to live my student life with them. But Mother would
plead: "Your father is so unhappy, why not come home, bring
your friends, have Gregory here for Sunday lunch? . . ." And
Mother was as hospitable to my college friends as she had been to
Kitty and Mollie and all my schoolmates. And, of course, I myself
wanted Father to be in on my new world and new relationships.
Then it would become a conflict for me again and I would argue
and resent, so that once Mitrany, an older Romanian student who
took a vivid interest in all our lives, reproached me: "Why don't
you leave home and live on your own instead of giving your mother
these constant pinpricks?"

I could answer that one. "She wouldn't let me," I flamed. "She
says people would criticize her if her daughter left home." Only
if you married, apparently, could this so desirable step be taken.

I wanted desperately to get out into the world, to "live," as I
thought of it, and the continuing war made it only more urgent.
And then one day, after America had come into the war, my tutor,
Graham Wallas, called me into his office.

"A good friend of mine has come to London on a highly confidential mission," he said, blinking through his steel-rimmed
glasses, "and asks me to suggest someone to help him. Would you
like to? Felix Frankfurter is a professor at the Harvard Law School
and Chairman of the War Labor Policies Board in America, and
is here to learn what he can from England's experience. Would
you like to work for him?"

At Claridge's Hotel I found a large, elegant suite where people
came and went, bells and telephones rang, and messages and cables
tumbled back and forth. I was shaking hands with a short, mercurial
man, with glasses and a cleft chin, who smiled, talked in quick
staccato phrases, flung questions at one, while attending to twenty
other matters at the same time. His smile showed a row of dazzling
teeth. Even at rest he seemed in motion. He was warm, friendly,
trusting, and assumed so immediately and unquestionably that I
would do this job, indeed that I could do anything, that doubt,
fear, hesitation vanished. Would I start right now, he had a couple
of cables to send, could I take shorthand? No? It didn't matter—
take them down in longhand and send them. "I want you to collect information for me," he said, with that enslaving smile, "tell

me whom I must see, or, better, arrange the meetings yourself. I'll take your word, I'm sure you know the people I should consult." And so I was catapulted into the heart of just such a job as I could have imagined only in my dearest dreams.

For three weeks I lived on Olympus. Code messages to Washington, urgent conferences behind closed doors, secret meetings in bedroom or bathroom, dinners, confidential discussions followed on one another's heels. At this time Americans were still rather mysterious in England; few Europeans had come into much contact with them.

Felix was bursting with exuberance and activity. He talked about America, told me of liberal causes and people he had supported, such as Harold Laski, laughed a great deal, and threw out questions, comments, snippets of information, gossip, personal experiences without letup. I had to do all kinds of jobs, but it all thrilled me. Had he asked me to get him the moon, I would have hurried to the nearest travel bureau.

Little chits were left for me daily. "Find X for me," "Invite Y," "Check on R." Occasionally Felix dashed in, busy, breathless, bristling with electric energy. "Have you any new ideas? Did Eustace Percy call? Laski? Balfour? Weizmann? Any cables?" And out he would rush again.

At last, it was November 11, 1918. With thousands of Londoners we milled about the streets filled with shouting, weeping people; buses hardly able to move, bursting with waving, screaming humanity mad with joy. It took three hours from Charing Cross to Aldwych, a seven-minute walk along the Strand, and it was the same all over London—a wild, hysterical jubilation. The war was over.

After a few dreadful weeks of waiting to hear from Rudi, we learned that all was well. He would not be demobilized for months, but what matter—he was safe, alive. And now the killing would stop.

For my father the war had always been unbearable: antimilitarist, pacifist, believing in reason and international brotherhood, he had had to live in a world in which his own family was "the enemy," a world dominated by nationalism, brutality, and hate. But one day, after the Armistice, while making his bed, I found under his pillow, where Mother said he clutched it every night, the award given Rudi for valor in the field, his Military Medal.

# 4

## PARIS, PEACE AND GLORY

"Postman!"

There was the usual wild dash down the morning staircase as each of us tried to be the first to reach the door.

"For you," my sister cried, disappointed, and threw the letter on the hall table. Late for class, I opened it on the run down the garden; I expected nothing and the letter was in a strange hand-writing, small and neat but unknown. I scanned the unpromising note, then stopped dead and tore back into the house.

"It's happened!" I shouted to Mother and Father, still sitting over their newspapers in the dining room. They looked up in alarm. "I'm asked to the Peace Conference. This letter . . . it's from a friend of Felix—he wants me . . ."

Only a few days before, I had been envying our students who were going to Paris as experts, technical advisers, secretaries. And I would miss it all! I fitted none of those categories, I had no chance—and how I ached to go.

Before I could say more to my startled parents, the telephone rang. "Well, young lady," said a pleasant voice. "This is Aaron Aaronsohn. Did you get my letter and are you coming with me?" I started to stutter something in reply, but he went straight on: "Felix is in a hurry, as usual, he's been in Paris a week and has no one to help him and for some reason wants you. Can I take you with me? I leave tomorrow." The voice waited. Tomorrow!

Mother had picked up the other receiver and was whispering at me urgently: "But you don't know any of the conditions! What arrangements are they making? Where will you live? What will they pay? Who will look after you? You need clothes—you can-not possibly be ready for weeks." For myself I would have slept on a park bench in an old gym suit and worked for nothing, willingly, but obediently I murmured for delay.

"Then Monday, but don't forget, Felix is in a great hurry, and as you know, he doesn't like to wait. Ask him any questions you need to know, he's at the Plaza-Athénée, I'll tell him to count on you, yes? *Au revoir* then, till Paris." The receiver clicked. I didn't even know where to reach him.

Just like that, the impossible happened. I would have taken the next train, but Mother was already there with a thousand questions, none of which I could answer. I did have misgivings. I must get some kind of permission from my college, at least inform them, and there was a difficulty: they expected me, as a star student, to win First Honors for them in the final exams at the end of this school year. It was an important consideration for the college authorities; with so many students away at war, the few remaining ones must make a scholastic record. In our year there were only two who were expected to achieve this, Herman Finer and I. I wasn't unwilling myself for this distinction, and if I went away now, I would be much less likely to win it. Nevertheless, "Opportunities are very sensitive things," that old school motto. I must not miss this one. I went to Professor Edwin Cannan, who had sounded me out about whether I would stay on after graduation as his assistant; he had paid me quite a compliment when, to the query of a friend of ours (Professor Sanderson, the blind Head of Oxford's Ruskin College) on what sort of student I was, he had replied, "Not as bad as most." "That's the highest praise I've ever heard him express," Sanderson had said, laughing.

Counting on that exaggerated praise, I was sure that Cannan would vote "No," and his first remark did nothing to dispel my apprehension.

"Nothing much in that," he mumbled, "don't see how it can help the world along much." I waited. Should I try to make clear to him how my work could make the difference between war and peace, a future for the world or none? But Cannan was going on through his beard: "'Course, don't know that it can harm much, either."

I took that for enthusiastic endorsement and ran off to my next obstacle. But Graham Wallas would be easier, he was more in this field, and, besides, he knew Felix. Tall, stoop-shouldered in his ample black scholar's gown, he walked up and down the stone corridor with me, biting his mustache, blinking his eyes behind those black-rimmed spectacles, as he listened to my outpouring. With his customary care he entered on an estimation, an analysis, a world view.

"If you go," he finished slowly, deliberately, "if you do go, you may get a Second instead of a First—but you'll have been at the hub of the universe for a while." And then he looked at my barely controlled impatience and smiled. He had hit my ambitious nail square on its head.

For the next week I scurried about at Mother's heels as she suggested, worried, warned; but she never bought anything as quickly as my new clothes, counting on the generous allowance English secretaries were granted. I got my first evening dress, yellow with tiny seed pearls; an afternoon black georgette with oval neck outlined in pale-blue beads; my first grown-up hat, a blond straw with a Mrs. Siddons ostrich feather—very fetching. I remember each garment—my first grown-up wardrobe, and not made at home. In fact one frock came from Debenham and Freebody. I had never thought of myself in such clothes, but there wasn't time to ponder this retrogression, though I was slightly astonished at my interest and self-approval in the mirror.

Finally, I was standing on Waterloo platform saying good-by to Mother, who was excited too, but tearful, doubting the wisdom of letting a young daughter go alone and unchaperoned to that wicked city. But I had no time for sympathy; I clasped ticket, passport, English money, French francs—French francs!—and listened inattentively to last-minute advice and admonitions. We were ordered to get in and the whistle blew.

"Don't lose your passport! Be careful of restaurant food! Look after your clothes! Have you got your fountain pen and glasses?" The train started. "Write!"

"I'll write!" I shouted from the window. "Don't worry." And then Mother, alternately waving a white handkerchief and dabbing her eyes with it, was only a dot. I sat back, grasped my purse, felt for my fountain pen and glasses ("You'll go through life losing your fountain pen and glasses," Father always said), rechecked my baggage on the rack. My two new suitcases were in order. Did I have the keys? I felt for them hysterically, then squeezed into my corner—trust Mother to get me the best seat—and dreamed the hour and a half to Southampton as the train's wheels beat their

tattoo into the future. The fields of Hampshire floated by, green
and gold. The new era had begun, I was riding into it in shining
armor. My mind repeated Bernard Shaw's war lines:

> So we lay down the pen
> So we forbear the building of the rime
> And bid our hearts be steel for times and a time
> Till ends the strife, and then,
> When the peaceful age is verily begun,
> God grant that we may do the things undone.

In Paris I hastened to Felix's headquarters and found myself
talking to Ben Cohen, a tall, slender, trembling young American
whose clothes hung insecurely on a diffident frame. His fingers
were long and skinny, and his hands didn't know what to do. He
had a long nose, straight brown hair brushed slantwise from a
broad white forehead above rimless glasses, and a shaking frightened voice. His quivering irresolution was due to a painful shyness.
"Mr. Frankfurter asked me to talk to you." He faltered on: "He
can't get in today, he's got so much to do, his time is so, er, he's
so, er, I'm to see if you're comfortable and . . ."
Three days later I sat at a desk, wondering how long before I
could get started. What was Felix doing? There was a constant
coming and going of the most unlikely people, old men with beards
and black hats, some in long black caftans, some looking as if they
hadn't shaved for days. They stood about in knots, and argued,
gesticulated, shouted. They talked in many languages, none of
which I understood except German, and it wasn't always the German I knew. And now the door opened and Felix rushed in, looked
at me a puzzled second, and then held out a warmly welcoming
hand. He was as gay and charming as last year, still a coiled spring
of energy, ready to bound to the next subject; but for the moment
he was concerned with me, giving me his full attention.
"So you got here! I'm so glad, I need you, are you settled? Are
you getting to know your way around Paris? Does your hotel suit
you? Oh good! Has Ben talked to you? Is he helping you? [Ben
had melted away.] He's a brilliant young lawyer from my Harvard
Law School, you must get to know him." He flashed his old dazzling
smile, showing the strong small white teeth; there was still the
dimple—the cleft in his chin—and he sat on my desk, like a bird
on a telegraph pole, ready to hop away.

"Let me tell you about the members of the Commission," he said. "There's Howard Gans, he's our businessman; Bernard Flexner, a brother of Doctors Simon and Abraham Flexner of the Rockefeller Institute, a very learned lawyer; and Judge Julian W. Mack.

"He's a great reforming juvenile court judge, Judge Mack. You're going to enjoy him." He continued as if he were a lecturer and I a young student. "He's done more for delinquents than anyone in America, he and Ben Lindsey, and they've achieved remarkable results. Make the Judge tell you about it." Later I found Justice Mack to be stout, fatherly, jovial, and friendly, but so addicted to good French food, including every variety of cheese, that it was hard to steer any conversation to another channel.

"The Zionist Commission is here to set up the Jewish homeland that Arthur Balfour promised Chaim Weizmann," Frankfurter flung out on another dash through the office. "You know, Doctor Weizmann won the promise of a homeland for the Jews in return for the work he did for the British on chemicals in the war. Now we've got the job to make this dry, barren, stony little country fruitful, able to support millions. Jews from all over the world have been waiting for years. They've come from Poland, Galicia, Russia, Estonia, Romania—all of Eastern Europe—to create their own country. They've been waiting centuries in ghettos for this moment, to get back to Palestine. It will end their persecution; they will be the equal of other peoples so that they cannot be ill-treated again." This was what Felix thought, what many Zionists believed, in 1919.

We listened to the loud disputations in the corridor. "They come from such different backgrounds, you couldn't expect them all to have the same views." Felix smiled. "What they do share is their one eternal tragedy." I wondered how deeply these differences must cut, since there was disagreement even as to whether Judaism was a race, religion, or nationality. "Some of their differences seem irreconcilable," Felix agreed. "But they have been debating them for years. Every conceivable—and inconceivable—plan and project is presented for consideration. That's good—everyone is concerned, is part of this moment they've been dreaming of."

"The world is divided into people who think they're right," I quoted sententiously, and Felix laughed.

"We can't be impatient," he said. "We all have to learn, and above all we in America must be humble."

There was a knock and I regretted the interruption, as I always resented our too-short talks, until I saw a broad-shouldered, good-looking, tall, imposing man greet Felix warmly with hands outstretched. He had thick black hair, a black pointed beard, and burning brown eyes, and his voice was the kind I always responded to, rich and resonant. A beaming Felix introduced Dr. Chaim Weizmann.

"Meet the most charming man in Paris, who can tell you anything you want to know—the man who made our whole adventure possible and who will be the first president of an independent Palestine." Felix's face shone with pleasure.

The men exchanged the gossip of the Peace Conference and discussed the vast problems ahead of them, the job to be done in Palestine: the irrigation projects required to help turn that arid desert into grazing lands, orchards, fields, crops. I listened enthralled, seeing water flow in the desert, canals fill, and bronzed men lead loping camels from the Dead Sea to these new oases.

"The Arabs will be our problem for a long time," Weizmann said, "it's not going to be simple. One day they may have to leave and let us have the country." And he added, in a gay kind of badinage, "They're ten to one, but don't we Jews have ten times their intelligence?"

Graham Wallas had been right, Paris was the hub of the universe. Pressures, passions, ideals met and tangled as statesmen clashed and haggled. The "movers and shakers" had come to re-establish a shattered universe, with promises and hopes dangled before millions, and millions trusted them, including me. I felt like those peasants in faraway huts we heard about, who prayed before Wilson's portrait, in gratitude to this strange man who would insure that war never happened again.

But the "old order" had flocked to Paris, too, and its representatives glittered at soirées and public balls, or met in hotel suites over confidential luncheons or in concealed, out-of-the-way gourmet haunts. Kings, prime ministers, and generals, bankers, businessmen, and politicians, with their "confidential advisers," pursued their separate interests behind the scenes. Advisers, lawyers, experts of every kind rationalized and justified—though we liberals and idealists did not see this so clearly yet. We still hoped.

Frankfurter had a foothold, or at least a toe-hold, it seemed, in about every delegation. He knew everyone and heard everything. People smiled when they talked of Felix—everybody called him that, so I adopted the habit, but not to his face. He was a magnet attracting politicians and statesmen, labor leaders, diplomats. As I went about his interests on practically a daily Cook's tour of the Peace Conference, I found friends, colleagues, and ex-students of his in almost every office. His name was an open sesame. My boss's strings were attached to British as well as Americans, his old friends Eustace Percy or William Ormsby-Gore of the Foreign Office, Arthur Balfour, Edmund Allenby. And Feisal and Lawrence of Arabia. The young, beautiful Prince Feisal was always followed by his group of tall, imposing, silent Arabs in long white robes and head dress, and by his shadow, Colonel T. E. Lawrence, also in native dress. Lawrence was short and fragile-looking, with a delicate, poetic face, but he appeared as much at home with the desert Bedouins and the prince he seemed so attached to as with European diplomats. Felix was as much intrigued by Lawrence's role in all the Middle Eastern politics as with his romantic appearance. In my perhaps too-fanciful imagination, Felix had magical influence, like Prospero, and I was his Ariel-Puck, helping to promote the practical measures that would remold the world. Often when he returned from a dinner or conference, he would sit on my desk and continue the discussions. No wonder I seemed to myself, from my ringside seat, to be wielding an actual hand in affairs.

I had also come to know, in fact had grown very friendly with, Lucien Wolf, the British Jewish historian who was in Paris to work on minority rights. He was strongly anti-Zionist, believing that the liberal attack on anti-Semitism should be to make all nations extend to their minorities, Jewish or other, the same protection under law, the same respect and dignity, as to the rest of the community. Wolf was helping to write the minority clauses into the peace treaty, and he kept his housekeeper-secretary, Margaret, a forthright, small, outspoken Irishwoman, very busy. She had been his housekeeper for many years and had to look after his physical needs also, since he was almost blind.

I spent all my available free time with them at the Chatham, their hotel. Wolf was a learned, humorous, all-round scholar, versed in politics and international affairs, and knew many personalities in British public life intimately. I did have some qualms at being so much with "the enemy" and dared not tell Frankfurter. Wolf was critical of the Zionist solution, and introduced me to Jewish leaders in Paris, Professor Sylvain Lévi and others, who shared his views.

Felix encouraged me, when he did appear, to learn all I could. Other members of our mission took me along to help buy hats for their wives—me!—and toys for their children, and consulted me on a bewildering variety of personal affairs, but they also invited me to plays, the opera, dances. One day Felix asked me to order an especially grand dinner for the whole mission and, after making his suggestions for food, added, "And, of course, you'll dine with us." It was my first Paris banquet: oysters, snails, champagne, frogs' legs—and eleven assorted cheeses for Justice Mack. At the Grand Vatel that night, Paris had gathered not only her beauty and her chivalry but the statesmen of our epoch. Tall, white-haired General Jan Smuts sat at the table next to ours with Lord Robert Cecil, lined, ascetic, troubled-looking, with his aristocratic hawk nose and ill-fitting clothes. ("*Ah, le vrai type ouvrier,*" Albert Thomas had characterized him in the House of Commons.) Eleutherios Venizelos appeared, and a brace of admirals, then Lloyd George, ebullient, expansive, with his mane of beautiful silver hair. Felix was, as always, full of stories. "I must tell you about your Lady Astor," he said to me cheerfully. "Last night at the Majestic [headquarters of the British delegation] she spied me, and left some British officers she was talking to.

"'Why do you Jews want Palestine?' she flung at me, without even a greeting, and then called across the room to Balfour, 'Arthur, tell these Jews they can't have Palestine!'"

In the next weeks I made friends with some of the young Americans—astonishingly young, it seemed to me, for such important official jobs—who were helping to set up their shining new universe. They really believed that that was what they were doing, and they were persuasive, too. I met the fresh, brash, independent head of American information, William Bullitt, just twenty-two, who made the daily reports to the United States mission. He had to read all the papers, know all the facts, keep abreast of world information and the work of a hundred committees. He had refused to come to Paris, Felix had told me, without his exquisite wife, Ernesta, one of the few American wives allowed here, and her beauty had become the toast of the American delegation. Felix also told me that they had had to get rid of their first information officer "because he couldn't impart his information; he wanted to keep it all in his own head." His name was Walter Lippmann.

Henry Alsberg blew in from Eastern Europe with shuddering tales of turmoil and starvation. The man in charge under Hoover —with the title of Director-General of Near Eastern Relief—was also a boy of twenty-two, Lewis Strauss, and he had responsibilities "we would hardly give a man of fifty," as I wrote home, but he certainly did not lack self-confidence. He told me he was trying to decide between a bank and public life; eventually he became a partner in Kuhn, Loeb, and Company, and later head of the Atomic Energy Commission.

Every day was a dancing dream, and I wondered how I would ever settle down to ordinary life again. Between the acts of a play Howard Gans, who treated me as a daughter, said, "You can't live all your life in the clouds, you know. Why don't you pick yourself a nice boy and marry him and settle down?" The usual suggestion of dear old uncles! This was said to me the very day I had written my name in a register at the War Office Library below those of Paderewski, Lord Milner, Keynes, Pershing; a day in which I had watched Clemenceau, Orlando, President Wilson, and Lloyd George walk into the Crillon to a plenary session, so close I could have touched them; a day when I had talked to Colonel J. H. Morgan at the British-delegation ball at the Hotel Majestic—our former lecturer in constitutional history, now a member of the British Military Mission. Me settle down!

Among Felix's little snippets of advice to me was this, as I thought, typical American one: "Use every opportunity to meet people in person. The English are not very enterprising. You with your zip and energy belong to the United States; you ought to go there, but take my counsel now, use every chance to make personal contacts. They are what count in life. You never know when one may become important." And that afternoon he bustled in with an errand. "I'm giving a dinner for some journalists. We'll have it at the Château des Iles. Will you make the arrangements? I want you to invite Charles R. Crane, our ex-minister to Russia, and Lincoln Steffens. The office will type the letters for you—and don't forget what I told you about personal contacts." He was off and I went for my hat, the fetching Mrs. Siddons straw with the ostrich feather.

"Have you ever heard of Lincoln Steffens?" Felix popped his

head in to add, and when I shook my head, he smiled at some picture in his mind.

"He's a great wit, Stef is, fond of saying things differently. He's an American newspaperman, much older than you, in his—oh, early fifties; he muckraked our cities, knows a lot about politics. You can learn from him, he'll give you a different picture than you got at the London School of Economics."

I didn't know what "muckraking" was. In England one regarded American journalists as rather vulgar and uncouth, who would do anything to get a sensational story. Questionable bits in the English press were called "American journalist stories."

Felix gave me the letters, with *By Hand* in the corner, and I saw with pleasure that the address on Steffens' letter was the Hotel Chatham, the pleasant old-fashioned hotel where my friend Lucien Wolf lived. I might lunch with the Wolfs instead of at a lonely Duval.

In the hotel lobby I asked if Steffens was in; the clerk looked up and mumbled, *"Numéro quarante-huit."* He was in. A disappointment, I couldn't run up to Lucien and Margaret. Well, I didn't *have* to deliver the note myself, I could leave it in his box—but I remembered Felix's advice. I went up in the creaky *ascenseur* to the fourth floor and walked, a little scared, to Room 48. As I knocked, I could see myself through Mother's eyes "going alone to a man's room." No answer. Relieved, I turned to go—I had done what I should—when a musical voice called "Come!" and the door opened. A figure stood in the door in a bathrobe. He wasn't even dressed!

The man was not tall, but he had a striking face, narrow, with a fringe of blond hair, a small goatee, and very blue eyes, and he stood there smiling. The face had wonderful lines. Jo Davidson once said, "Men spend a lifetime making the lines in their face." There was something devilish—or was it impish?—in the way this figure stood grinning at me.

"Hullo, nice girl," the voice said, and melted all my anxiety; it was soft and mellow and somehow humorous and it charmed me. "Come in." He stood aside for me to pass.

"Oh no," I said quickly, embarrassed to be standing at an open door with a man not dressed. "Thank you very much I won't come in, thank you, I haven't time, I've just brought you . . ." And I held out my letter.

"A love letter?" He chuckled. There they were again, the Americans, making fun of you before you even knew them, taking love so lightly—like Ralph Hayes and Lewis Strauss and the others. And now this one—who was so much older and ought to know better.

I answered rather formally. "I've brought an invitation from Professor Frankfurter for you. He wants—I was going to leave it downstairs, but . . ."

"But you decided to come up and call on me, so why don't you come in? I have a bit of my usual bronchitis, that's why I'm working at home. I find I learn more when I stay in my hotel; the other reporters come and tell me things."

His voice was so friendly, so unthreatening, and his smile so warm that my fears vanished. I walked into his room. It was large, pleasant, and sunny, with books strewn about, a large leather suit-case open on the floor, and clothes lying untidily around. A black velour Homburg hat hung on a rack; on the desk a tiny portable typewriter had a sheet of paper in it.

"I'm afraid I've disturbed you at your work," I said, my heart beginning to pound again.

"Why did you want to run way when I opened the door?" He chuckled with that musical laugh. His voice was so attractive; his blue eyes smiled in such a friendly way behind gold-rimmed glasses. His interest flattered me, but I shuttled between ease at his teasing and dismay at my temerity—alone with a man in a dressing gown in a room with an unmade bed. Think of Mother. I got up.

"Don't run away," he said. "I'd like someone to talk to." I paused uncertainly, while he read his letter.

"Felix giving another of his parties?" That impish grin again. "To meet the most important people who'll very importantly tell him what's unimportant?" Then he talked as I'd never heard anyone talk. When I looked at the clock, it was two. I had been here my whole lunch hour. I jumped up, stricken, and rushed back to my office—and safety.

Though my personal fairy tale and the glamour of Paris continued for me, the world's high hopes were fading. Now people were asking, "What has happened? Where are Wilson's promises? What has become of our expectations?" Faith and trust were turning into dismay and disillusion. Wilson was the universal topic. Would he hold out this time, on this line, that point? Or would he sacrifice everything for his League? We all believed in "the inevitability of progress," even if it might sometimes not look so inevitable and occasionally not like progress; but with this developing reaction I was swept along on the tide of disquiet.

War must never happen again, and I had come to Paris to help see it didn't, to work however infinitesimally for a peace that must last; but it was turning into a peace of vengeance, hate, a sowing of dragon's teeth for future war. What had gone wrong? I longed to ask someone the questions.

Until my last few days, I saw Steffens only fleetingly after that first meeting, once when I was hurrying down the Rue de Rivoli under the colonnades on my way to the Crillon. He was lolling outside the Press Club, and I didn't notice him until I heard that ironic, melodic voice.

"Hullo, nice girl." And immediately the banter: "What's the hurry? Are you afraid the Peace will run away? Why don't you stop and talk to me?"

"I'm taking something . . . er . . . for Felix"—he laughed and I finished furiously—"a document for the Mandates Commission."

"Palestine will have to learn about British rule," came his comment. "Too bad the Jews must go through all we've just begun to get over. They deserve better." I was afraid he would say something I should not hear and rushed away, the draft of the Mandates section written by Whitney H. Shepardson clasped tight under my arm.

Another time was in the Bois de Boulogne and I could have killed him. I had met an American, tall, intelligent, excessively handsome, a Rhodes scholar from Oxford, who was working on the League of Nations draft. The moment I met him I said to myself, "Now *this* one," and he had reciprocated with some interest in me. At the tentative, tender beginning of a possible relationship he asked me to dinner in the Bois. I had flirted with Lewis Strauss and Ralph Hayes and other young men in Paris without being particularly drawn to them, but "Shep" was different.

We were sitting under a chestnut tree, when a boat drew up to the bank filled with chattering people, and gazing idly, with my mind not on them, I was shocked to recognize Felix, Bullitt, and his beautiful Ernesta, half a dozen other people—and Lincoln Steffens.

Shep was embarrassed; his friends had caught him, and Americans always mocked a boy and girl alone together. He folded like a pocket knife, and murmured quickly, "Let's join Felix when we're finished." I had the impression that he did not want them to see us together—was it that I was "only" a secretary? It spoiled the dinner, of course; neither of us ceased to be aware of that other group. We got through the meal somehow—my precious tête-à-tête —with practically no conversation, and Shep suggested, "Let's have our coffee with them." We crossed over to gentle smiles from "them": they were busy listening to a foreigner whom Bullitt introduced to us as Alexander Kerensky.

"He's come to get help against the revolutionary violence of his colleagues," Steffens chaffed, with the banter I had come almost to dread. No one knew that Steffens and Bullitt had recently returned from their highly secret mission to the Bolsheviks; they were still trying to get to Wilson or Lloyd George with their report. I didn't know anything about Kerensky except what everyone was saying about this "middle-of-the-road" Russian trying to bring order to his country, the one man the Great Powers trusted. But no matter how politically fascinating the talk, it could not overcome my personal discomfiture. I was too acutely self-conscious. I could not talk, I could not listen, and then suddenly I could no longer bear it. I had to get out, to make it clear there was nothing between Shep and me and that I was going home—alone. I got up during a moment's lull and asked of no one in particular, "How long would it take to walk to the end of the Bois?"

"That depends," Steffens quipped in a flash, in that maddening, mellifluous voice of his, "on whom you're walking with."

It was the end. Scarlet, confused, abashed before Felix, who laughed, and Bullitt and Ernesta and the others, who sniggered in happy, appreciative malice, I swore I would never, never speak to that beastly man again.

# 5

## PETER!

And then, by a fluke, during my last days in Paris Steffens and I became close friends. I had had supper with Lucien Wolf at the Chatham and was going home, deeply melancholy. After much discussion and conflict I had decided I must go back to London and cram those last months for my final exams. But I could not bear to leave; I was in love with Paris, with my life there, I wanted it to go on forever. The Commission, however, was breaking up. Frankfurter was preparing for a long-postponed visit to Palestine; there would be only office routine now. And the heart had gone out of my lovely Peace Conference—the struggle was over. It was all set: the Germans were to sign a hard, vengeful, unforgiving peace of retaliation, the opposite of what we had so desperately hoped and worked for. No ideal had been realized, hardly even the League. Both personally and politically, I chafed at the descent from the clouds.

I paused outside the hotel door to drink in the warm, caressing, but already nostalgic, evening air—the very breeze was asking me to stay—when I became aware of a small dark figure leaning against the wall of the hotel, hands in pockets, black hat on the back of his head, apparently as melancholy as I. And then a caressing voice, not bantering now, not mocking, fused with the quiet magic of this dying spring.

"Where're you going, nice girl?"

"Home, just home." I must have sounded as sad as I felt.

"Mind if I go with you?"

As we strolled, Steffens told me about Jo Davidson the sculptor and Jo's sitters, for it was at his suggestion that Davidson was making busts of the outstanding leaders at the Peace Conference.

Stef was Davidson's closest friend. "I thought an exhibition of busts of this era's big men would make Jo's name. Jo jumped at the idea, but stipulated that I must be in the studio while he worked, and talk to his sitters, so they'd be at ease and not 'pose.' It gives me the chance at the long, slow interviews I like, which are almost impossible to get here." And so, Steffens told me, he could "explore politics and history and the plans of such different people as Herbert Hoover, Clemenceau, Bernard Baruch, Maynard Keynes.

"And so you see, bright girl, I can be one ahead in understanding the people who make our world."

The clocks of the city struck midnight, then one and two and three, and we were still walking. I poured out my aching heart to my sudden companion, the beauty and the wistfulness of this glorious spring. And the bitter, creeping disillusion: I had not, after all, made a better world. Stef listened, and he was not teasing now and he did not laugh at me. He listened and said things in that magical voice, and though I did not grasp it all, I somehow began to feel lightened. It was as if someone had put cool fingers on a burning ache. I was held, interested, fascinated.

"What happened to the Conference?" I asked. "It started out so well, how could it all drain away like this?"

"Do you ever ask about the causes of things?"

"That's my college motto—*rerum cognoscere causas.*" But I was startled.

"Do you follow it?"

I had a quick answer ready, but I saw that that wasn't what he meant.

"All liberals have the same illusions," he said. "When they lose them, they're disillusioned. They don't ask 'why,' only 'who.' "

"And you?"

"I?" He smiled. "I get myself a new and better illusion."

"But if Wilson had been stronger—"

"The same forces would have been at work; a man twice as good couldn't have made rivers flow uphill. Wilson's fault was his refusal to admit 'They' were too much for him."

"If he had, one would have been even more upset, more at a loss."

"People would have known where to look for *what* was wrong; now the tide just sweeps away their good man."

We walked by Notre Dame outlined against the dark-blue sky.

The river swirled below; dark trees loomed against the dark stone walls. We leaned over the parapet and watched a solitary fisherman cast his rod into the silent water.

"My businessman friend, E. A. Filene, says he's never seen a Seine fisherman catch a fish," Steffens laughed. "They just sit there and fish."

A couple came along hand in hand, a young man with fair hair and a very pretty girl, graceful and small with curly hair lightly blowing. She had on a blouse and dirndl skirt and her face was all alight. They stopped in surprise.

"Why, Stef," they cried, and then turned curiously to look at me. Steffens introduced me.

"Griffin Barry, a young newspaperman just beginning where I'm leaving off, and Rosalind Fuller, a dancer who still makes up dances instead of dancing life." Both laughed; I felt shy and stood tongue-tied. For a little while this strange man had been close to me, my friend, and now I saw him as a stranger with people I did not know and a life quite alien to me. But Steffens was already teasing his friends.

"Why do all you girls love Barry?" he complained to Rosalind. "Why don't you love me?"

"He needs looking after," Rosalind shot back over her shoulder as they walked on, "that's why all we girls love Barry."

We strolled back to the Hotel Quai Voltaire, whose wooden door was long closed, and I knocked till the porter sleepily opened, gazed crossly—and, I thought, disapprovingly—at my companion, and let me in.

But next night the same thing happened. I had dinner at the Chatham with the Wolfs, and at coffee Steffens came to our table. Wolf had met and liked him. We all talked together a moment, then I said good-by, but Steffens accompanied me. Again we wandered the streets of Paris, in and out of winding, dark, narrow gulfs between buildings, and by the banks of the Seine. We crossed the river into a maze of ancient little streets threading in and out of this oldest section, the Rue St. André des Arts, the tiny winding Git-le-Coeur, the Rue de la Harpe, Rue de la Huchette. And across the boulevard farther into the heart of the old city, past the age-old tiny church of Saint-Julien-le-Pauvre. The streets were silent. Even in Paris everyone had gone to sleep. But I was still trying to find my intellectual bearings.

"Perhaps what has happened in Paris had to happen to show what we're up against," he said, quite gently for him. "We must learn to be scientific about politics; the human race *can* become conscious."

"But a lot of people did know what they were up against, and still fell into a trap. What was it?" In my puzzlement I was argumentative.

"We don't have to go on making the same mistakes and excuse them with the same explanations. Do you know why the League isn't what you liberals expected?"

"I can tell you what Felix and his friends say," I retorted. " 'There's been too much to do, you mustn't be impatient, the people will correct the Conference's failures, you can always alter clauses, at least it was a start. Rome wasn't built . . . There has to be compromise—ever read Morley's *On Compromise?*' That's the question they always ask, but Felix denounces Wilson for compromising on principles."

"And that's bad." He smiled. "They'll always take half a loaf."

"The English are as bitter," I said. "My friend from the Board of Trade told me what they say of Wilson. 'He came over to make peace and brought nothing but a phrase.' Jim thinks me a bit disloyal to have worked for Americans. 'Your Yanks with their high ideals always manage to get their practical interests attended to,' he says, and 'You just can't work with them on committees; they're always either abstract or negative.' "

"We're a very moral people," Steffens jibed.

"Wolf says the Americans didn't know what they'd be up against. 'Self-determination seems to be an article made exclusively for export,' he chaffs. 'There's only one thing greater than knowledge and that's stupidity; we can read and write but not think.' He believes the British were the most cynical." I quoted Lucien's favorite Conference *bon mot:* " 'Balfour knows but doesn't care, Bonar Law cares but doesn't know, and Lloyd George neither knows nor cares!'

"But wouldn't someone," I went on, "I mean like House or Smuts or Lloyd George or Bonar Law—all those people who have so much power and can surely do anything—would they not be able to fix things better?"

"They are fixing them the way they want them. They know it's a struggle between what the people need and their own privileges.

So they talk about what the people need and they arrange quietly, secretly, to go right on dividing the spoils."

We had reached the Seine again. We stopped on a bridge, and I listened to the water lapping. "Is there anything wrong with ideals?"

"They can't rise any higher than their source," Steffens replied. "You've got to stop wishing and hoping and saying 'if.' History is scientific. I believe man acts scientifically and for reasons that can be discovered and that are predictable. You see, I've seen something new under the sun. I've seen some answers to the questions that plagued me all my life. Not perhaps the best answers, nor, as Lenin said, the only answers, but—answers."

"It sounds idealistic," I said. "And idealism is out, isn't it?"

"You talk like an American businessman." Stef laughed. Was he laughing at me? But he went on. "Who made this mess? The practical men. You don't have to own another country to buy its raw materials. . . . But we're arguing and I don't like to argue. You must 'see through' what they're trying to do—that's your job as a social scientist or a reporter, isn't it? Or as an artist. To see and understand."

I warmed to that; did he guess my innermost ambition?

We shifted to talk of Lucien Wolf again, I was full of him. "Lucien isn't as hard on Wilson as the rest," I said. "He's a bright spot, he thinks, 'he failed, but he tried,'" and I quoted Wolf again, this time on his beloved Voltaire. "'There's one person more powerful than Monsieur Voltaire and that's Monsieur Tout-le-monde.'" I was pleased with Wolf, Voltaire, and a little bit with myself, and went on with Lucien's comment: "'But what can you expect, with all the rascaldom of Europe let loose in Paris?'"

"Bad men again, you see," Steffens mocked. "The French are more logical; Clemenceau expresses the French perfectly. Old and tired and cynical and he cares only about France. That's bully. He doesn't pretend to be setting up a new world."

Steffens stopped by the bridge and started stroking his hands. "Let me tell you a story. Clemenceau wears gray suede gloves that he never takes off. So he sat there with the Big Four in his gray gloves, a little apart, almost dozing, not very interested in their scrambling and grabbing.

"'Is it peace you want, gentlemen?'" he asked, so quietly that they were startled. Yes of course they wanted peace, that's what they were here for, the whole world was crying for peace. Clemenceau ignored them. 'If it's peace you want, gentlemen, you know what that will mean. You, Mr. Lloyd George, must give up your rivers and ports in other lands, you, Mr. Orlando, will have to stop looking over to Africa for colonies, while you, Mr. President, you must sacrifice your manganese and potash and tin and quinine. Italy must cease wanting parts of Austria, England must give up her sea routes, France must stay away from Syria, the United States . . .' There was a moment of stunned silence and then a horrified outcry. Not that! That was impossible, absurd! No one could expect it. . . . Clemenceau continued quietly stroking his gray suede gloves.

" 'Ah, then it isn't peace you want, gentlemen,' " he said calmly. 'It is war. And if it's war you want, you must go on dividing up the world as you are doing now, to each country what she can get. And then France will have her colonies, her Syria, North Africa, her share in reparations. That's all right, gentlemen, if that's what you want. As long as you are clear that it is not peace you want, but war.'

"They protested, they didn't mean that. That was absurd. Everyone had to have colonies." Steffens stroked his hands.

" 'You don't mean you're willing to give up concessions, you don't want to change anything? Very well, gentlemen, if you mean war, France knows what to do; France understands that. The time for us French to make war is—now.' And slowly the glove stroking stopped."

I gasped. "Are you saying—" I started, but he interrupted.

"That's right, I'm saying it to you."

"But—" I stuttered again. "That's what I learned at college, from the Fabians, from Brailsford's *War of Steel and Gold*—that's what I grew up on. I know that!" Was everything coming full circle? Was "making the world safe for democracy" really only a phrase about coal and oil?

"There's a difference how we know things. You know it with your pretty head, but not with your hips, and that's where you must really know things, in your hips."

He had to explain his philosophy again and again, answer my objections over and over—it was all so bottomside up. "Can you be the only man who is right and everyone else out of step?" Yet what he said sounded so plausible—if you just threw out everything else you'd ever believed. And he told it all with such graphic illustration, so many tales and anecdotes from his own life and experiences. I must store up what he was saying, to take it out and look at it in the long gray hours when all this would be over. And then he started to tell of that other world he had just visited, that no one as yet knew anything about.

I was aware of the horror and atrocity stories out of Russia, of the "baths of blood," people butchered, the violence, the terror. That was not Steffens' picture. He described for hours, as we sat or walked and wandered, what he had actually seen over there, what they planned, how they were changing a world.

Again and again I marshaled everything I had learned, my whole liberal Fabian philosophy, even Professor Cannan's summation of Marx: "Nothing much in that." It did not impress Steffens.

"The difference between Lenin and Wilson is the difference between the two cultures of our era" was his summing up. "You'll see more of that than I, but let me show you."

We climbed down the stone bank to the edge of the river and sat there.

"Lenin had a definite plan: 'That's the way we'll go,' he said. Then the Bolsheviks met difficulties. Straight Communism couldn't work, not in the mess the war had left, so 'We can't introduce Communism yet,' Lenin said. 'Let's go back a bit, we must have some private trade—some capitalism.' They introduced the NEP— New Economic Policy—and had some private trade, private capital, and concessions."

"Giving up what they set out to do?"

"No. Lenin admitted this temporary setback. 'We've left our straight line and gone around at an angle of forty-five degrees,' he said. 'It's not what we want, but as long as we know it, we can get back on the right path again.' "

"And Wilson?"

"Wilson won't admit he's had to give up any of his Fourteen Points. Not one. 'Did you win your points?' we asked him, we correspondents. We asked him three times, and three times he made the same reply: 'I got what I came to Paris for.' The President has to justify himself; he can't say, 'I failed, but I know why. I can do wrong now, because I'm forced to, but later—' " Stef broke off. "We're a very moral people," he repeated. "We can't face doing wrong knowingly. So Wilson won't ever go back to his original Fourteen Points."

"Not even if they're what he really wanted?"

"Every step has to be justified; he can't face that he failed."

I thought about it a long time. Then I asked, changing the subject, "But why did we have to take such petty revenge? Like that milch-cow clause—so many milch cows to be taken from Germany that a whole generation of kids will grow up with rickets." I quoted Lucien Wolf again. " 'It would have been more logical to have taken a shipful of prosperous Germans and torpedoed them.' "

"But Wolf is able to laugh," Steffens said gently. "That's a very great gentleman." And, after a pause, "Don't they teach you to laugh at all at the London School of Economics?"

"A girl can have a career," I flared, but suddenly challenge didn't seem appropriate. I felt I was saying good-by to a whole world—and, like Orpheus, looking back just once more as I clung to my old certainties. "There's nothing wrong with caring about what goes on in the world, is there? Wanting, for instance, not to have another war? And look what they've done!"

But Steffens was not bitter about Wilson, the way Felix and Ben and the others were.

"I'm not a Liberal," he said, "I leave that to you intellectuals, you and your Purpose, your Felixes and your arguments, your heavy burden of the world all wrong." He was silent again, and then he seemed to say something quite different. "Look at the river, little girl. Don't you have any room for beauty? Don't you ever just look and enjoy? What is the river doing? Look at those lights— where are they going, what is *their* heavy purpose?"

There was that yawning chasm again, some boat ready to carry me right away—from what? From some secure haven? I looked at the red and white reflections, tall, wavy, wandering.

"A dancing Seine-light night," I murmured.

"Ah! That's what an artist would see. So you *do* have it in you; I was afraid for a moment you were all brain, all set to see things wrong. . . . You do see that those lights care nothing for your heavy thoughts. They dance, they delight in being—for fun and joy. A cabbage doesn't work to be a rose, and the rose is content, too, isn't it, just to be a rose?"

"But one must work!"

"Work that is play, and play that is work," he responded. "Don't miss life, Frau Professorin, while you work, don't go through it with closed eyes. Gaze at it, see it, love it."

I tried to look into the reflections he was throwing into the river. Very gently he put his hand over mine. I woke and drew it away quickly.

"Oh!" I said, as my mother rushed in, "Oh!"

It had been so wonderful. I thought he had cared for ideas—and here he was putting his hand on mine, and my mother struck.

"So you're a rotter like all the other men," I heard my voice mutter, incredibly. I did not know whether he heard. We went on walking, I more than ever sublimating into intellectual talk anything I might have felt. The dawn was beginning to match the gray stones of Paris as once more we reached my hotel. The porter opened the door and yawned. He wasn't even surprised. I was a hardened case.

We had one more night. We talked and walked so long that at its end I was almost in a trance. My universe was topsy-turvy, everything jumbled, confused, unanchored. What would I be going home with? A churning, questioning, uprooted world of ideas I had never thought before. Would I be able to communicate with my old friends at all?

I must have said something like that because I heard Steffens say: "Your whole life will be one of unlearning, little girl. They do that to us—they impress their picture on our mind as tightly as a corset—as they did to me; it has taken me all my long life to undo. It may be too late for you, you're older than I; for though you're young and curious and you could discover, you know it too firmly. You'll pass your exams, you'll serve Them, you'll do it all correctly. You won't commit a crime."

He was talking as I had not heard him talk; he sounded blue, depressed. Should I be a criminal?

Then his voice brightened, upsetting it all again. "But you will commit crimes, you must, a person like you must break out. Only, when you've committed your crime, make it conscious, compre-hended, yours; don't justify it and call it 'a mistake.' That way you'll never know what it was you did wrong." He was oddly serious again; his voice was almost husky.

"I think all your life you'll search. Where is it you want to go?" he went on after a pause, and I hesitated. Did I know exactly what he meant, or was I always too literal?

"All my life I've dreamed secretly of the Amazon," I ventured, "so far away, so strange, exciting and unexplored, it means Magic and Adventure to me. . . ." Stef seemed to understand.

"You may never get there," he said slowly, "but always remember it's the journey that counts. Just keep those big brown eyes of yours on the road. I have an Amazon too, you know, but it's right here. It's called—the Seine."

We both gazed at that river in a long, long silence that Steffens broke, again in his bantering old voice: "But what shall I call you, Frau Professorin? You must have a name."

"But my name is—"

He brushed that aside. "I can't call you what They call you. That's your world's name, the name of the girl that's going to do what They say. I want a name for what I see in you, what I like to call the Divine Purpose. It has a hard time breaking through the argumentative Fräulein who goes along with the dubs, but I see someone—who could break away."

A solitary barge, blacker than the water and the night, sailed slowly up the river. Once more the realization came with a sharp pain—I was leaving all this. "I want this never to change," I almost sobbed, "I want it never to stop."

"That's my girl," Steffens suddenly said happily, his old and laughing voice quite re-established. "Who was it who wanted never to grow up? Who stayed a wise boy always?"

"Peter Pan" was my low answer.

"Peter!" he exclaimed. "That's your name. Peter! A boy!"

# 6

## MAYBE, PERHAPS—BUT

I might never have seen Lincoln Steffens again, but on the Channel boat, the same chuffing little Channel steamer that had brought me over so many aeons ago, I was overcome by the feeling that I must not lose him. But what could I write? I watched the gulls scream, fly and scream back, catch their fish in mid-sea, gobble and wheel. I tasted the salt spray and said sternly to myself: "Get your feet on the ground, you've been warned you can't go on living in those clouds."

"It will take a lifetime to digest," another me whispered, and then there was a comforting afterthought: "No hurry: look, see, enjoy." I had used one of his phrases. I sat a long time, then fished a pencil out of my purse—no, I mustn't lose him. I wrote simply that I hoped I would see him again.

And then it was back into harness and cramming for four months to make up for that lost time—constitutions and commonwealths, wages, profits, no diminishing returns, economic laws, and books in small print; no magic and poetry, but facts, facts, facts.

The trees turned yellow, leaves drifted down, it grew foggy and cold. When the week-long examination started, I warned everyone I must have no interruptions, must work every night, sleep ten hours, see no one. At the end of the first long day, as I dropped onto my bed, exhausted, Mother brought me a telegram:

ARRIVING LONDON TONIGHT    NEED NEW CLOTHES    STEF

Once more the telephone rang. Oh, I did like that voice!

"I had to come to London, only London tailors make my clothes right; will you have time for me? I want to talk to the English, find out what they're thinking. Will you dine with me tonight?"

Under Mother's astonished look I dressed and ran out of the house.

It was midnight when I returned. Every evening of that crucial examination week I dined out with Steffens, slept six hours, and never opened a book. (Nevertheless, a month later I had made my First.)

I took a job, when my examinations were over, with the American commercial attaché—rather a dry piece of research, but they paid me, and I was still working magically with "the Americans." I could contribute at home—and I would be independent. Every day Stef walked up and down in front of the embassy, waiting for me for lunch or dinner, and the attaché, a rather jolly fellow, was tickled.

"Steffens waiting downstairs for you," he would call out, "been stalking around for twenty minutes." I was glad now that Americans took "all that" so naturally, without the criticism or disapproval that always awaited me at home.

I took Steffens to Fabian lectures and we talked with the Webbs, Wells, Bertrand Russell. We went to tea on the terrace of the House with Ernest Thurtle, George Lansbury's son-in-law, and Josiah Wedgwood, an old single-tax companion-in-arms. I liked the mutually appreciative relationship of Stef and his British friends. The handsome young writer Francis Meynell had returned from Russia with crown jewels romantically hidden in chocolate creams, and I listened to him and Steffens talk endlessly of the new Russian world. Or we would get for dinner Ivy Low, now married to the Bolshevik Maxim Litvinov, and her tall, red-cheeked sister Letty, animated, vivid, bold-eyed, who lived in the bohemian world I envied. They introduced Stef and me to some of the early psycho-analysts, who entertained us with their case histories.

My father went away to Germany, but I was able to bring him and Stef together once. We invited Marion Phillips, and all went well at first while Steffens related in detail the story of the McNamaras, which he could tell so movingly because he was so deeply involved. They were the labor "dynamiters" condemned for blowing up the Los Angeles *Times,* whom Stef and Clarence Darrow had saved from execution. Father listened fascinated. But when the conversation turned to the Russian Revolution and Bolshevism, the evening, to my dismay, exploded into astonishing hostility and bitterness from Marion. Like the official Labour party, she was implacably opposed to the Russian Revolution, but it did not occur to me that her enmity and personal rudeness may have been partly due to her realization that she was losing me.

However, it was another signal to me that I might not be able to make Steffens acceptable to my circle. When at his invitation I took him to lunch with my college friends, to whom he talked as he had talked to me in Paris, I thought they would be equally bowled over; but all they said to me afterward was, "You're not thinking of marrying him, are you?" And Stella Morel added, "Youth should mate with youth." I was astonished at her assumption.

All the same, feeling was growing between Stef and me. We wandered around London, as we had Paris, walked and talked, but now more and more about ourselves. Stef told me about his early life in California, his boyhood with his pony, his student days at Berkeley, in Germany, and at the Sorbonne, and then the saga of his becoming a famous reporter in the early days of the century and his sudden rise to fame—or notoriety—as a "muckraker" of American cities. This was the name President Theodore Roosevelt had applied to a group of journalists and sociologists who exposed organized bribery and corruption in American life. These exposures had made Steffens' reputation and skyrocketed the circulation of his magazine, *McClure's*, "so that," he told me, still wondering at it a little, "I couldn't travel in a train without seeing someone reading one of my articles." Stef had stopped being a "reformer"—he disliked the moral implications of the word—but his reputation as one persisted.

Stef talked to me a lot about Jack Reed.

"Jack is practically my adopted son," he reminisced lovingly, "a genial, joyous poet, who can 'see,' as I think you do, Peter. He went to Russia and was bitten by a bug—he found a cause and grew serious, a fanatic. I love Jack." He told me about Reed coming home from Mexico "with so much stuff that he didn't know how to write it, and I sat whole nights with him editing him into articles, him, not his stuff; I showed him what he had."

"Another Peter?" I suggested, with a little envious stab.

Stef glanced at me, then grinned. "Another Peter—in a way."

We spent all our free time together, and his American friends seemed to expect to find us together. I liked that, I liked not being just a daughter-at-home any longer. Every night we went to a play, dinner, the opera—just two people, not a family group. It would have been unthinkable not to be together. Yet something loomed, some menace. "I ought to be going," Stef would say. "I have my new suits, my interviews are done, I've seen my friends." But he did not go. We discussed our relationship, and Stef kept reassuring us.

"Leave it to me, Peter, trust me. I'll see that no harm comes to you." Or "What is it, Peter, loving friendship, friendly love? Categories—pah! The Greeks ruined us with categories, but we don't have to accept them; we can make our own rules." He took the responsibility and wove his magic, and I trusted him, as I trusted "authority"—in this case not only to do nothing "wrong" (in my mother's sense) but also not to "break my heart." I had romantic notions about love; one loved once and forever, so if this was not that, because it couldn't be, it must be something else. What it was, I left to him; he was the older and the wiser one. And, of course, I should not marry one so much older.

Yet, walking down Kingsway after that Soho lunch with my college friends, I was very silent.

"What's the brown study, Peter?" Stef asked. "Are your friends afraid I'll do something wrong to their friend?"

"Have you any children? Are you married?" I suddenly asked. It had come to me all of a sudden that I knew nothing about his private life.

"No, but why do you ask, Peter?"

"Did you ever have any?" I pursued.

Long afterward Stef told me that this was the moment when he thought, Perhaps . . . no . . . but maybe . . . an impossible dream . . . I might give him a child, the child he had always wanted and had never had. What he told me at the time was that his wife had died years ago, that he had been rather solitary since, except for a relationship that still existed. "She expects me now in Paris," he said. "I have an obligation—it's an old relationship, Peter." He was reluctant to talk about it—as he apparently preferred not to use her name—and I did not press him. He told it in his own way.

"I want to be fair to her, Peter, as I want to be fair to you," and he related in outline a situation that could only rule out any possibility of a permanent relationship for us. He had been engaged to a fellow student, "G." In the years in Germany he jilted G for Josephine, who "remained my wife for nineteen years, till her death. In that time, G married a man she did not love, who, through a dreadful accident, became an invalid in a wheelchair. And then, a few months after Josephine's death, when I was lonely and unhappy, by sheer accident I ran into G on Fifth Avenue." He paused in his story, a little painfully.

"And then and there," Stef continued, "we picked up where we had left off twenty years before. G did not feel she could ask her invalid husband for a divorce, and she spends only vacations with me or the periods I'm in New York." It had been like this for eight years. She still loved Stef. She expected soon to retire from the college where she taught, and then hoped to be able to share more of Stef's life. "I cannot do the same thing to her twice," Stef objected, and I agreed. So, apart from my own considerations, anything but our odd companionship was out of the question. Singular, anomalous, irregular it might be, unusual, but I could not break up that relationship with G, and Stef obviously felt bound by it. "I'll manage it somehow," he affirmed.

It was Mother who flashed angry eyes and grim questions at me, "offensive and insulting" questions, as I told her, but to which there were, in her terms, no answers. When I did quote anything that Stef said, she was contemptuous: "Words, fine words! What are his intentions?"

The charmed month had to end, the magic strap itself back into its box. Stef had to leave. That first telegram of his seemed a century ago, from another universe. Everything had changed.

I went with him on the train to Dover and waved to the Channel boat till it was a blurred speck. Going back, I could only stare out of the train window, and then I found a little note he had written the night before, in London.

Sweet Peter:
  You thought I was gone, didn't you? Yes. And here I am saying "good-bye," just as if I hadn't said it afterwards and wouldn't say it before. And I'll be saying it again, and you'll be taking it seriously. No sense of humour. Yes. I know it's foolish, but let the fools be wise. No goodbye is goodbye, not when we so want to say Hello. So—as I said before—hello, Peter, dear, dear Peter.

I read it many, many times, then went home and crawled into bed; I was spent, I wanted only to be alone. Instead, Accusation sat down at my side.

"What did he say? How did you leave it? Is he coming back? What has he asked you?" She sat stonily, my accusing mother, and I could only turn to the wall and weep.

"Is he fair to you? Did he say—did he say what he intends?" And when I did not answer, she was angry.

"It doesn't help to lie there silent. I suppose it's different because it's you, I suppose no one has ever met a man before. You're an exception to all rules."

"It isn't like that," I could only sob weakly. I knew I had to fight, alone, but with what weapons? And it wasn't like that.

Then came the old, old charge: "You know the whole thing is only an idea." My mother could still exert her influence and she was very emphatic. Besides, there was G, in Paris with him now.

"Did he kiss you?" The question shot out. "Oh, he did? How did he kiss you? Like a father?"

I wrote Stef every day. I poured out everything, but after days of inquisition, like Thomas I doubted. "If we must say good-by, let us say it while we love," I wrote. "We may have to lead our lives apart." G was there, with him, so I had no right. I could, I had to assume, get over it, somehow, someday. If we had to live our lives apart—as we did—let us be close, intimate friends. One of the things Stef had said to me was, "When you marry, as one day you will, Peter, I will be your friend and the friend of your children —they will be partly mine." Perhaps, but I would never marry now, I was sure. Instead, I would bury myself in work.

I learned that life went on, one looked the same on the outside. My job at the American Embassy continued, but I was more than ever determined to get to America, and studied carefully the stream of Americans that flowed through the London School. Felix sent me students, ex-students, and friends. Lewis Mumford came to edit the *Sociological Review*, Felix Morley, brother of Christopher Morley, to study postgraduate Economics (so that, as Cannan's assistant later, I corrected the essays of the future editor of the Washington *Post* and president of Haverford College). Ordway Tead, later president of the New York Board of Education, and Carter Goodrich, another professor-to-be, came from Harvard. Beardsley Ruml arrived with seventy-five million dollars to spend for the Laura

Spellman Rockefeller Foundation and asked me to "advise him how to spend it." (For a brief moment I took the question seriously.) I saw Ben Cohen often. He had become increasingly devoted, but inside myself I was marking time.

Then came Opportunity. The Society of Friends (Quakers) had relief missions in many countries, and I was thinking of joining one, when a letter arrived from Stef saying that he would be in Vienna with his friend E. A. Filene, the Boston businessman. "Why not come, Peter? Filene is looking for a secretary to take back home, and you might be the person."

It was still a Steffens who had decided with me that marriage for us was out of the question. So I was a little disconcerted, on arriving in Vienna, to find him at the station. I could do no more than greet him; the Quakers, who were also there, looked askance at a new recruit meeting a man. They whisked me off to a large apartment in the Sixth *Bezirk* that had belonged to a wealthy family, with parquet floors and marble sunken bath; and next morning Hilda Clark and Kathleen Courtney assigned me to three "depots" where I must dole out meticulously rationed food to five thousand hungry people.

Long lines of thin, desperate women shuffled up or wilted in queues for the carefully weighed few ounces of cocoa, sugar, or rice we could give them. "We keep the books of desperation," an Austrian woman helper said. "I must get my husband to a sanatorium," a woman with a baby whimpered, "he spits blood." A gaunt creature with stringy hair stood with a paralytic boy. I dealt with such burned-out lines of people all afternoon, and, seething with its horror, burst in on Filene and Stef that night, sitting at dinner, in a warm, brightly lit room at the Bristol Hotel, with bankers, industrialists, and diplomats, both American and Austrian. We ate four courses of luscious food—game, cakes, whipped cream; this was how black marketeers and foreign visitors lived in Vienna. Filene was constantly called to the telephone to advise, or make more appointments with, "leaders," the Chamber of Commerce, businessmen utilizing Vienna's misery. I had to go home early and had no chance to talk to Stef alone.

The musician lay on a straw pallet in a cold bare room. Large eyes stared from under thin red hair in a white face; a bony, creased woman stared, too, and three ragged children shrank back with their huge eyes fixed on me. The man lay emaciated and motionless on his matted straw.

"I haven't eaten for three days," he said weakly, "if I could get work—just enough for a little food. I burned my last manuscript for warmth." His dull eyes closed wearily.

This was a typical scene, one result of the war and the peace I had watched "us" make in the glamour and glory of Paris. "Self-determination of peoples" meant the break-up of the corrupt old Austro-Hungarian Empire—the phrases had sounded good, but this was the reality. Vienna was cut off from the countryside that had provided it with food and milk, city and country were hopelessly divided, and a million people in Vienna starved.

The worst were the children. Legs so crooked with rickets that the child could no longer walk were operated on, the bones broken and reset; and a month after, the child was back in the hospital, its legs deformed as before. My visits to the Pirquet Clinic appalled me. Whose was the responsibility? The owner of Kafka's castle was not more difficult to locate. The Quakers could not make much of a dent; a million people went on starving.

One day in that first week I saw Filene at his hotel window embracing a girl.

"That's the one he's hired as secretary," Steffens, who had come out to meet me, remarked sadly. "I'm sorry, Peter, I didn't know when I wrote you what he was really after." And that was that, as far as a job in America went. I felt ill at ease in the luxury hotel, eating that black-market food when I was seeing such daily misery; besides, the Quakers disapproved of my evening absences. I could not talk to Stef alone; it was not the same, the circumstances were wrong—I did not know what it was. Had G come between us? Had I killed it? I found out later that Steffens, too, believed he had settled a war within himself. We believed we had made the proper, rational decision. I was almost relieved when he and Filene left.

I threw myself wholeheartedly into my work, and kept going all day. I undertook mercy jobs on my own: found a sanatorium for this tubercular old man, a bed in Doctor Pirquet's clinic for that skin-and-bone baby. I sought everywhere a job for a starving teacher; brushes or canvas for a painter; drugs, bandages, anesthetics, surgical instruments for hospitals now operating without them, or straw and cardboard for makeshift bandages. I haunted the clinics, talked to everyone who might help, arranged at least temporary palliatives. I wrote to friends in England for money, clothes, and food, and worked on a dozen possible schemes for help, like exporting Viennese manufactures, lace, embroideries, art, or arranging for our universities to adopt students. I wrote articles, stories, appeals for English and Viennese papers. And amidst all this I struck up a close friendship with one Viennese family, the Schreibers. Regina, the oldest, was serious and musical, and a medical student like her tall, earnest brother, Sigmund, lately returned from two years as a war prisoner. Emmie, the youngest, strikingly beautiful, was vivacious, irreverent, gay, sparkling, and always up to something. She could wheedle anything, from opera tickets to a weekend boating trip. "Why not?" And she would laugh mockingly. "They like it, and they're all racketeers anyway." I spent many evenings with them and took them to concerts, plays, lectures, the Staatsoper, the Burgtheater.

The family had been wealthy; their father had owned a factory. But they were Jews, and it had been "sacked by the Poles." Now they had nothing. The three lived in two tiny unheated rooms, and the girls said, "We've had no clothes for seven years"; but they did not lose heart, were gay and *echt* Viennese. Emmie always had some fascinating adventure story to make my eyes pop.

"Last night we slept three in a bed," she said casually one evening. "And did I have to keep Husband on his good behavior!" Or, "I went with three girl friends to an orgy, strictly for the dinner, of course; rather hot, but I kept my purity." Luscious Emmie, so frank and outspoken, with her black hair, large dark-blue eyes fringed with black lashes, and her camellia skin, charmed me with her constant escapades on the razor's edge.

In the contrasts of Vienna, where wealthy black marketeers rubbed shoulders with the destitute, I was witnessing the disintegration of a whole society. Social groups and classes were disappearing like villages under lava. Yet there was an unexpected vitality in this flickering phantasmagoria. The Viennese theater was extraordinarily alive; people were as hungry for art as for food. I went to concerts and chamber-music evenings, and haunted the caustic political cabarets I loved. We sat through ravishing performances of Richard Strauss (early performances of *Ariadne auf Naxos,* and *Die Frau ohne Schatten*) , Ibsen, Shakespeare, Hugo von Hofmannsthal. I saw the first incredible performance of *Heartbreak House* in German, went to Arthur Schnitzler's comedies and the sizzling sex dramas of Frank Wedekind. I couldn't believe my eyes when, in *Schloss Wetterstein,* an American "dollar king" offered a girl a hundred thousand dollars to tell her life story, tortured her with her degradation, and when she stabbed herself in front of him with his knife, he writhed wildly on the stage.

"*Lustmord,*" remarked my friend Emmie, matter-of-factly. "Some fun, eh, kid?" Well! It wasn't everyone could see a murder of lust on the stage. I tried to imagine Mother seeing me at this play.

Because of my knowledge of German, I was assigned to liaison with the Austrian press. Otto Pohl, the head of the Press Bureau, sharp-featured, small, cynical, was a radical critic of everything, in the best Viennese style. (Later he became editor of an Austrian newspaper in Moscow.) His assistant was a highly intelligent, well-informed Russian boy of seventeen, Constantine Oumansky, who wrote on modern German art and later became Soviet Ambassador to Washington and Mexico.

I visited often with Karl Kraus, an original, prolific Austrian Swift, the owner-editor of the satiric *Die Fackel.* He was a pacifist, poet, essayist, and playwright, and devoted a lifetime to excoriation of corruption in politics and the press. I heard him read Shakespeare alone on a stage to packed audiences. Central European intellectual rebels seemed to have this mixture of biting wit, cynicism, and poetry, like Bertolt Brecht and Peter Altenberg, Kurt Weill, Georg Grosz.

Dr. Karl Renner, the gray-haired Chancellor, wanted me to help him publish articles in foreign newspapers. He sat in an old palace chamber, with polished floors and brocaded chairs, smoking a large cigar, and seemed to have plenty of time. I asked him his views on *Anschluss.*

"My dear child, why talk about *Anschluss* when we are alone?" Then he would wave his cigar at me. "It is not your interest in these subjects that attracts me, or your mind or intelligence, dear young lady, but . . ." He asked me to help him translate his books, *Austria's Rebirth* and *Marxism, Socialism, and the Internationale,* but still ended with the same old suggestion. "What about spending a week somewhere together, translating my books if you will. . . . No, I suppose it would be all over the papers. I can't afford that."

It did not seem to strike him that I might not be able to afford it (let alone want to), but when I entered my objections, he argued: "Everything is permitted to artists and poets."

"I'm neither, alas."

"Ah—and journalists," he amended.

Almost every Austrian made a play for almost any woman, especially an adventurous, eager girl like myself, whose particular brand of rather eccentric innocence may well have appeared to them like something else. Married businessmen took me, more or less discreetly, to *chambres séparées* in restaurants, sure that no girl ever said no. I did not intend to "tease," I was merely indoctrinated to believe that every man acted like that; so it became to me an amusing kind of game, and I liked the attention, even the risk and the temptation. The romantic love I was looking for did not look like this; this was just fun—surely permissible fun?

I did lose my heart every now and again. The person I liked to run around with was Frederick Kuh, then correspondent of the *Daily Herald,* a hard-working, intense young newspaperman. He allowed me to run occasional errands for him or go with him on assignments, and he was the one young man our strict Quaker directors did not frown upon, since he helped them in many ways. Once he sent me secretly on a lifesaving errand to Budapest, where, with my uniform and Red Cross armband, I could take letters unnoticed. I was told nothing about the nature of the errand, and was happy when Kuh later told me I had saved the lives of several young men involved in the Bela Kun uprising, who were to have been hanged.

Felix Frankfurter came to Vienna on his honeymoon. Tall, delicate, willowy, Marion was as quiet, slow, and serene as Felix was fast, excitable, and energetic. He was looking for articles for a liberal magazine his friends had recently started, the *New Republic.* Felix told with gusto of visits, talks, interviews with "leading personalities" in every country, Beneš, Masaryk, Stinnes, Einstein.

"What a charming fellow, Einstein, so other-worldly. We reported to him that Haldane is studying his mathematics all over again to better understand relativity, and the old boy was delighted: '*Aber was sagen Sie? Aber wirklich?*'"

Marion took up: "His wife said, 'You wouldn't believe how absent-minded Albert is, he goes to class with only one sock.'"

"And about that railroad ticket," Felix interrupted. "He paid a ten-mark bill for a fare of nine seventy, and the clerk suggested he give him another seventy pfennigs. 'But I've already given you more than the fare.' When the clerk explained he could give a one-mark bill for change, Einstein thought a moment and then broke out in a radiant smile. '*Gott, wie einfach!*' he exclaimed."

"We're going to offer Freud ten thousand kroner [about twenty dollars] for an article for the *New Republic*," Felix rattled on, "d'you think that's enough?"

But Freud was not in Vienna, and Felix asked me to take the message to him when he returned. I did, too. I bearded the old man timidly; his study desk was littered with objects, and the room was close and stuffy. Freud sat at his desk, rather sullen, and when I told him my errand, he burst out: "Why do they think we should write for the layman, who doesn't know anything about the techniques of psychology or brain processes or functional diseases? They wouldn't ask a physicist to write magazine articles for laymen, would they? It's the same for our science!"

What I had liked best about their honeymoon visit was the romantic love of Mr. and Mrs. Felix. They made eyes at each other, squeezed hands, pressed feet under the table, were upset when they were apart for an hour. It was like a book.

Before I left, I called on Doctor Josef Redlich, the finance minister whom we had studied at college, and who wrote Kaiser Karl's speech of abdication. He traced postwar politics for me in fascinating detail, and said he had known Lenin in "the old days."

"What do you think will happen now?" I asked him.

"All Europe is going to be anti-state," Redlich answered. "Bureaucracy, state interference is a last spurt of the old candle. Bolshevism is a small, unimportant stream and will peter out." He had obviously seen the future and, like so many, did not want any part of it.

Home from Vienna, I traveled in northern England, lecturing on the starvation, the misery, the ricketty legs of the children. I wrote articles appealing for help, and was even fairly successful, but it was a drop in an ocean. This was 1922, and still the Allied blockade, which had been maintained around Germany since the end of the war, continued. Something more fundamental than the Quakers' good works was needed to re-establish Europe; my six

Viennese months had led me no nearer to knowing what this might be.

I was still groping, searching, too, for a passionate relationship. Since I was of my time, it had to be Passionate with a Purpose, like Wells's *Joan and Peter* or *Ann Veronica*. I examined every young man with the unasked questions, not only "Is this he?" but "Would our ideals, our purposes, unite?"

Marion Phillips wanted me to work for her; I declined. The Sidney Webbs asked me—they were always on the lookout for bright students. My visit with that remarkable couple was one of those extraordinary afternoons so many people have written about. They sat at either end of the tea table. Mrs. Webb asked a question, and while she poured tea, Sidney finished it; he started some comment, and when he was called to the telephone, she continued. Embarrassed anyway, I did not know which one to answer. They were very complimentary to my "scholar's reputation," very persuasive —and most disappointed when I refused. But how could I sit day after day over such problems as municipal tramways or the rate of interest on local bond issues?

When Graham Wallas asked me to be his assistant, I was appalled at the prospect of being "locked up" in a college. "But I want to live!" I exclaimed to that rare and understanding teacher, and he understood.

In Germany on holiday I wrote for a London paper some articles on Baden-Baden's black marketeers eating whipped cream while babies starved. I was so proud to have broken into print that I sent copies to my friends—who took the wind out of my sails by upbraiding me for giving ammunition to those "who opposed the liberal line of helping Germany recover."

I tried other journalism, but newspaperwomen were still a rarity in England. At the *Daily News* the editor looked me over. "You're young," he said curtly. "What experience have you had?"

"None—so far." My voice sounded weak and unimpressive, not at all like my fantasy of bearding the dragon. "But some job has to be the first," I defied, but rather timidly.

"We can't take the time to train people."

"Maybe I'm too young now," I said, "but one must start sometime. When I've had enough experience, I'll probably be too old." But Bouverie Street was not convinced. When I went to George

Lansbury, the radical editor of the *Daily Herald* and Stef's good friend, I fared no better. He listened, biting his false teeth. "You might write on fashions," he said doubtfully, "women on newspapers write on fashions or cooking." I thanked him and walked out.

Felix Frankfurter had said to me, "Your energy and vitality make America the place for you." Steffens had once asked Graham Wallas what he thought I was "cut out" for, but when he suggested writing, Wallas had countered, "But why make a writer out of a first-class executive?" What should I do? I could not just go to the United States without a job. Surely something would come down some pike.

So I went back to LSE and taught Economics for a year as assistant to Professor Cannan. I lectured for the WEA (Workers' Educational Association) , explaining to tired clerks and office workers the magnificent benefits of socialism and nationalization, which they could not have cared less about. I did six months' research on nationalized industries for a body of Conservative M.P.s. Sir Arthur Steel-Maitland, who owned the profitable Rio Tinto copper mines, told me to be objective, but they wanted proof that nationalization did not work—Lloyd George might bring in a bill to nationalize coal. When Lloyd George did not do so, my work and the committee petered out without a whimper.

Then I took a tutoring job. Lady R. had asked the School for "someone to help my demobilized son bone up for a Parliamentary career." I went to see her in her Mayfair flat.

"James should serve his country," she elucidated. "Our tradition is to govern, but James has not been interested so far. I want you to create interest for him, explain in attractive terms the issues that will come up and how he is to vote—as a Tory, of course." She looked at me doubtfully. "Aren't you a little young?"

I took on James, who knew nothing about politics and who yawned as we took up housing.

"A lot of people don't have decent places to live," I started.

"Really? Too bad. Why don't they get them?"

When we had covered housing, unemployment, and other domestic issues, he complained: "But the Labour party takes the common-sense view; I'm supposed to be a Tory M.P. What do the Tories say?" And, when I told him, "But that's not as sensible as the Labour party, dash it all."

Soon his mother sat down ominously to tea with me. "My son

feels that he is not getting a sound basis for a Conservative platform," she said. "He complains that the clearer you make it, the
more socialist he becomes."

"I've been as neutral as I could," I defended.

"There are two sides to every question," Lady R. retorted. And
that—once more—was that.

I wanted to be on my own and make my own living, but I kept
turning down jobs, all sorts of jobs, and wondered why. Had Steffens
disturbed me too deeply? Had Paris, the experience of being taken
up to the heights, spoiled me for more mundane opportunities?

# 7

## "VERWEILE DOCH . . ."

Among this succession of jobs I undertook, none of them related to another. One was reading for a time to a blind woman at the British Museum. She asked me to talk about myself.

"May I tell you something?" she said suddenly one day. "I have been studying you, you're a strange mixture—intellectually very mature but emotionally quite undeveloped." I was astonished. How could she tell? "I can tell," she said, "even if I can't see."

So I continued my search, in the British Museum, in jobs, in people and books. I found a saying by Walther Rathenau, which seemed to give me a clue: "The stronger the personality, the more isolated it is from life and the more it requires love." Love was certainly what I needed, but you couldn't order it.

Father had been ill and depressed from blood poisoning. On my return from Paris I saw him one day crying, and though the doctor explained that blood poisoning did that, I had never seen him cry and felt it wasn't only the illness. The war had wiped out my father's universe, and he foresaw more horrors, predicting, "They'll take it out on the Jews." He sat in his armchair reading war books day after day.

But something else was wrong, and an operation was undertaken; he did not recover properly and was operated on a second time. His doctors assured us there was no trace of any growth, the pathologist's report was negative; but the wound did not heal. His convalescence dragged on and prevented his working. When he got no better, Mother took him to another doctor, who reported cancer. The original pathologist had made a mistake and all the treatments over two years, including electric massage at Wiesbaden, had been wrong. The doctor gave him six months.

Mother found a villa in Belsize Park, in a dull little street with no view and no garden. I never regretted anything so much as the loss of the Finchley Noris. Father sorely missed our house with its country fields, view, and sense of a home.

Mother said he must not know the truth; we must not show our anguish. Father's parents had both died of cancer, and when the pain became unendurable, he might guess. I ached then for Mother, and I suddenly saw clearly and with a sympathy I felt too rarely for her how the kernel of her life was the man she loved so deeply.

About this time Heinemann, the publishers, asked me to translate a German best seller, *The Diary and Letters of Otto Braun*. Braun was a brilliant young boy killed in the war, a precocious scholar, poet, and critic, who even in boyhood had given promise of being a considerable person. I thought of this as a gesture to repay some of the debt I felt I owed the young men killed; it might also show that not all Germans were the atrocity beasts of the war propaganda.

Havelock Ellis wrote the preface and I visited him a few times. He was an astonishing old man, extremely tall and imposing, with a large head, white hair, and a bushy square beard. He lived alone in a small flat and, to my surprise, made the tea and carried in the tray. Men were not supposed to be domestic, I thought.

"My wife lives in another flat," Ellis explained, "we feel that's better for our relationship." When he discussed marriage, I kept very still lest he stop, but I was uncomfortable because he kept his eyes glued on the opposite wall and did not look at me. He developed this habit, I supposed, when he interviewed women about their sex lives for his *Psychology of Sex*. Presumably one talked more freely that way, but it gave me an eerie feeling. He did not ask me about my sex life. I was rather hurt.

I wanted to leave home and be on my own, and my odd jobs did not afford this. A chance came when Sir Charles Myers offered scholarships for his Institute of Industrial Psychology. This new science of practical, applied psychology set out to discover under what conditions workers could work better and faster, and so cut fatigue. The charge was made that employers would then speed up production and cut wages, so workers were suspicious of "time-motion studies," but I told myself that improvement in methods might increase welfare. And psychology of any kind could be a door for me to understand more about people and life, and was not that what I wanted? So when, after an interview, Sir Charles offered me a scholarship for the Psychology Laboratory at Cambridge under F. C. Bartlett, I accepted. I could be no help with Father, but I would come home weekends. And I would be getting to my romantic college spires after all.

I stayed in Cambridge a year. I rented an attic, just large enough for bed, table, bookcase—but mine. I was lonely, but at last I had a room of my own. I was seeking for the meaning of the universe and my place in it, but my scholarship and Professor Bartlett specified "data on the co-ordination of hand and eye." So I must find other avenues for philosophic answers, and sneaked into Sir Arthur Quiller-Couch's lectures on literature (sneaked because only registered English students were permitted). These were stimulating talks on the art of reading and the art of writing, famous lectures that jammed his auditorium and were later made into books. Every student who hoped to write followed "Q" eagerly, and for that hour I could feel I belonged to the elect. I also watched in awe the tall, spare, ascetic figure of A. E. Housman, in cap and gown, stalking, head down, along the Cambridge streets. I knew *A Shropshire Lad* by heart and felt I knew him, but I never dared break into his solitude. He looked such a gaunt, haunted ghost, I thought, that had seen something too terrible to tell.

I longed to see Steffens again, but he could not get back to England—he was denied a visa. It was a mystery who was keeping him out or why, and he bade me, through Josiah Wedgwood and other British friends of his in and out of Parliament, to try and find out. For a long time we had no success, but the trail finally led to Lloyd George; it appeared that he was afraid Steffens might embarrass him in England with the truth about the Bullitt Mission. Having authorized it, he had, when called to account by several hundred irate members of Parliament, denied any knowledge of it. Anyway, Steffens was prohibited from visiting any part of the British Empire for four years; he joked later that but for this Pete might well have been four years older than he was.

In my little attic I sat down to write. Thoughts, moods, ideas, words crowded one another, but how did one put order and form into such a welter of emotions? When I was at my loneliest and most lost, my friend Ena, whom I had taken a great liking to during my last school year, suddenly asked to come and stay with me. She was a blue-eyed, fair-haired girl who had come on a scholarship and whose father was a tinker; she had no mother, was very independent, and at school had made fun of teachers in a way we would not have dared. I discovered her again, after several years, in a tiny Chelsea basement room, writing poetry, and she had told me of her lonely bohemian life. I introduced her to a friend on a newspaper, whom she married, but now she had been ill and was up against it; could she stay with me in Cambridge?

Could she! I ran around and found a larger room at the top of a tall narrow house leaning over Little St. Mary's Lane, where a dour landlady looked me over and said we couldn't bring men up to the room. "I usually rent only to students. I prefer men. You say you aren't students, and you aren't men; but I like having young men— young men students, of course I mean—and you are not young men, are you?" I essayed an adequate reason why we were not young men, but the landlady, pursuing her own thoughts, could only repeat, "Of course, if I let you have the room, you can't bring young men up here." It was a blow, for I had thought, with Ena's help, to achieve exactly that: to have wonderful, ecstatically eligible young men up here, make cocoa for them, talk, make friends and— who knows? So I challenged propriety. "Why not?" I said.

"You can't pretend it isn't a bed," she responded.

The room was not beautiful, with its black cooking ring and an old-fashioned washstand, but the crooked little lane was a Middle Age relic, and our view was over an ancient cemetery filled with lichen-covered slanting old gray headstones.

We lived a gay life together, enlivened by Ena's mocking humor, which could be expressed in satirical drawings, odes to our jug and basin or the aspirations of Man. We shared our young men, the beauties of King's Chapel, walks along the river, and the endearing old botany professor who had taken up Freud, needed a "patient" to practice on, and picked me as his guinea pig—with no appreciable result.

Our lane was an extraordinary place. We used to pass a child playing in the gutter, rather unkempt, but of no particular interest until we learned she was the issue of a father-daughter relationship. Her parents lived with many other relatives, whom we never disentangled, in a yellow walking stick of a house even narrower than ours, whose crenelated top leaned even more dangerously toward the cemetery. Every day I came home from my rather dull research cheered at the prospect of some new prank of my irreverent Ena. I had someone for my loneliness at last. But the big interest in our lane was a man who remained for a long time an intriguing enigma and the subject of endless mystified discussion. Jason (as I shall call him) was a middle-aged, lame, quaint eccentric, who blushed easily, wore a perpetually embarrassed look, a green Norfolk suit with short pants, bare knees, and leather sandals. He lived alone in an artily furnished studio, with bright rugs and cushions and woven curtains. A long wooden refectory table, and diverse smaller ones, were strewn with photographs of a rather beautiful young woman always nude. Jason spoke of her constantly, especially of her physical beauty, but it was months before I found out she was his divorced wife. Men and girl students dropped in any time of the day or night to talk to Jason confidentially, mysteriously, and privately.

After months of this unsolved riddle, Jason told us "older women who can be trusted" that his purpose was to teach uninitiated, inhibited, inexperienced students about sex. He not only explained, he demonstrated with "field work" in the woods. "I only take out exceptionally stubborn cases that might benefit," he said, "only the quite unversed who find grave difficulty. . . ." The sexual revolution, encouraged by the work of Havelock Ellis, Freud, Wells, and the First World War, was still new enough in England for puritanism to exact its toll and for "Victorian" problems to flourish, and Jason's tutorial aid may well have helped many a frightened soul. I rather admired him.

My own problems were not so easily solvable. Besides two serious proposals of marriage—which I spurned—the subject had come up several times with an odd assortment of people. The first was Ena's father, who appeared one day, a little unshaven man with work-gnarled hands, and took me punting. In the boat he said quite simply, "I would like it if you would be my wife, you're so pretty, young, and full of life, I can't imagine a girl I could love more." He was so earnest and wistful that I was moved and told him I was already engaged. He accepted this philosophically. "I'm not surprised," he said. When I got home, Ena chuckled. "Did Father propose to you? He does to every young girl, you know; I forgot to tell you. He's got no idea how old he is."

Then there was Harold, a geologist who was writing "a great work" and preparing to devote his life to mathematical geology. He talked about that pedantically and then, once more in a punt, quite suddenly changed his subject.

"I have something I should like to bring up," he began, solemnly, and I assumed it would be again his incomprehensible science, but no. "I have been giving my considered attention to my personal life, and I think you and I might gain from a combined enterprise." Had I heard properly? There was no emotion. "You must not be surprised," he said, "I have thought about this. You would contribute quite usefully to me; you see, you are my Solveig complex." "But what complex are you of mine?" I queried. "At least such a bargain should be reciprocal." When he insisted on a serious answer, I could but intimate that I was looking to marry a man, not a complex.

At a Psychological Congress in Oxford, where Professor Alfred Adler played a leading role, I came to know a young poet, George. Köhler and Kafka were presenting papers on the new *Gestalt* psychology, but I had wanted to hear Adler, largely, I think, because he came from Vienna. I translated for Adler; I liked his fat, good-natured easy manner and willingness to talk freely, so different from Freud's irritated aloofness. One of his remarks stuck in my mind; talking of a child's relation to its parents, Adler ruminated: "First they stand about the crib adoring each darling little gesture, the waving fist, the little pink toes; then the child grows older and where has all this loving admiration gone? He commits a fault, is slapped, sent to bed, stood in the corner; the indulgent, glorious world he has known vanishes. He cannot adjust. Will he ever find it again?"

George was in the group around Adler and asked me to his rooms to listen to his poems. We talked till midnight, and all next day; I was attracted, although he was a little unimpressive: blond, gray-eyed, compact, but the features a little too small. Still, you couldn't have everything. My last night we had cocoa very late and—something must happen. It did.

"I have to tell you . . ." George began. "I've been meaning to tell you, it was difficult. . . ." My heart beat. "We've had such a very good time, you are so understanding, there's this extraordinary sympathy between us. . . ." He paused. "I must tell you," he said, "that I am engaged."

I had given up my room, the last train had gone, I could not bring myself to ask if I might stay on his sofa. I wandered down the railway embankment and shivered all night in wet scrubby grass between old tin cans and piles of refuse.

Finally, there was black-haired, blue-eyed Frank, extremely handsome, again, with a head too large and heavy, I thought, and flat feet that turned out like a penguin's, but Ena considered him an answer to all prayers.

We went for a walking trip to the Peak District with another boy, Jerry, and I pretended it was Jerry I liked so that Ena could have Frank, but alas, Frank liked me. He was going to be a sculptor and entered for the Prix de Rome. I sat around his studio and posed for him, occasionally in the nude, but I could not fall in love. When we spent a night together, I made him promise even in bed that platonic friendship was preferable. Was it sublimation or was it something else?

What was wrong with me? Why couldn't I fall in love? Stef, of course, was a class apart.

Toward the end of my Cambridge year, H. G. Wells ran for Parliament as Labour candidate for London University, and asked some LSE students for help. The constituency consisted of London University teachers and students anywhere in the world, present and past; the campaign was carried on mainly by mail. I had known Wells slightly, but never before seen him troubled about the effects of his well-known unconventional behavior. Had we not regarded him as the apostle of women's rebellion and women's freedom? I was disillusioned when he wondered whether he ought to send out a letter justifying, possibly excusing, those actions. I was also surprised to find how little he knew of, and how childish he seemed about, practical politics.

He was defeated in the election, but what most humiliated him was the fact that he ran third to the Conservative and Liberal candidates.

I stayed in London for that 1923 election to canvass votes also for a favorite School of Economics teacher, R. H. Tawney, who was running in North Tottenham, then still a slum section of London. My friend Jean Flexner, niece of the Bernard Flexner of our Zionist Commission in Paris, was doing postgraduate work at LSE and wanted practical experience, so we canvassed together. We bought fish and chips and ate them from greasy newspapers as we knocked on peeling, dilapidated doors. Tired, worn, often sour-faced mothers, with hostile or listless eyes, would appear with five or six open-mouthed children clinging to their aprons, listen apathetically as we extolled the glories of life under a Labour government, and wearily shut the door. We grew lyrical in our efforts to keep those front doors open: "Labour will give you a decent house, a holiday with pay, a bathroom!"

Only once I elicited an excited response. A woman with four ragged children asked, "Will the Labour party abolish lords?" I hadn't boned up on this one. "I—er—imagine, when all the reforms are brought about, everyone is fed and housed and clothed, there'll be greater equality in general. I assume there won't be any need for the aristocracy."

"Then I wouldn't vote for you—I like lords," and she banged the door.

Father did not get up any more. The morphine successively lost its power and we must watch the face we loved contort with the effort to control the pain. He was always so pleased when I came home and told him everything that had happened to me that it was increasingly hard for me to accept the truth. When pain prevented talk, he would ask me to read to him, and I covered, in German, the whole of *Faust*, both parts, a lifelong love of his that we discussed when he could talk. I read Heine and Schiller, too, and *Der Trompeter von Säckingen* with its moving

*Behüt' dich Gott, es wär zu schön gewesen,*
*Behüt' dich Gott, es hat nicht sollen sein.*

One Saturday morning we were discussing some aspect of Faust's difficult philosophy. Father was not in pain; we had a wonderful talk, in which, to his amusement, I unexpectedly asked him the somewhat unphilosophical question "Have you any illegitimate children? I don't want to pry or anything, but I would like to know if I have any other brothers or sisters in the world."

Father enjoyed the idea of a daughter asking her father this. "It wasn't the way I was brought up," he laughed. We felt intimate as Father told me that, as far as he knew, no—he would gladly tell me if he did know of any. At this moment Mother came in and asked me to run an errand, but, not wanting to break into our mood, I asked if I might wait. Mother unexpectedly flared up.

"You just want to stay in the room alone with your father, you two always want to be alone!" I saw her cheeks go scarlet as she realized what she had said, and she ran quickly out of the room. I did not know if Father had noticed—nothing was said about it, then or ever—and I continued reading: *"Verweile doch, du bist so schön."* But I had gained an insight that might have made me feel more generous to Mother—too late.

I kept feeling I ought to have some last conversation with Father, about things I would regret forever not having discussed with him. But the pain grew worse. The doctor held him down so that he would not throw himself out of bed in torment. No drug helped, and when one evening he fell asleep, as I thought, I was momentarily relieved, till Mother uttered a strangling cry. "This is the last coma, he won't open his eyes again!"

She spoke the truth. At the end he suddenly cried "Tetrazzini! Tetrazzini!" and then the Cheyne-Stokes breathing began.

I took Mother to Brighton. I hoped sharing our grief would bring us together. Her loss was greater than mine, but perhaps I also resented the years she had had with Father, so much closer to him than I. And I felt unable to talk about my own life, so we walked along the waterfront in silence.

A trivial incident broke the tension. In the small bedroom we shared, a ceiling lamp hung too low, and as I vigorously brushed my long hair, one swing landed into the globe. It broke with a crash and Mother broke with it.

"Can't you be more careful, must you be so clumsy? Can't you watch what you're doing?" she scolded angrily, but my shattered self answered as sharply.

"Must you always scold? I'm grown up now, d'you think I did it on purpose? Did I want to break that lamp? Don't I regret it as much as you?" On and on. Then Mother burst into tears.

I did not feel I could give in and I would not apologize, but that night, as so often when I felt guilty or self-reproachful, I faced my meanness and hated my unkindness. What blocked me from expressing my real sympathy for my mother? When would this bitter struggle between mother and daughter ever end?

Soon after, I undertook an adventure inexplicable to myself. After Father's death I was ill with a mixture of migraine and misery, and Mother called in the substitute doctor of Father's last week. He thought there was nothing wrong with me that couldn't be cured, and shortly after this, I received in Cambridge a letter telling me he would like to spend the weekend. Reading between the lines, I tried to create romance. He was interesting. Should I let him come up, was he attracted to me? I tried to pretend he was, and when he arrived in his little car, I had almost convinced myself. When he told me he did not live with his wife because she suffered from heart trouble, I rationalized that I was also helping someone with a desperate problem.

We drove through beautiful country to a distant village inn. But when I went to register, I discovered the last name in the book to be that of a family acquaintance. Suppose she were downstairs now, eating dinner at this very moment? Of course I could not dine downstairs.

A dinner was sent up, lamb and "two veg"; I sat and shivered and could not eat. There was a step on the stair, his? No. Should I wait, undress? I arranged some flowers in a vase I had surreptitiously brought in my suitcase. I took out a book, then I rearranged the flowers.

Finally he came. He told me in detail what he had eaten, asked perfunctorily about my dinner, and did not wait for an answer. I did not know whether to talk while he undressed. I wondered whether to change, perhaps, from my blue pajamas to my pink nightdress, which I had also brought. Should I ask him? I fetched the flowers and put them on the night stand. "I thought perhaps— do you like Michaelmas daisies?"

"Why not?" he said. Unaware of my total inexperience, he began to grow irritated, and I more worried. How did one broach the question in my mind? He must know what I was worrying about, he was a doctor. But when he said nothing, I stuttered: "But how—isn't there—shouldn't—?" His annoyance grew at my nervous fears, and he assured me impatiently he would "look after everything, take care of everything."

Then, very fast, everything happened—as far as he was concerned —and, satisfied without my participation, he turned with a deep sigh of what sounded like contentment and fell asleep.

With no one in the immediate vicinity apparently concerned with me, I got up on tiptoe and sat silently by the window—until dawn.

And that was certainly not that.

Cambridge was coming to an end. One day I stood in a bookshop, depressed and aimless, when a small, compact, bizarre-looking young man addressed me. "I'm editing a series of scientific books with

I. A. Richards," he said. "I'd like to talk to you. Will you come back with me to my room?" It was C. K. Ogden, a writer, and editor of a well-known scientific series.

We climbed a narrow rickety stair above a fried-fish shop to a small dirty room. The dusty walls were plastered with yellowed newspaper clippings; used coffee cups stood about, piles of books lay untidily on floor, chairs, and table, and in a corner stood a shabby red plush sofa with its springs and stuffing hanging out.

"How do you like this room?" he asked.

"Are you serious?"

"You only think it's ugly," Ogden said fiercely. "That's the tyranny of conventional aesthetic ideas. This may be a beautiful room."

"And the sofa?"

"Beautiful," he said. "You only think . . ."

"I don't only think I smell fried fish."

"But you think you don't like that smell."

The conversation seemed to be like my life, getting nowhere. Then he said, "You translated a German book rather well. Would you have a go at another? We have a book about experiments on anthropoid apes by a German professor, Wolfgang Köhler, who has founded a new school of psychology, *Gestalt.* Richards and I want it for our series."

"And?" I stalled.

"You'll find the experiments absorbing. Köhler was a war prisoner on Tenerife and found these anthropoid apes there, so he experimented with them for six years. On the basis of his results he's evolved this new theory."

I said I'd think about it.

And then, on Father's birthday, Steffens came back.

## PART II

# THE THIRTIES—ACUTELY

# 8

# THIS TIME TOGETHER

This time it was different.

I had accepted that it was over, that our relationship would be some kind of friendship, "nothing more." Yet how wonderful it was to see Stef again! And his pleasure was evident. Dinner was gay and warm. The heaviness lifted before we had begun to talk, and how we talked. There was so unbelievably much to say. He had been all over Europe, back and forth to the United States; his letters had grown few and unsatisfactory, and I had lost track. I had never imagined his return.

"I had to come for some new suits." Steffy grinned. "I do need some, Peter. I told Jo I had to get new clothes and he looked at me with malice, Jo did, and said, 'Peter—Peter, Stef.' He can be so wrong, Jo."

Well, but he wasn't wrong, malicious old Jo. When I went back to Cambridge next day and listened to the sound of my train, a decision had been made. We didn't know it for a while, but the decision did.

"*She* arrived that Christmas on the *Rochambeau,* you remember," Steffens said. He never used her name to me. He called her only "G." "And she wasn't well. I didn't tell her about us, not then, not at first. One day she kicked open a suitcase I had left half open, and your letter fell out, that long sad letter in which you discussed 'us,' all about us, and said you thought we ought not to go on perhaps except as friends. I told her it was all over, but she didn't believe me; she sensed the truth before I knew it."

"It was true all this time, then?" I asked, astonished. There was so much I had to understand.

"I tried to go back to the way it had been between her and me,"

*95*

Stef said. "At first I thought I might. We spent the winter in France and the summer in Italy, and then we went to the Riviera, but I had to leave Monte Carlo, Peter. I couldn't stand it. It was different, something had gone out of our relationship and she knew it. We were no longer lovers." I was sorry for G then, and I kept silent.

"Logic doesn't work in human relations, I guess," Stef said wryly, after a pause. "I try to understand myself as I tried to understand the bosses in my muckraking days. I 'got' them, but not myself. I don't know anything about myself. I'm as much a dub as any man can be about personal relations. They ought to teach that subject in school." But he did not regret much. For Steffens what was done was done.

We spent a month around the English countryside while I finished writing up my Cambridge research. We stayed at one old pub in Sussex that was once a smuggler's hideout, where Stef wrote in the guestbook, "Forty-eight doors to escape by and you don't want to escape." We had a happy get-together with old Lucien Wolf, now married to his Margaret. The Wolfs at least had no rules about what was "right" or "wrong" for us, and were delighted. Stef and Lucien taunted one another as of old. We told no one else; we were illicit, illegal, and deliriously happy.

But it was winter and Stef wanted to get away from England's wet and cold and fog, which settled on his chest. Louise Bryant, now married to William C. Bullitt, begged Stef to come to Paris and "talk about Jack" (Jack Reed had died in Russia of typhus). "Louise is going to have Billy's baby, and she wants to talk about her first husband, Jack." Stef laughed. "Okay, let's go." I had to have an excuse, of course. What explanation would I give my family, my friends? My research job was over. I looked up C. K. Ogden and told him I would do the translation of the ape book.

So Stef and I went to Paris, this time together.

Stef took me to his hotel, "where they know me," the tall, narrow Richepance on the corner of the Rue Richepance, a stone's throw from the Madeleine, the very heart of Paris. We took two rooms; I must preserve the proprieties. Then we went to call on Jo and Yvonne Davidson.

Jo Davidson had come once to London to arrange for a show and at Stef's request had agreed to "take a look at my girl." As we sat in the Cheshire Cheese, I was embarrassed and nervous. I had put on my sister's hat and, I think, a motoring scarf of my mother's. Jo grinned maliciously into his malevolent black beard. Seeing me look so grotesque, stupid, and tongue-tied, Jo must have said to himself, "He'll get over *her*." I was so inattentive to clothes, and how abashed and gawky! Stef told me later that that was about what Jo felt, and, in addition, he reported, "her nails are not manicured"—he had observed my uncosmetic student appearance. But Jo had reason not to want me in "the family": he loved and was possessive about his friend.

Both Davidsons adored Stef. Since he had helped Jo at the Peace Conference with his famous sitters, world leaders like Smuts, Hoover, Wilson, House, Lloyd George, Pershing, Jo had come to value Stef's judgment, and Yvonne found him a wise counselor both in her work and in the upbringing of her two rather difficult sons. Yvonne had recently started as a *couturière*, with her own shop, doing her own designing; with her rare creative taste and knowledge of American needs, she looked forward with some elation to making her way as an independent businesswoman. She had gone through the bohemian days of the artist—poverty with Jo, "not knowing where the children's next meal was coming from," and sometimes being thrown out of studios—so that independent financial security seemed to her a boon much to be desired. Yvonne's was an old French family, De Kerstraet—her aunt was the novelist Bis; she had grown up in France but gone to live in America. One day, at eighteen, she had asked a big New York department store for material and scissors and, to the firm's astonishment, designed a stunning "collection." Her ideal, she told me, was to make for mass production dresses as pretty and suitable as only wealthy individuals could then afford. "Why shouldn't a girl in Woolworth's look as chic as Mrs. Rockefeller?" she asked, at a time when this was less possible than today.

Yvonne became my great friend in Paris and helped me immensely, those first months, to climb out of the narrow chrysalis of my upbringing and find myself in this new world. Tall, striking-looking, graceful and artistic, with long sensitive fingers and hair pulled back in a low knot, and warm affectionate eyes, she was a "wise" Frenchwoman, interested in everything, forthright and outspoken. We made a constant foursome, the Davidsons and Stef and I. We went to operas and plays that were a revelation to me—some about subjects I had only read of in Havelock Ellis. *La Prisonnière*

(*The Captive*) was the story of a Lesbian relationship; *Le Secret*
by Henry Bernstein had a girl in a brothel in her slip, the man
talking but not wanting to go to bed with her. *Le Tombeau sous
l'Arc de Triomphe* (*The Tomb of the Unknown Soldier*) presented
a night-long discussion between two lovers and the girl's father as
to whether they should use the time to be "legal" and marry or
spend together the night the doomed boy was sure would be his
last—and when they decided on the latter, they had it on stage. And
*Le Cocu Magnifique,* with a husband so distraught at the possible
faithlessness of his wife that he made her expose her breast before
visitors, and I goggled to see her actually take it out of her blouse
and stand thus through a whole act. Distinctly these French believed
in Life. Yvonne discussed the plays with me with fervor and vehe-
mence, as real experience—to be thought about, digested, and
learned from.

Yvonne would call in at our hotel on her way to work. Once,
in my first weeks, she came before we were up, so I kept her
waiting while I rushed into my own room to rumple the undisturbed bedclothes. "What on earth's the matter?" she called impatiently through the door, and when I finally let her in, burst
into laughter. "But Peter, this is Paris—really, you English!"

I had for so long been preoccupied with the problem of when
I was going to begin to live, and now here I was, living. "This
is it," I told myself, fortunately aware that one of life's compensations is to be conscious of the moment. *Verweile doch.*

Mother kept writing, "What are you *doing* in Paris, what *are*
you doing in Paris?" I asked Stef what to reply. "Say you're living,"
he said, chuckling, and I did, at which Mother asked our family
dentist what he would do if his daughter had gone to Paris with
a man and had written she was "living"? "I'd tell her to come right
home," the dentist advised, and Mother wrote me just that—seriously.

I went to Sylvia Beach's bookshop and met Jane Heap and
Margaret Anderson, who ran the *Little Review.* We dined at Web-
er's on the Rue Royale with William Bird, a tall, thin, sardonic
newspaperman, who explained to me, when we discussed adultery,
that unfortunately he could never find the time, there was always
a deadline to meet. Guy Hickok ran the Paris office of the Brooklyn
*Daily Eagle,* a rendezvous for visitors and the resident American
colony. We dropped in at his office every day for news and gos-

sip. Jo would stop by, or George Slocombe of the *Daily Herald,*
or the new young American writer Ernest Hemingway. Stef had
already told me about this "big, handsome boy" with a half-
limp; "a genius," Stef said, "who'll make his mark." Hemingway's
talk was always about boxing, shooting, skiing, or the six-day
bicycle races he was passionate about. He sat slumped in an armchair, mumbled and grumped, got up and practiced sparring shots
on the air, or took aim at a bird as he talked. "Stef, come with me
to the gym and watch Zora train. That guy really stinks, it's hardly
worth watching him, but I can get a turn of my own in." He knew
boxers and wrestlers in the darkest corners of the town. He also
talked endlessly about writing.

Stef had been sure of "Hem's" genius since he had read his war
cables from Greece. "He's fascinated by cablese," Stef said, "sees
it as a new way of writing." Stef loved anything new, original, or
experimental, and he especially cherished young people. He was
sending Hemingway's stories to American magazines and they were
coming back, but this did not alter his opinion. "Someone will
recognize that boy's genius," he told everyone, "and then they'll all
rush to publish him." At this time Hemingway had published only
*Three Stories and Ten Poems,* but he worked all the time, above
the noisy sawmill in the Rue Notre Dame des Champs. He wrote
for the Paris little magazines, *transition,* edited by Eugene Jolas,
and *Transatlantic Review,* edited by Ford Madox Ford. Their contributors formed a group with similar objectives: new conventions,
form, and typography—e. e. cummings, Robert MacAlmon, Sisley
Huddleston, Ezra Pound. Stef contributed an article on the NEP
in Russia to *Transatlantic Review.*

Stef and Jo took me to Gertrude Stein's. The apartment was
crammed with *"objets,"* furniture, and paintings I did not then
appreciate. I was intensely shy and, hoping to be ignored, petted
the little dog, Basket. But black-haired, unbeautiful Alice Toklas
concerned herself with me—as she always did with the "nobodies"
—while Miss Stein talked to Jo, whom she loved. I was intolerably
embarrassed when Stef asked Gertrude Stein, "What would you
advise her to do if she wants to write?" The Buddha looked me up
and down. "Write," she said, and turned back to the important
people.

Ezra Pound was thin and tall, and his pointed beard wagged as
he uttered his remarkable opinions with undaunted assurance.

"Hem is lost," he said with pity one day, "lost to us, it's too bad, that boy had something, he could have been a writer, but now he's finished." When Stef wanted to know what the calamity was, Pound sighed. "He's sent us a story with a clear meaning."

I made friends with Hadley, Hemingway's first wife, who had straight fair hair and small teeth, and appeared somewhat bewildered and out of things. She tried hard to be a good wife, to ski, fish, shoot, and attend prize fights with her husband, run a household on very little money, as well as care for their bouncing baby, "Bumbie." He was large, blond, good-natured, and loved by everyone. Stef had an anecdote about this baby's coming. During a discussion on birth control in the *Eagle* office, Hemingway suddenly got up and announced grimly, "There *is* no sure method." "So I knew he was going to be a father," Stef commented, with his malicious grin.

We were almost always with Jo and Yvonne. The Davidsons appreciated food in the French manner, and discussed and selected restaurants all over Paris for their specialties. Their thrill at discovering a new *bistro,* or a sauce at Chez Pierre or Le Commerce, was a curious experience for me, with my London memories of three-and-sixpenny ABC lunches, and I must confess I was at first somewhat dismayed at so much fuss about mere food.

Steffens discussed with Yvonne and Jo whether he had the "right" to marry me.

"She may stay with you only five years," French Yvonne told him, "but they'll be worth it for you, Stef, and as for her, she'll get more out of five years with you than a lifetime with a younger man, inexperienced in life. Of course take her, Stef." This influenced me—and Stef.

Stef asked Yvonne to "dress" me. They stood me up like a mannequin and tried on the different models while Jo, Yvonne, and Stef discussed which ones suited me and why. I was allowed a voice, a very small one, but I felt too ignorant to say much. Since I had always considered clothes a waste of time, this was a shattering new experience, but I adjusted with a speed and, yes, enjoyment, that surprised and dismayed me. The frocks were so bewitching that I was delighted even while scandalized. Stef and Yvonne taught me taste, and shattered forever my "intellectual's" supposed superiority to such matters. Stef had positive theories on the subject. "When a woman walks into a room, everyone should

say, 'What a beautiful woman,' " he remarked, "then look again
and say, 'Ah, it's the dress.' " That was one of them. "Dress to your
good points" was another; "you have small shoulders, don't hide
them; you have a small head . . ." and so on. Madame Jeanne,
Yvonne's fitter, dealt with my less happy points. *"Fausse maigre,"*
she would murmur as she pinned the material on my more ample
hips.

We saw much of Louise and Billy Bullitt, Louise very pregnant
in an Arabian Nights maternity gown of black and gold that I
thought could have been worn by a Persian queen. Billy hovered
over her like a mother hen, and one night when he returned to
find Stef reading aloud from Joyce's *Ulysses,* which had just been
published, he was furious. "Think of the baby," he shouted, "our
child—what will it turn out to be if it hears language like that?"

After a few months of this exhilarating Paris, when I had begun
to wonder "What now?," Stef suddenly announced: "I've had
enough, Peter, let's go and get some sun. I want to write now; I
feel like writing."

We found a *pensione* at Ospedaletti, a small village just over the
Italian border from France, and soon were lazing in the sun—by
Browning's dark cypresses, red-rusted. The English lady tourists of
the *pensione* must have decided there was something odd about
us; we preferred our own company. Sitting on the rocks by the
ocean, I translated my ape book and learned Italian. Stef was
writing about the new light shed by the Russian Revolution on the
story of Moses. He wrote with delight, regularly; in the afternoons
we walked or sat by the sea.

I had been feeling a little sick, and we called an Italian doctor,
a stout, affable, kindly man. He examined me rather carefully, asked
some pertinent questions, and then remarked casually, in French,
*"Peut-être que c'est quelque chose intéressant."*

It was. It was Pete.

"I have now what I have wanted in my bones all my life—a
baby," Steffens wrote his sister Laura. All the same, the news was a
shock to him. What would a baby do to his life? "I saw, stopping
the route of every ship that sailed, a baby—a muling, puling,
bawling tyrant," he wrote, and he asked me, "Can I ever travel
again?" But that was not what was upsetting me.

I was stunned. A baby had not occurred to me. What was to be

done? How could I face a child, domesticity? And what about
marriage? This was not how you should feel when you first hear
you are to have a baby! The title for the novel I was thinking of
starting came to me: *Nothing Is Like That.*

The *pensione* seemed to have become dark brown, to have filled
with smells of cooking, so we moved south to a little town with a
wide white sandy beach, Alassio. We settled in a beach hotel, with
verandahs on the Mediterranean and spent six weeks there. We
bathed, walked, worked, roamed over rocky hills that straggled with
olive trees, and—to consider for a moment only me—worried. I
vacillated between shock, anxiety, incredulity, concern. We rambled
among the terraces of vines and carnations, millions of carnations
staked in neat stringed rows for the flower markets of Europe, while
I questioned, debated, deliberated. The village had one cobbled
market street lined with stalls; the perplexing problem followed
me among the laces, tomatoes, toys, and *pasta*. There were only
two months to decide. Suddenly books and stories had become real
—Tess, Marguerite. Absurd. It didn't happen like that—it didn't happen to you—yet it was happening, and to me. Stef had quite other
thoughts.

Stef's two oldest and closest California friends, Charles Erskine
Scott Wood and Sara Bard Field, were in Florence and Stef wanted
to "show me off." They were also good friends of his sister Laura,
who was not happy at the turn of events, at the unknown, new
wife. "You used to be a genius," Laura had written bitterly, "and
unique, now you're going to be a father and there are millions
of those." Stef deeply loved his sister, and was troubled about her.
Sara and Erskine, he thought, might help.

In the carriage from the station to the *pensione* on the Arno
where the Woods were staying, I felt apprehensive and nervous,
but as soon as Colonel Wood welcomed me with arms outstretched,
all anxiety vanished. They were enchanting. The Colonel was a
large expansive man with a wild gray beard and flowing white hair,
and he wore a wide black silk bowtie flowing untidily from a soft-
collared silk shirt. Sara Bard Field was also white-haired, but soft,
gentle, effusive, a poet too, much younger than Erskine, but as
demonstrative. We had, curiously, two things in common: the
difference in their ages and the fact that they were not married.
In no time at all, I was not only accepted but enveloped in the
loving friendship of Sara and Erskine.

Sara had had a tragic experience I only learned of later. When she left her husband, a missionary in India, for Erskine, who was a married man, her husband denounced her and prophesied the wrath of heaven for her sinful act. Not long after, driving along a muddy road in California, her car skidded, overturned, and pinned beneath its wheel her young son, who died there. Sara's hair turned white overnight; her husband charged the "murder" to God's vengeance. Erskine had undertaken this first trip of theirs to Europe to help her get over the tragedy.

We spent an unforgettable time in Florence, the four of us, Stef and Erskine introducing me to the world's great art and encouraging me to look at it for myself and enjoy what I liked instead of admiring what an inward duty monitor dictated. At the Uffizi, Stef said, "Go through once fast and take a quick look, then come back and take in at leisure what you most liked."

"You don't mean I'm free to like or not like?" I marveled, and years of gallery boredom fell off my shoulders. Stef freed me with those few words to enjoy art. We became the slaves of Florence, the four of us.

"Where've you kept this girl hidden all this time?" was all Erskine wanted to know of his old friend. Erskine Scott Wood had led a remarkable life. After he had served, as a young lieutenant, against a tribe of Indians, he befriended them in defeat and they made him a member of their tribe. Home in Portland, Oregon, he married, had six children, and became a celebrated attorney. But he had a second, secret office, to which came poets and artists, and where Wood wrote poetry and the humorous satires, such as *Heavenly Discourse,* for which he became famous. He was an unusually well-read man and full of poetic lore as well as encyclopedic knowledge, but what one warmed to was his passion for all life, for beauty, people, food, art, nature. He hated sham and hypocrisy, conventions and injustice; he was both *bon viveur* and an artist of life. One felt at once more alive in his presence. Erskine and Sara made me feel better about my possible future.

That summer in Italy was a charmed time, except for the big decision I still had to make; in view of all my mother's warnings, it was ironic enough. Stef wanted that baby, but not to be again a married man. "I'm an anarchist, I don't want the law to dictate to me," he said. Illegitimacy, so dread a concept to me, meant nothing to him; in fact, he regarded it as rather an advantage. "Love-children have always been the best," he insisted, "Michelangelo, Leonardo, Erasmus." He almost convinced me, but if we did not count on a proper marriage "forever," I argued, what of the child? *If* we separated, we would both want it.

Did we know what we were really talking about? We were both, I suppose, afraid of the difference in our ages; I wanted a career, I had never contemplated not working, of being tied to domestic life only, while Stef was afraid of the mere possibility of the end of a relationship to which he was giving more and more of his monogamous self.

My mother was writing desperate letters, using every argument. She even wrote that she "could not have an illicit child in the house because of Rudi and Rosa" (who were both in their late twenties).

Then Stef hit on what to him was a possible solution. "Have the baby," he argued, "and give it to me. You can be free. I will look after it—but I want it. You may have other children—let me have Pete." I didn't accept this, but one day as I lazed in the hot sun on the gray stones in Bellagio on Lake Como, a lizard darted out of a crevice, lay motionless and sunned itself. I lay as still, and suddenly in some incomprehensible way, after being so deeply troubled, a pall seemed to lift from me, and I felt that somehow everything would work out all right.

However, Billy Bullitt then came from Paris and sketched for us the disadvantage of traveling to America unmarried; to travel together would be "moral turpitude." And in America the situation might be uncomfortable. Gorki had been thrown out because of a wife he was not married to. Reluctantly we considered jettisoning all "anarchist" plans and being regular after all.

Another decision loomed. G was coming to Europe and Stef felt he must try and comfort her. He had, after all, treated her badly a second time; he had tried to cheer her up by letter, telling her it was not "another woman," but a baby that had come between them, but in vain.

"And so," said Stef one morning, "since I must go to Paris, we might as well get married there—but just to get that document. As soon as we're married, let's turn around and get a divorce, secretly." He could thus have it both ways—almost.

In Paris Yvonne designed for me a cape to hide the six-month child. We were married with much merriment in a registry office, where officials kept demanding documents we didn't have: the death certificate of Josephine, Steffens' first wife, who had died twelve years earlier; a certificate of my birth, registered at the French Consulate in Melbourne. "But my mother had no reason to register me at the French Consulate," I objected.

"*Tant pis,* madam, but under those conditions you are not legally born and we cannot marry you." Stef discovered that each objection required only a sum of money to be cleared up.

Afterward, we had a gay wedding breakfast with Louise and Billy Bullitt, Jo and Yvonne, and James and Nora Joyce. Jo made drawings on the tablecloth, which the waiters carried away to keep, constantly bringing fresh cloths for Jo to draw on again. Joyce sat and smoked in amused, ruminative silence. I hoped it was not the hazards of marriage that he was contemplating.

I went to London to spend at home the month that Stef would dedicate to G. "If you need me, Peter, I'll come," he promised. "Write me three times that you need me and I'll be there." I was heavyhearted when we separated, and in London I was so miserable alone, after the glorious months together—we had not been apart for almost a year—that I was now sure of the rightness of our decisions. I stood it as long as I could, and eventually I wrote him three times and he came.

"I tried to make G see I hadn't really done anything bad to her. I tried to tease her into a good humor, but she wouldn't play," Stef reflected resignedly, shaking his head at human "unreasonableness," at the obstinacy of a woman's heart, which would not obey logic. But he did not worry long. He wanted to get into the Italian sunshine for the coming event, and found a villa in San Remo, a small seaside village on the Italian Riviera, where we settled for the next year.

# 9

## PETE

Our second morning at the Villetta Margherita, a small, squat, grizzled woman, clothed in black dress and apron, walked into our kitchen unasked. She was very wrinkled and almost toothless, and she neither greeted me nor asked any questions, but went right to work cleaning up the kitchen. After a while she announced to me, "My name is Giulia, I shall work for you." She looked me over a little severely and added, *"Lei giovanni,* I shall tell you some things."

Giulia did not have a very high opinion of the *signori inglesi,* who were cranky, tart, stand-offish, and did not like to spend time gossiping. Her social life and her friends were downtown in the market, where she could scold, argue, bargain, shake her head over the lack of *lasagna* or the latest scandal. Her own home was among the ancient houses that clung steeply to the rocky hillside above us, with crooked crevices for streets, deep and narrow, joined above by bridges. No foreigners climbed into old San Remo. It was dirty, decaying, it smelled, and only Italians lived there, natives.

On the third day Giulia capitulated to our odd household. When she found out a baby was coming, she took over household, baby, *signora,* and all. She gave herself to us completely—including old wives' tales.

"I can tell you everything, *signora,* I know about babies. I have had eleven and lost nine. What midwife will the *signora* take?"

"None, Giulia, I'm looking for an English nurse."

"'Nurse,' what is that? I know our midwives from Bordighera to Pisa. There is Sister Theresa, but she has already a *bambino* to deliver. Sister Ursula . . ."

"And an English doctor, if I can find one."

*"Un dottore! Un dottore!* What good will he do? What do men know of babies?"—agreeing a little with Mother, who had written, "Of course you will come home, one has a baby in a London hospital, properly."

"The baby will be born in Italy," his papa had replied quite as firmly, "and what's more, at home. I want to start right away on my education of Pete, and all the books tell you it's the first weeks that count."

Finally, we did discover an English maternity nurse, cockney but experienced, who had brought "thousands of babies into the world, mostly from workingwomen." She had also looked after little Scotty Fitzgerald, the Scott Fitzgeralds' three-year-old daughter. "Very spoiled" was her tart comment, "opens the door to guests and offers right away: 'Champagne or highball?' " We hoped Pete would not pick up cockney or alcoholism in his first six weeks.

I discovered to my surprise that I liked to knit. I sneaked onto his father's nightstand some minute garments, even a minuscule glove with five separate fingers, for age three weeks. "Are their hands that small?" Stef asked, and kept the glove by his bedside table a year. I never made the second.

We unearthed an English doctor who hadn't brought a child into the world for ten years, but thought he "could manage." "We won't need him anyway," Nurse Fraser commented tartly, agreeing for once with Giulia; "men are only in the way when it comes to childbirth."

The days followed one another and we were all impatient—and surprised at the end when Pete came a week early. During the night I had a stomach-ache. "This may be it," I said. "But it might be a false alarm," Stef suggested, "the doctor warned about that." Two hours later the pains were coming fast, but they were not as bad as I had expected—no ten-minute intervals, the way the books said.

"Suppose the doctor comes and it is a false alarm?" I asked. Stef had telephoned a very sleepy and irritated physician. "It can't be yet," he asserted. So Stef went next door and asked the Contessa Maggiolini, our old Scottish neighbor, to come over. She stumped across the garden, sat down by my bed, and then announced, "It's the real thing, you've skipped the first two stages." Then everything happened very quickly. The nurse took one look and gave quick orders: "Hot water, basins, towels, sheets." She whirled about, re-made the bed, told me what to do, telephoned the doctor, who came scurrying. But, seeing everything done, he did what the nurse had predicted—walked out and sat with my husband, "with a bottle between us," as Stef told me later.

Then came a loud, strangling wail.

I remember exactly. I said, "I've made a human being!" I lay still with happiness.

Stef peeked in, took a look at the bawling red bundle, kissed me, and looked again. "He doesn't look at all like Little Pete," he said, disconcerted.

In the morning I awoke to a new universe. It contained Pete. We whispered, not to wake him in the next room. Finally the nurse brought him in and held him to my breast. He nuzzled close but did not suck—he did not know how. She put honey on the nipple but still he cried. No book had warned me of this, and after a futile five minutes the nurse, red-faced, took him away, but I was more mortified than she.

There was another crisis. We had warned Giulia and Giannina, the young, pretty maid Giulia had brought into the household, about our "no nonsense" British nurse, but they still resented her sharp orders, her contempt for Italians. In the morning Stef stuck his head in my room and announced, "Giulia wants to talk to you."

"I don't want my patient disturbed." Nurse Fraser rose up, but Giulia pushed past her and stood before me with disheveled hair and red-rimmed eyes.

"I have to go, *signora*," she said. "I wish to leave at once."

"But, Giulia, what's happened—with your *signorino* just arrived? What is it? Is it the nurse?"

"I do not like her, but that is not why I must go."

"You've been up all night, you haven't slept, you're exhausted." I almost wept. There was wine on her breath. "You can't go, Giulia."

Tears came to old Giulia's eyes. "*Lo so*—I know it, I am sorry, I did not wish, but *si può vedere*—you can see."

Later Giannina came in with broom and duster, looking guilty. "Giulia has given notice," I said. "Giannina, what's up?"

"I know," she answered, busily dusting.

"Have you two quarreled?"

Giannina burst into tears. "I must do the same, *signora,* I must go, too. I love the *signorino* already, but how can I remain in a household where I am falsely accused?"

"Giannina! Who accuses you? Nothing has disappeared. What story is this?"

"Not stealing," Giannina whimpered. "It is Giulia who falsely accuses me of coming up here early to see the *signorino* first, when she has not seen him at all, but it is not true *signora,* I saw him only when the *inglesi* nurse called me and wanted something. I did not steal up just to look at him when I should have been dusting."

I realized I had to be Solomon.

"You get Giulia up here," I said very firmly now, "and bring the nurse, too." The three came together.

"I told you no excitement . . ." the nurse started to scold professionally. "What d'you suppose your son will get for milk?"

"There's going to be a new regime, nurse," I interrupted. "Every morning, as soon as our son has had his breakfast, he's going to hold a levee. He's starting early, but he must get acclimated; and Giulia and Giannina will come up and pay their respects." The nurse would have exploded, but a look at my face kept her silent. Giannina broke into her radiant smile, and even Giulia's old face creased into a reluctant acquiescence. I had weathered my Italian crisis.

The only other was concerned with my own clumsiness. I was bathing Pete for the first time, when I dropped the squirming little body and screamed that I had drowned him. I shrieked for that wonderful, blessed nurse, and she came and fished him out and held him upside down till he could get his breath again.

Then she said to me, in her most withering tone, "What *did* they teach you in that London School of Economics?"

The next seven months were very domestic. Pietro went downtown to market, and the village adopted him; he was their *bambino.* He kicked in the sun and lay in his pram under the waving palm leaves. His father talked to him about life and men and politics. A clergyman came to baptize him, and Stef dismissed the clergyman with a sermon on Good and Evil. "Pete knows neither, and I am not going to start him on such man-made conceptions now." Mother spent a month at our villa, loving her grandchild and disapproving of almost everything we did. Jo came in answer to Stef's letter and sang Italian songs, and Yvonne brought me a present of a mink-trimmed red velvet housecoat—to wear when I nursed the baby.

On another visit, Jo brought Mrs. Harry Payne Whitney, one of America's millionaires and a sculptress herself. Nervously, I gave our new maid a description of what Mrs. Whitney's New York and Long Island homes were probably like, and told her to serve everything "as nicely as possible." When the meal came in, I was horror-stricken: the cook had selected "the best porcelain" in the house, which happened to be the soap and toothbrush dishes from the washstand. "They were decorated," she explained.

Steffens was eager to tell his son what he had learned from his own life, "to save the boy learning things that aren't so, the way I did," he said. "I want to save Pete the long road I had to travel."

He kept coming back to this thought in our second Italian year, when we had moved to a lovely old house full of cracks on a hillside in Alassio. "He can start way ahead, knowing all I had to unlearn." He watched the little boy crawl and climb, stumble, fall, pick himself up laughing, try to puzzle out our prohibitions. He read his own childhood into Pete's behavior, and his memories came alive. One morning he said, "I think I can start my Life now."

Publishers had been pestering Steffens for years to write his autobiography. He had talked about it, but the job seemed too vast. He had recently been working on an article on "Oil and Its Political Implications" for *Century Magazine,* but it was rejected.

"I don't seem able to state my truths so that they'll be accepted," Stef complained. "I must find a new form." He had finished *Moses in Red,* an account of Moses as a typical revolutionary, on which he had worked off and on for years. He talked about a life of Jesus, for which he had collected a large library. He also wrote several chapters about Satan, who was to go with him on all sorts of muck-raking and other adventures. He was discouraged because publishers were not interested in these projected books.

"Editors are afraid of me," he lamented, "since I took the McNamaras' part ten years ago. I was condemned by everybody—you should have seen the trunkfuls of clippings." No magazine or newspaper would send Steffens to Paris for the Peace Conference. He had printed one article on it and that under a pseudonym.

Ray Long now cabled to San Remo for an article for his *Cosmopolitan* magazine:

. . . ON "MOST WONDERFUL THING IN THE WORLD—A BABY" AND WHAT IT MEANS TO PHILOSOPHER-TRAVELLER YOUR AGE MUST BE STEFFENS TALKING FROM THE HEART.

Stef did not want to do it, but I persuaded him, using the almost daily letters he had been writing to my mother from little Pete, which I thought amusing and original. And of course I wanted my baby written about. Stef spent two months over the article, "Radiant Fatherhood," which Long turned down. (It was later published in French in *La Revue Hebdomadaire* in 1926, and in English for the first time in *Lincoln Steffens Speaking*, after Steffens' death.)

But now, settled in this distant, quiet Alassio garden, with a new future before him, Stef began to feel he might be able to start on the story of his life. "I want to call it *A Life of Unlearning*," he said, "to show how I gained my picture of the world, how firmly They plant it in your mind so that it becomes almost impossible to change it." He was daunted at the size of the job, and kept putting it off, discouraged. I cudgeled my brains as to how to get him going.

Stef told stories dramatically, and illustrated any discussion by vivid, witty anecdotes from his own experience. I had always loved those stories, from the time I first listened to them along the Seine; and I loved to watch his listeners "get" them. That gave me an idea. Sitting behind a stone pillar that was topped by a broken-nosed angel, I started to take down these tales as he told them to our many callers, and one day brought him fifty pages. Stef read them and was astounded.

"But that's 'written,'" he said. "I would hardly have to change it. It's all down! That's how I ought to write my Life!"

"Why don't you?" I said. My ruse had worked.

We arranged the large tiled bare room on the top floor as a studio and he went to work. Every morning he climbed up there and wrote. I had started a novel, so we both devoted mornings to writing. I had also started writing regularly for the *Manchester Guardian*—articles and sketches on life in Italy, the baby, the garden, the big frost, "The Egg Gentleman and the Garden Lady." The editors like them and to my joy printed all I sent.

The baby went with Rosa, the cook, to market, or crawled along the terraces and ledges of the wild old garden, learning about insects, learning about ponds and stones, too, by falling into or over them. Or Stef carried him about the garden telling him about the world, America, politics, or crooning an Italian ditty he had made up:

> Piccolo Pietro,
> Andiamo
> Nel giardino,
> Faciamo passegiata.
> Nel giardino,
> Piccolo Pietro.

Rosa watched father and son in wonderment. *"Ho mai vista un bambino così pel suo papà,"* she exclaimed to everyone who would listen.

Stef wrote on small pad pages by hand, wrote and rewrote, unwilling to leave a paragraph "until the prose sings," he said. I would steal upstairs when he was not there and find twenty or thirty of his small pad pages with the same phrase or paragraph rewritten and written again, sometimes with only a word or half a sentence changed.

"Aren't you polishing too much before getting the record down?" I ventured.

"I can't leave a paragraph until it's perfect," Stef replied. "That's how I trained myself to write."

He was getting discouraged again, and I was afraid the constant revision might hurt the spontaneous freshness of the story, as well as discourage him, so I asked if I might send it out to be typed. "No," Stef said, "it isn't done yet."

I decided to be bold, stole a chapter, and sent it to New York to Miss Ford, the typist who had typed Steffens' articles for thirty years. "Miss Ford can read my writing," Stef had told me. "Only people who love me can read my writing." Which was true. His writing was atrocious, small and cramped. He didn't cross his *t*'s or dot his *i*'s or join his syllables, and he misspelled. I knew how difficult his handwriting was, and I suddenly thought, in a panic: If Miss Ford died or gave up working, who could read the manuscript? That gave me the courage to steal it, and luckily Stef did not look, did not know it had gone till the day it came back in type. Then he was so gratefully astonished that he let me send out other chapters. Again, the strategy had worked.

The next time he despaired, as writers do, I sent some chapters, again secretly, to Marie Howe. Stef valued her judgment, but the first he knew of it was an enthusiastic, delighted letter from Marie, which encouraged him so much that he continued the rest of that winter, with Marie reading each chapter and returning it with hosannas.

It wasn't the first autobiography submitted to Marie for judgment. Her husband, Frederic C. Howe, Commissioner of Immigration and Housing under Wilson, had written his life in *Confessions of a Reformer*. Marie had told us with wry irony that when she had finished it, she handed the manuscript back to her husband. "But Fred," she said, "weren't you ever married?"

"Ah, yes," her loving husband responded, quickly and contritely, "I'll put it in." When he handed his wife the amended manuscript, there was this line added: "For the beautiful Miss Jenney was by now my wife." Marie, a great feminist, was at this time living in Europe and writing the life of George Sand, and she remarked to me a little sadly, "Imagine a woman writing her life story and paying that much attention to her husband."

Pete's second summer I took him to London, which was going through the general strike; we watched university students drive the trains and buses in place of the striking workmen. Tension, excitement, and anger raged in the streets, argument and discussion, and bitter was the disillusionment when Ernest Bevin "sold out" and allowed the strike to be broken. I hurried back to Stef in Carlsbad; Filene was with him, and we spent the rest of the summer there and in Salzburg, listening to concerts in and out of doors, spending time with Fritz Kreisler and his American wife, watching the crowds alternately gorge themselves on whipped cream and take stringent cures. Pete developed his musical talent by conducting the military bands. Kreisler was taking the waters and struck up a friendship with our infant musician. Grace Hegger Lewis, Sinclair Lewis's first wife, was there, vacationing with her small son, Wells (who was killed in World War II). She talked of her troubles with her husband, "Red," who was then falling in love with an American newspaperwoman, Dorothy Thompson.

One afternoon, walking in the hills, we stopped to talk to an acquaintance of Filene's, a stout, gray-bearded man puffing heavily along the trails. "Know who he is?" Filene whispered before he introduced us. "That's Lomonosov, the engineer who was in charge of the train that carried the Czar and his family to their doom. Railroad officials wired him all along the line asking what to do with their precious cargo; when they got no reply, afraid and at a loss, aware their passengers might be rescued, they took them off the train and, torn between awe of the royal family and their new revolutionary loyalty, shot them."

In Salzburg we were taken to Schloss Leopoldskron, to one of the fabulous Max Reinhardt evenings that followed a performance of *Jedermann* with Moissi or *Turandot* with Max Pallenberg or a Goldoni *commedia dell'arte* featuring the gifted Thimig family. Helene Thimig was a brilliant actress and Reinhardt's mistress. Morris Gest, the American impresario, was choosing new young talent for America and had already picked the young dancer Tilly Losch, whom Filene was making much of. Lily Darvas was acting in Hungarian comedies by Ferenc Molnár, her husband. Rudolf Kommer, Reinhardt's near alter ego, presided over it all, particularly the great Leopoldskron banquets that were like something out of Lucullus or the Arabian Nights. American and British stage personalities, writers, composers, poets, dancers from all the world mingled in the great halls under stone walls covered with oil paintings or tapestries, and buzzed around the laden trestle tables. There were whole lambs, boars' heads, suckling pigs, game of all varieties, and feasts of talk, too.

In the mornings we heard Mozart, Bach, Bartók; in the afternoons we walked in the hills or rode on the blue lake; and every evening a new exhilarating entertainment indoors or in the open air— an enchanted time.

We wanted to get back to work, and while we wondered where to go next, we stayed in Paris, where Jo made a statue of Pete, now twenty-two months. Every day, when undressed, he would scratch his stomach, so Jo made the statue with the two little hands doing just that. It is one of Jo Davidson's best. Stef called the statue, with its bowlegs and the little stomach sticking out, a "human being only just erect."

For our last winter in Europe we went to Bêcheron, the Davidsons' newly acquired old French *manoir* in Touraine. Yvonne had made it over with great taste, but since Jo was to be in America and Yvonne had to work in Paris, it stood empty. It was a lovely old stone building around a courtyard, with two giant elms in front, and across the road a French kitchen garden running down to a river. A few miles away was Saché, with an old castle where Balzac had lived and worked. But the weather was as gray and leaden as in England; we missed the Italian sun, and there were few people to break the isolation. And Stef was developing a growing nostalgia for "home"; he talked more and more to me of California, his family, his friends, the countryside, "the boys" in San Quentin. "You'll see the fog drift in over Tamalpais, Peter—San Francisco is often buried in fog—but there are long, hot days, as in Italy. The view from Laura's house over the bay, and Dot's ranch, thirty thousand acres of burning yellow ranges—you must see them." He dreamed about California. And then fuel was added to his eagerness when Jo returned and told his stories of what he called "the astounding new America."

"It's got to be seen, Stef. I tell you it's something new under the sun; the country is bursting its seams. Everybody's in on it, everybody's making money, but they're building, creating, experimenting —in art, too. The whole damn country is alive with a new vitality, and you can find a lot of it in my new friend, E. W. Marland— the phenomenon of Ponca City. He's one man you've got to see— in his three-hundred-million-dollar setting."

By the spring Stef had determined to go with me to see this new America. The last week, Pete and I went to London, where we hired Anna, a gentle Welsh woman, whose one dream had always been to get to America. Stef joined us on the boat at Le Havre. I was sitting in the dining room with my back to the door, when I suddenly saw my son's face flame beet-red, and when I turned to discover the cause, he and his father were in each other's arms crying and laughing by turns.

# 10

## GOLDEN GATE

I was bowled over by my first impressions of America. We had had a stormy passage across the Atlantic, Pete being almost the only passenger who dared to go on deck. He thought the ship was playing games with him when its rolling knocked him down. "Bo-at!" he would cry, and roar with laughter. On an early misty Sunday morning the storms subsided, and the Manhattan skyline came into view. A cynical newspaperman, Robert Dunne, an old friend of Steffens, leaned over the rails with me. "Not bad, eh?" he muttered.

Another surprise came on the way from the boat to the hotel. I had expected noise, bustling traffic, jostling crowds. Instead, there was a wide, clean, silent street, not a man or a dog to be seen; the city seemed asleep. An organ pealed from a brownstone church; it must be some outlying suburb, I thought, and looked at the street name: FIFTH AVENUE.

Marie Howe had engaged rooms for us in a tall, narrow hotel, the Marlton, in Greenwich Village, on a street with quaint, individual shops—nothing mass produced here! And around the corner a green park, watched over by a gray stone arch like the Arc de Triomphe, nestled among painted brick houses with pink and blue shutters. On the way to the park we passed a narrow cobbled mews. The Washington Square section, the Greenwich Village I explored the next few days, was not so different from Chelsea, and I hadn't been prepared for that.

It was lucky to have Marie Howe in New York to help me feel at home. She had a basement apartment on Twelfth Street, with a tiny back garden enclosed by brick walls. It was also like a Chelsea basement, with brightly colored wall hangings and rugs and books

strewn around. Marie was president of Heterodoxy, a New York
club for professional women who kept their own names even
after marriage; they were known as Lucy Stoners, after the first
American married woman to keep her maiden name. Marie asked
me to speak there.

I sat with her at the speakers' table and was introduced to some
of America's "leading women." There was Signe Toksvig, the blond
Swedish novelist and wife of Francis Hackett; Katharine Anthony,
biographer of Margaret Fuller; Frances Perkins, later Roosevelt's
Secretary of Labor. I met Elizabeth Irwin, the head of the first experimental progressive school in the public-school system, and Ruth
Hale, dark, small, and brooding, a writer married to Heywood
Broun. "She's made a life's battle of her feminist views," Marie
whispered. "I think she's harder and more aggressive than the
others." I felt a camaraderie among these women ("girls," they
called themselves), an understanding almost like a secret that could
be shared because men weren't around.

I had not spoken in public much, except as a lecturer, and as
I looked at these faces around the long table, I felt intimidated
—they seemed so self-assured. I took a chance that what they
wanted to hear about was their old friend Steffens, the "bachelor"
they knew who had fought battles with and for them. What was he
like with this change in his life, domesticated, a husband and father
—on their level now?

So I told them stories of our Italian household, of Giulia and
Giannina, their quarrel the night of the baby's arrival; of how
Stef had warned the child that if he continued wetting his pants
he would not be fit for Harvard but would have to go to Oxford;
and how the ex-muckraker explained the causes of political corruption to his year-old son.

When I sat down, I was surprised at the eager applause. It went
on and on, they laughed, cried, wrung my hands—these "career"
women! "We'll want you here every year," Ruth Hale said. "Why
didn't they tell us about you?" It was my first success on an American
platform and gave me the thrill an actress must feel on an opening
night.

We crowded people and places into those three weeks. The
*New Masses* gave us a lunch that was gay and serious and full of
laughter, with friends I had met in Europe, Max Eastman and his

Eliena, painters and artists, poets and caricaturists and writers. Art Young, the cartoonist, rotund and cheerful with twinkling baby-blue eyes, told stories of Stef and "the old days"; Floyd Dell, the novelist, quiet, dark, and shy, more solemn than the others, blossomed like a sea anemone when I compared his story of adolescence, *Moon-Calf,* with my favorite, *Sinister Street,* which we read at sixteen with delicious shock because it had a prostitute and "W.C." in print. Michael Gold the socialist barked antagonistic questions at Stef the liberal, his homely dark furrowed face sarcastic, his mobile mouth seeming to slant with pain. Another day we met the "liberals." They seemed to make a bigger distinction than we did between liberal and radical. Stef talked to the *Survey-Graphic,* which Paul Kellogg edited, to the *New Republic,* and at the Cosmos Club in a rapid trip to Washington.

Anna Louise Strong came to see us in New York, a huge woman with cropped gray hair, china-blue eyes, and a manner so impersonal that I wondered if she would go on talking if one went out of the room. She had lived in Russia for years, and before that had been through strikes and labor troubles in her home town of Seattle; she talked about Russia and gave Stef the latest news. We saw much of Robert Minor, a friend of Stef's. Minor, an artist and member of an aristocratic old American family, had joined the radical movement and drew cartoons for the *New Masses;* but he was beginning to regard this as an "indulgence" and felt he should only write and organize, which he did not do as well. It was apparently his form of hair shirt. He had distributed antiwar propaganda among United States troops in Germany after the war, and when he was caught, and discovered the penalty to be hanging, had begged Stef to save his life. "I wouldn't mind being shot," he apologized, "but I can't face the idea of being hanged."

Clarence Darrow, craggy, broad-shouldered, slow-speaking, and humorous, told stories in a voice as mellow as Steffens'. I was tremendously drawn to him and he was eager to know his old friend's new young wife. Darrow had a great interest in women.

"You know why we get on, Ruby and I?" he asked about his wife. "It's easy, we both love Darrow." He told us in fascinating detail about his cases, the Leopold-Loeb trial and others, and so I now heard about the McNamara case from him. Stef could not forgive himself for the failure of his well-meant "interference" and never stopped trying to get the men pardoned or paroled. I had started corresponding with J. B. McNamara in Italy, telling him all about our Italian life and the baby. He had asked for snapshots and sent back enlargements he had made in the prison workshop.

Stef liked to bait Darrow. Like a fox terrier at the heels of a slow, ponderous hippopotamus, he darted all over the lot. When we went with Darrow to Baltimore to call on Henry L. Mencken, whom Darrow admired, Stef was disappointed. "But he doesn't get at the deeper issues," he said, and blurted out at Mencken, "You believe a lot of the things you accuse the dubs of thinking! I expected you to see through all that, but you make moral judgments —in politics!" Darrow laughed his deep rumble. Happily cynical, cheerfully pessimistic himself, he mocked Steffens. "I admire your illusions," he told him, "but I can't share them." And, turning to me, "He still thinks you can improve man."

"We held a debate once across the country," Darrow told me. "What a dirty trick Stef played me! The title was 'There Is Good in Good People.' " Stef finished the story: "I merely argued that there is so much good in bad people, there must be *some* good in good people, though I admitted I'd never seen any."

"And he expected me to contradict that," Darrow muttered. "How could I? Very unfair."

Darrow was as picturesque as he was fascinating. His huge head dropped sideways, as if too heavy to carry. His face was carved into deep and wonderful lines, his hulking frame hung loosely inside his clothes, and he hunched his head deep into his shoulders when he made a point, so that you saw no neck at all.

"He handles himself as if he were a musical instrument," Stef said. "He has fought the greatest battles of our day and won them. He can't bear to have a client executed. We call him the attorney for the damned, and he says life isn't worth living!"

"Had I known what life would be like when I was born, I'd have asked God to let me off," Darrow said. He shared with Steffens the belief that social evils were due to "the system," and he had an absolute and unshakable need for and faith in individual freedom. As he listened to Steffens' tales of Petrograd and Moscow, he shook his head with a cynical smile. "They'll end up like all the rest," he prophesied.

Stef was impatient to get to California, so we moved on. I sat for hours glued to the train window. At wayside stations with fascinating place names—Des Moines, Omaha, Cheyenne, Sioux Falls —Pete ran up to the locomotive engineer to be lifted for a blissful moment into the engine cab, which he thought they said was called a "caboose," a word he happily chanted all across the country. Stef sat on the observation platform and pointed out to his son and me, with an endearing pride as if the land belonged to him, the great grassy endless plains, Iowa fields turning yellow, the Nebraska desert, and the red-ribbed canyons of Utah. I was not prepared for such a breath-taking panorama: the Great Salt Lake, with the train crossing mile upon endless mile of water on a trestle running taut and straight, the railway lines converging into infinity.

Then a flat day of desert under a blazing sky, sand and heat, cactus and scrub. In the night the train climbed, and we needed extra blankets against the cold. We rattled through long, hollow, echoing wooden sheds—the snowsheds of the Sierras; all night we shivered through those snow mountains and in the morning woke to sun again, shining on giant trees with dark glossy leaves, golden balls hanging between them.

"Our orange groves!" Stef cried, excited as a boy. The train puffed for a day among the shining gold and green, through meadows of blue cornflowers, mauve lupine, purple wild iris, and then it slid into the Sacramento Valley, glowing with its yellow California poppies.

"My boyhood valley!" Stef was scarcely able to talk. We glided into the open and the Pacific Ocean glistened before us. We boarded a ferry, broad and matronly; Pete pranced and danced in his French gray goatskin coat, which was too heavy and too hot, but his father had determined that this was the garment in which Laura would first set eyes on her late but newest nephew.

The ferry docked. Stef pointed to a tall figure standing alone on the pier, well set-up, with a square jaw. "That's Uncle Allen," he cried to Pete. The boat was made fast and Pete ran on to the pier.

"Al-len," he cried. "Au-to. Bo-at. Choo-choo." In five seconds Al-len was Pete's. How grateful I was then for baby prattle. At the front door of 850 Francisco Street, a square stone house atop a steep hill, Allen stopped a moment, put on his dignity, and took Pete by the hand. He didn't have time to insert his key in the lock before the door opened and a short, fair-haired, blue-eyed woman, with Stef's olive skin and low quiet voice, stood there.

"Len," she said.

"This is Pete," Len said.

"Bo-at," Pete said. "Choo-choo, Lo-la, long choo-choo."

When he saw through the big bay window overlooking the Golden Gate the beautiful harbor full of steamers, sailboats, ferries, tugboats, he climbed the sofa and stared, oblivious to all but that fairyland.

Pete did the job of making it up. The months and years Steffens had worried about Laura's reactions vanished in one short afternoon; the family battle was over.

"Not that stubborn Laura will admit it," her husband, Doctor Suggett, said to us privately, "but I can tell you she's his slave. In fact, she doesn't think you give him a break."

We went to the *Call-Bulletin* office to see Fremont Older, one of Steffens' oldest and most intimate friends, a courageous, "crusading" editor of the old type, independent and fearlessly outspoken. An extremely tall, powerful man sitting at a wooden desk piled high with books rose as we came in. He had huge hands, a big head, a face carved into deep lines of character, and his voice was full of kindliness. He wore a soft green tweed suit and plus fours. "Lincoln," he said as he shook and held his hand. "So, you're married now and a father." He paused, then shook hands warmly with me. "We're old friends," he said simply. A little to my surprise, and perhaps to hide his emotion, he pulled a small pink book out from the untidy pile on his desk. "Here's a marvelous new book, Lincoln, it's my new Bible. It explains the things we never understood." To my joy, it was a book I knew well, Bernard Hart's *Psychology of Insanity*, still one of the clearest, simplest expositions of psychiatric mechanisms. Older, I found, always had some new book he believed in and made everybody read. "It's a book we've been waiting for," he said now. "After this They can't condemn so easily, or even judge."

A few days later we drove across the bay on my first visit to San Quentin, my first visit to any prison. Our road led along the blue and gold coast at the foot of steep curving hills. The sea shone, and the sun glittered on the waves and rocks right up to the heavy black barred gate. A wide asphalt drive bordered by flowers ran along the coast, and convicts in gray uniform were working in the gardens. I wasn't prepared for flowers. We were taken to the warden's private office while they sent for J. B. McNamara and Matthew Schmidt (J. B.'s brother, John, had been released after serving eleven years).

The McNamaras had been militant labor leaders in the early 1900's when unions were making little progress by accepted union methods. The two brothers felt that violence was the only way to draw attention to working conditions and force employers to raise wages. They had embarked—with official labor's support, it was charged—on a campaign of dynamiting. As soon as a new bridge or dam or building was finished, they blew it up.

A strike at the Los Angeles *Times,* which was strongly open shop, made that building the next target. The McNamaras were chosen, or volunteered, for the job. Others helped in different ways, but the two Irish brothers and Matthew Schmidt were the leaders. The building was blown up. Then it was revealed that on the appointed day some workers had remained after hours and all had been killed. The brothers were caught, and the charge against them was murder. (Matt Schmidt eluded the police and private detectives for years, but at last he too was arrested, at the house of Emma Goldman, the anarchist leader; he was given away by a boy in her house for the reward.)

Union labor believed the McNamaras innocent and hired Clarence Darrow to defend them, but as the trial proceeded the prosecution's mounting evidence against them made Darrow doubt he could win. Steffens still believed reason could lead to justice, and was anxious to try out a long-cherished plan to get labor and capital together. He wanted a "new deal" for labor, and hoped that the employers, rather than punishing individuals, would sit around a table and enunciate new principles. But time was short, the employers were too angry to listen, and the fear grew with Darrow and Steffens that the men might be convicted and hanged. Stef finally persuaded J. B., over the prisoner's fierce objections, to change his plea to "guilty." (The argument that finally won his grudging consent was that his elder brother would hang, too.) No client of Darrow's had ever been executed and, Stef told me, Darrow could never bear to face that possibility.

The labor movement was nonplused and infuriated, for despite the concession Stef had wrung from judge and employers of relatively light sentences and no castigation from the Bench, J. B. was given life and John J. fifteen years—and a sizzling indictment from the Bench. Stef was reviled and mocked, attacked by friend and enemy. His protégé, Jack Reed, wrote a satiric poem called *Sangar*, jeering at Steffens' naïveté. Stef had described to me the trunkfuls of denunciations that reached him; from then on, no magazine would publish him. I had the impression that he never ceased to feel a certain self-reproach, and he had worked tirelessly for the men's release. His "interference" had satisfied neither side, had not helped the men or made "capital sit down with labor." Stef admired the courage these men had shown throughout the whole case, especially at its end. Whenever we saw Tom Mooney at San Quentin, Stef would comfort himself by teasing Mooney: "I'm not interested in your case, you're innocent."

J. B. and Matt Schmidt came into the warden's office. They wore faded blue trousers and shirts, and they sat down at once and talked quietly in low, almost monotonous, voices. J. B. was blond and spare, with blazing blue eyes and a silent secret smile that showed gold in his front teeth. "Schmidtie" was dark, stout, jolly, a Micawber type; he kept smiling as he made his sarcastic remarks.

"So this is your girl," J. B. said, with a pleasure that thrilled me. "You'll go on with this case when the old men have gotten tired, won't you, Peter, and, after you, Little Pete."

J. B. wouldn't talk about himself. We knew from Older that in the jail he befriended young lost boys who came in angry and truculent, and fought for justice inside the prison. For years men came out of San Quentin telling what J. B. had done for them; they almost worshipped him. J. B.'s prison job at the time was feeding the condemned men on Death Row, but he would not talk about that, either. For years we called on J. B. whenever we were near San Francisco. This particular warden was friendly to Older and let us visit with the men in his office; later wardens made me sit on one side of a caged counter, with glass between, all the prisoners together in a room and a guard watching.

Steffens appealed to every governor for a pardon; he wrote to conservative labor leaders, editors, politicians, to the Chandlers, who owned the Los Angeles *Times* that had been blown up. It was all fruitless.

When J. B. McNamara died in 1941, I said a few words at his memorial service. He had been sent to Folsom, a harsher jail, as punishment for helping other prisoners, and he had also been deprived of his few comforts—slippers, books (including Steffens' *Autobiography*), and a strip of carpet he had used for more than a decade. I had gone to Folsom and kept up my visits to J. B. until, after thirty years behind bars, cancer finally ended his life.

In Santa Monica I met Jack Black, a former highwayman and burglar, now a close friend of Older's and Older's prize illustration of his belief that "there is no such thing as a criminal." Jack was hard and straight, a painfully thin man with bony hands and a tragic face. He had been tortured and flogged, laced into a strait jacket before that particular torture instrument was abolished. One could not be "phony" with him. It was a novel experience for me to know a thief as a friend.

He told me a good deal about his life, though not all at one time. As a milkboy he had been collecting bills in a brothel when the house was raided. "They took the madam and the girls off to jail and scooped me up with them," he related. "I didn't even know what the place was. A few days later the girls were bailed out, but I was a kid, nobody's business, and I was forgotten. I stayed in that jail a year, and the only people who treated me decent were the yeggs and tramps. They made a pal of me, and when I came out and ran into one of them, Smiley, a burglar, who had been decent to me, he asked me to help on a second-storey job. I couldn't refuse, could I?" That was the beginning; after that Jack Black lived a burglar's life for thirty years.

He was not "reformed" now, he said, and distrusted any burglar who claimed to be. "How is it you don't steal now?" I asked. "When Older got me out of jail and trusted me, I quit stealing, that's all."

"I cured myself of dope because Older asked me to," he said another time. "That was hard. Older had told me, 'You'll have to cut it out, Jack, or it'll make a bum of you.' I put in six hard months, but I had to do it; Older trusted me."

In his book, *You Can't Win*, Black tells how he broke himself of his opium habit:

I had been using opium steadily for ten years. Now I made up my mind to quit. I found I had to pay back every second of sleep, every quiet restful moment I had got in the whole ten years. I could stick the daytime out. I read, or ate, or walked around the room. I did not dare go out in the daytime, for fear I would be recognized by the police or some stool pigeon. It was the small, still hours of the night that got me. But the last words of my friend who had rescued me [Older] were always in my ears. "Lay away from that stuff, it'll make a bum of you."

Hundreds of times it was just that memory that tipped the balance, and I would take only what I had allowed myself, no more. I believe now I quit because he said that to me. I felt that if I could not do that much, and it was the only thing he ever asked me to do, I wasn't worthy of the friendship of such a man.

That was Jack Black's law of life—someone trusted you and you lived up to it.

Before we met, I had wondered what to talk about, but the moment we shook hands I felt at ease. He was so pleased to see Steffens, and so obviously delighted with Pete, so happy that there was a Pete at all, that we were soon like old friends.

I asked the burglar what habits had stayed with him from his housebreaking days. He thought only a minute. "I never go into my house before walking all around it to case the joint. And I count ten before I talk to a cop."

He never got over his hatred of the police. I was driving with Jack up the Bay Shore Highway once, when a police siren blew.

"Your driver's license," a traffic policeman challenged, at which Jack broke into a furious tirade at me.

"I told you not to drive so fast, I kept telling you you were speeding, why couldn't you watch the speedometer?" I was abashed before the policeman and drove on in silence.

"I had to talk to you like that," Jack said. "If I hadn't, I'd have exploded at the cop."

I asked Jack once how to prevent burglaries. "Get a dollar-and-a-half dog," he said cynically. And another time, when asked, "Could you imagine ever stealing again, Jack?," he answered in a flash: "If Older asked me to." He was interested in my visit to San Quentin, but when I expressed my surprise at the gardens, he shamed me with a muttered "Yeah, *gardens.*"

After seeing Jack in Santa Monica we went north to the Hollister Ranch, the ranch Stef had daydreamed to me about. His sister Dot and her husband, J. James Hollister, a California state senator, met us at their small railroad station of Gaviota and drove us for an hour along a narrow, rocky precipice road that made me nervous all the way lest we slide down the craggy side. It ran between grassland and huge trees, the wild oak and lilac I was already coming to associate with California; after a hairpin turn we came full upon the ocean—lying blue and sparkling, like the Mediterranean. The dazzling white beach ran empty for seventeen miles—"seventeen miles of private ocean," they said.

Dot differed from Laura. Small and blonde too, she talked in an endless stream. "I suppose you've got ideas we won't approve of, we're landowners and reactionary of course, but it doesn't matter, we don't agree with Len's ideas either. You're an intellectual, my children aren't, I would have liked them to be, like myself when I studied at Göttingen, where Len took philosophy, but none of them are except perhaps Janie. . . ." On and on. It delighted me, and then around the last bend there stood the house—a white frame building, large and old-fashioned, set in lilac, laburnum, and loquat trees, with a swimming pool before the door.

Jim Hollister was the opposite of his wife. He was also of a pioneering family, tall, bronzed, square-jawed, with weather-beaten, leathery skin that showed his outdoor life. He rode the range from dawn to dark with his cowboys, who, to my surprise, called him Jim. He was as slow-spoken and deliberate as his wife was quick and jerky, and it surprised me, knowing England's gentleman-farmers and remembering my experience with the Misses Debenham, to see two such large landowners work along with their help. For Dot was also at it all day, with one Chinese "boy" to assist her; managing house and farm, orchards of grapefruit and oranges, avocadoes and walnuts, which she made yield a handsome profit; keeping up with scientific agricultural knowledge of soils, wells, rock deposits. She suspected they might strike oil, which was making fortunes for Californians then. My experience at the ranch gave me my first view and an appreciative insight into "grass-roots" American egalitarianism and lack of class feeling.

The month passed quickly. Stef felt at home and grateful to have Pete become a member of his wider family, his American uncles, aunts, and cousins. Pete himself went off delightedly on horseback with Janie or "the Sentator," taking in roundups and brandings of calves and lambs and learning to kill rattlesnakes with his cousins. It was exactly the life his papa had hoped for.

# 11

## TOO MANY LAMPSHADES—BY THE SEA

We came to Carmel by chance. We needed to settle somewhere temporarily for Stef's work before going back to Europe. So we drove down to Carmel.

Pete was hardly on the beach before he went native, stripped off his clothes and ran into the water. "Why don't you stay here for the summer?" Laura suggested. There was one small frame house still for rent, on the road that ran along the beach; we could have it for six weeks. So we rented The Sandbox.

Stef wanted a home, a place of his own. We hadn't yet had one. "In my bones," as Stef put it, he wanted to settle. He had got to the muckraking section of his Life, which bored him. "I don't believe in that kind of action any more," he complained, "how can I put my heart into something with which I no longer agree?" Once he tore up two chapters by mistake and stopped writing for a year. The job seemed just too much, and he cried often, "I've lived too long! I can never finish this book."

Then, as happens in California, we ran into a real-estate agent, John Kenneth Turner, a lanky old newspaper colleague of Steffens, who kept bringing us suggestions of houses to buy. His zeal amused me, it was so useless; of course we would be going back to Europe, where I belonged.

But one day Turner took us to a house on San Antonio Street, a romantic place that looked handmade and, in fact, was. A great studio room had five high windows with book shelves underneath; a few steps up, a wide balcony overlooked the sea. On a level with the lowest floor, an irregular garden stretched all around. The house had been built by two artists, Jessie Arms Botke and her Dutch husband, Cornelis Botke, who were now moving to Los

Angeles; it was full of hand-painted furniture they had constructed themselves. There was an outside studio with a solid carpenter's table, away from the house—an ideal place for work for me; and on the garden level, also separate from the rest of the house, a downstairs room that would serve as a study for Stef.

Without telling me, Stef made what he thought an impossible offer, more to tempt himself than with a thought that it might be accepted. But very early the next morning Turner ran up our garden path waving a telegram. "You've got a house," he cried. "They've accepted your offer."

"But we're not going to stay in the United States," I exploded. I went down to the beach and lay on the sand and tried to digest it. We had a house. We had chosen a place. We were not going back to Europe. I was going to live in America. This is the way important decisions usually happen. You don't "make" them, you haven't made up your mind at all and are not clear what you really want—and the decision has taken place. "Life is a violin that you learn to play as you go along."

I was now a householder I didn't want to be, in an America in which I was not going to stay, in a small seaside village that my wildest dreams had not foretold would be my home for nine years.

Carmel had been created when a real-estate man decided to enhance the value of his land by developing it and offering free lots to any artist who would build. The general public would follow artists, he knew. Among early settlers were George Sterling, the California poet, Jack London, Mary Austin, Ambrose Bierce. Stef himself had been offered a lot. Now Carmel was an "artists' colony," with painters, writers, musicians, photographers living in little wooden or stone cottages. But it was also a haven for the retired. "When they've died and gone to heaven, you find them in Carmel," Stef wisecracked.

It was an unspoiled, uncommercialized community. Special meetings decided whether a pine branch could be lopped off or a street paved. Roads went around trees. There were three traffic policemen and one judge—who hated to fine traffic violators—two hotels, one movie house, and a few shops with hand-painted signs: CORNER CUPBOARD  *  VANITY BOX  *  CABBAGES AND KINGS.

You went down the main street, Ocean Avenue, with its line of trees down the middle, steeply to the beach. Our town lay in a valley in the midst of hills and woods, facing the ocean, along which stretched a white, wide sandy beach from Point Pinos to Point Lobos, usually overrun by sandpipers and kelp.

Small as it was, Carmel had three separate personalities, as a university town is town and gown. We had the shopkeepers and builders, estate agents and businessmen; there were the socialites, wealthy retired families living either down the Highlands or among San Francisco millionaires in luxurious Pebble Beach or along the Seventeen-Mile Drive; and there were the bohemians and artists of Carmel proper, most of whom were unsuccessful, though there was a sprinkling of reputations. Robinson Jeffers, the poet, lived at Carmel Point, the writers Harry Leon Wilson and Gouverneur Morris over the hill in Monterey (where fish was canned), and John Steinbeck, who came later, in Pacific Grove, three miles away, in the dunes, a section that provided a meeting place for religious groups. As our local wisecrack had it, "Carmel-by-the-Sea, Monterey-by-the-Smell, Pacific Grove-by-God."

The serious artists worked; the arty hangers-on hung on. Stanley Wood, the painter, once summed up the difference for me. "Yes," he said, "the arty work, but in between working they yearn."

We had now to make a garden and find a name for our home. I eagerly took care of the first, and Jack Black gave us the second. "The thing a burglar needs most is a getaway," Jack said, and Stef jumped at it. "That's it, we'll call our house 'The Getaway,' a refuge for any poor s.o.b. in a jam." Now, as soon as we were settled, Stef wrote and invited his friends, all his friends, to come and stay with us. It was a habit of his to get far away from everybody, out of civilization, to be alone, and then invite the world to his door.

An old newspaper colleague of Stef's introduced us to Robinson Jeffers and his wife, Una. On their gate was a wooden plaque: NOT AT HOME TILL 4 P.M. Their low-walled granite-boulder cottage was called "Tor House," because Una loved everything Irish. To one side of it was the thick-walled square Irish tower built by Jeffers of boulders he laboriously rolled up from the beach each afternoon after four, when he had finished work. Una was a great believer in physical effort for her lean, powerful, long-limbed man. "It will keep him busy," she said in her incisive way, "the work I've got laid out for him, till he's eighty."

Robin was always the same tall silent man, painfully shy; but one could content oneself with just looking at his weather-beaten, handsome, rocklike face. One eye was violet, one blue. His gestures were timid and he kept his long arms hanging, his big hands uncomfortably unoccupied except for his pipe, as if he did not know what to do with them when they weren't rolling heavy boulders up cliffs. His shirt was always open at the long bronzed neck, and he wore breeches and leather gaiters. His voice was so low that it was hard to catch what he said when he did speak. When he talked to the twins, his boys, it was like a foreign tongue or a secret language.

The twins were part of Una's carefully nourished legend. "I wanted twin boys, I intended to have them, and when my first little girl died soon after she was born, I knew it was meant that I should get them." Donnan and Garth, then about twelve, were as handsome, blue-eyed, and silent as their father.

Una was a great contrast. Small, gay, lively, full of energy and an iron determination that life should yield what she wished it to, she was indefatigable in fashioning it. She had an insatiable curiosity: if new guests wore dark glasses, she ordered them to remove them: "I want to see your face." She elicited everyone's story, did the talking and entertaining for all the family. She offered you their homemade wine, made you feel at home, and fussed over you while she asked you a hundred questions. "Have you come to stay? Do you like it here? We've lived here seven years and we're going to stay forever. I don't believe in a telephone or electric light, do you? I like kerosene lamps, they're more work, but I prefer them. No, the boys don't go to school, I teach them myself at home, they waste so much time at school. Did you know anyone in Carmel before you came?"

I loved our visits and loved Una and Robin. They did much to reconcile me to this village the other side of the world. Una was always on the go, like a rushing bubbling brook. I admired—and a little envied—her unquestionable assurance about everything; she knew exactly what she wanted and usually got it. "I don't like grays, I like everything black or white," she asserted. She did the shopping, driving uptown in her old Chevrolet twice a day, to collect the mail that we fetched at the post office with the day's gossip, and to gather the latest news and the legends of the region, which she brought home for her man's epic poems. She also collected myths about her beloved Ireland from Ella Young, the wild-haired old rebel poet.

Sometimes Una drove over the hill to Monterey for wine or olive oil, and once in a while to get her men haircuts. She wore always the same kind of loose green tunic tied with a cord at the waist and white mocassins on her tiny feet. Her hair, which came to her waist, was wound in a thick braid around her head. This she always washed in rainwater collected in a special cask outside the house. In keeping with the legend Una joyously fostered, her first husband built a big house nearby on Point Lobos, and Una proudly related how "Teddy never turns off his lights at night till he sees my candles go out." Edward Kuster ("Teddy") remained a good friend of the whole family.

Visitors flocked to the Jeffers', poets like Witter Bynner and Arthur Davison Ficke from Taos, Edna Millay from the East, Ben Lehman from San Francisco. Robin's equally tall, silent brother, Hamilton, arrived occasionally for a wordless visit. Una told how once the two brothers had some business to transact about an inheritance, and how they sat silent a whole afternoon. "And when Hamilton left it was done." Robin's work was Una's religion. She managed all his correspondence with publishers and friends—he never wrote letters himself—read the reviews of his work, which he always denied doing, was his mouthpiece for the outside world. She also kept him at it. "I listen at the foot of the stairs," she told me, "and when I don't hear Robin walking up and down, I call up, 'Robin, pace!'"

I liked the story of Jeffers and the White Russian princess who called at Tor House the same weekend we, at the other end of the village, entertained Ilf and Petrov. They were the Soviet satirists who wrote their American impressions, including Carmel, in their book, *Little Golden America*. The Russian princess was telling Jeffers of her escape from her homeland, when they had to leave everything behind. "We came with nothing, absolutely nothing," she emphasized indignantly.

"You had your lives, didn't you?" Robin murmured.

But not all of Robin's admirers were welcomed at Tor House. There was, for example, a pretty Hollywood movie girl with green eyes, named Marcella, whom Una found when she came back from her shopping sitting there alone with Robin, before 4 P.M.—the sacred hour before which the poet must not be disturbed. Una chased her out of the house, then went back and vented her anger. "I've spent a lifetime making this house, our lives, everything," she cried, furious, "and I won't have that woman come here and break it up, I won't stand it!" And as she spoke she tore at the balustrade, and pulled out balusters one by one. As she continued her tirade, her two sons, with masklike faces, carefully and silently fitted each baluster back into place again.

I managed to steer a rather safe course between my warm friendship for her and my admiration for Robin, which I took no pains to hide. He liked us all three ("Pete is my friend," he said once), appreciated our visits and Stef's stories of the revolutions, my talk of England or Italy, of books or our work—though Jeffers never discussed his. He liked to hear any stories of that outside world he so seldom visited, and he preferred natural people. But though I was as circumspect as possible, I once ran afoul of Una at a cocktail party at which everyone had had perhaps a little too much to drink, for suddenly she burst out at me out of the blue: "As for you, I know you've never touched Robin or he you, but there's something between you all the same."

Robin's response was typical. When in my dismay at Una's challenge I appealed to him standing there in his usual embarrassed way, smoking his pipe: "But Robin, you know there's nothing, absolutely nothing like that, why don't you tell Una?," he merely smiled constrainedly and went on smoking.

On occasion Una could become irritated by our political activities, of which she had no understanding. Her only political feeling was that of anger as their house taxes mounted. Once she even asked me, "What's so wrong with Hitler? He doesn't smoke or drink or go with women." Politics was not Una's strong point. Individual lives were her delight and enthralling interest, and she knew every legend of every writer and poet practically throughout the ages.

Something was always going on in Carmel that seemed to me lunatic, though I took part in it out of curiosity and fun. Susan Porter, of the mahogany voice, and old Mrs. Blackman set up a God Circle. "Only those can participate who've had Authentic Experience," Mrs. Blackman bubbled. "We must share it fully and honestly. That will be reaching Beauty. Have you had an Authentic Experience?" We actually met for several months in Mrs. Blackman's Victorian-Iowa faded living room, with her thick chintz curtains, brown with yellow cabbage roses, and her batik lampshades that enveloped everything in a halo vague and blurred. In our ceaseless self-examination, "What's wrong with Carmel?," one answer remained in my mind: "There are too many lampshades."

We had our share of callers, too, and among The Getaway's early visitors were Ben Lindsey and his wife, Henrietta. Lindsey, small, wiry, pugnacious, had become famous for his methods of dealing with young offenders. Steffens had written about him in his muckraking days, a series of articles called "The Just Judge," in which he told how Lindsey did not sit on a dais above but on the same level with the little culprit and talked to him man to man —it was new then to trust a small delinquent. Lindsey made a practice of sending a boy alone to reform school, merely handing him his train ticket. "Only one boy betrayed me," he boasted. Ben told me stories of the illegitimate children of Denver's "best" daughters, which he had happily and secretly (and somewhat triumphantly) arranged for their own mothers to adopt.

James H. Causey came from Denver, too. He was, even for an American, unusual. Stef had told me about him in England, how he had gone to the Ruhr after the 1914 war "to see how I could help." Germany was starving, the Allies were still thinking in terms of punishment and revenge: "Hang the Kaiser"; "Make Germany pay." And Causey was aghast.

"I was looking down from my hotel window wondering what I could do," he related, "when I caught sight, in a long queue of waiting women, of one who looked like my mother. I imagined my mother having to queue up for potatoes like that, and I couldn't bear it; I knew at once what my job must be—I must feed the Ruhr." And he did. Alone he raised the millions of pounds to do it, until truckloads of potatoes rolled into the Ruhr, all marked, as he described, "James H. Causey, American, Essen."

During our first months in Carmel, Laura and Suggett came down often. We drove with them to a newly opened Yosemite "luxury" hotel, the Ahwahnee, very much directed to adult wants, and as I tucked Pete in bed one night, he complained to me in verse:

I want to go back to my house
My house is crying for me
I don't like this Ah-Wah-Nee
I don't like this Yo-sem-pi-ty
I want to go back to my house
My house is crying for me.

So we went back to Pete's Getaway.

Visitors of all kinds to our distant village came to lecture, and some stayed on, frequently for quite a time. A. R. Orage, the English editor who helped discover writers like Katherine Mansfield and Michael Arlen, remained a year. Krishnamurti, the Indian sage, handsome, black-haired, and slender, with a beautiful voice, whom Annie Besant had chosen as the reincarnation of Jesus (until he repudiated this role), came often. He traveled up and down the coast, from his Ojai Valley, lecturing on his gospel of individual responsibility. Stef and I liked him and enjoyed listening to his talk, even when not quite sure of its import. One of our Carmelites thought she knew, though: "Is it not true, Krishnaji, that you are saying, 'Life is a wheel and we are all spokes'?"

Mabel Dodge came from New Mexico with Tony Luhan, her American Indian husband. Tony was still married to an Indian wife and under United States law was not allowed to divorce her, so every Friday, Mabel told us, "I plait his long black hair with bright-colored ribbons and send him off to his wife." Tony was broad-shouldered, square, brown-skinned, and wore Western clothes, with cowboy boots and a colored Navajo rug, togalike, over his shoulders. He was illiterate and childlike, and liked to play darts or gather shells on the beach with the children. He brought his big Navajo drum to parties, and when he got bored, would take it out and thump on it an Indian lament. When I saw him silent and seemingly unhappy at these cocktail parties, and asked Mabel if she thought he understood what they were chattering about, she responded, "Oh, he gets it through his skin."

Tony accompanied Mabel everywhere, driving their long black Cadillac while she sat dignifiedly in the back with a stout white bulldog. When the limousine swept down the little winding Carmel streets, they looked like three bulldogs sitting together.

Mabel was square and squat like her husband, and though her face was broad, she wore her straight dark hair cut short in a bang. She was a strong, dominating woman who had always been wealthy and who used her money to make a personal bohemia. She created settings for artistic or odd individuals—the "movers and shakers" she liked to have around—the latest being a hundred-thousand-dollar luxury ranch in Taos, New Mexico, which she built when she shed her painter husband Maurice Sterne in favor of the Indian, Tony. "I like to make things 'happen,'" Mabel said, and she did; she experimented with drugs, treating her guests to mescaline parties. She mixed couples for the fun of "making trouble," and did not hesitate to destroy in the process. She even made trouble between Una and Robin on one occasion.

I admired her intense vitality and energy even while I distrusted the anarchic uses to which she put them. When she told me about her famous "salon of radicals, anarchists, and poets" at 23 Fifth Avenue before World War I, and I remarked what fascinating discussions there must have been, she commented dryly, "Oh, I never *listened* to what they said, I only watched the interplay of personality." Her literary friends wrote about her—Max Eastman, Jack Reed, with whom she had had a celebrated affair, Carl Van Vechten, D. H. Lawrence (*The Woman Who Rode Away*)—while she herself recounted in six volumes her *Intimate Memories*. When Lawrence "unfeelingly died," as Steffy, who was a very old friend, put it, Mabel decided on Jeffers for her "next lion," and came straight to Carmel.

Mabel was frantic when Jo Davidson chose to sculpt Robin on our balcony instead of in the house she had especially rented, and sought daily to lure me away from artist and model on any pretext. She would drive by in that domineering Cadillac and peremptorily order me to accompany her uptown—on one occasion to send fourteen telegrams inviting guests to Carmel, only to cancel them the next day. "How boring if they should all show up," she wailed. And a scowling Mabel showed up at the studio party to which we invited all Carmel to admire Jo's finished bust. Jo took one look at her face and whispered gaily to me, " 'We' are not going to like the bust." He was right. "He hasn't caught the spiritual quality in the eyes," Mabel announced, "or the poetry of the nostrils," and none present dared oppose.

# 12

# TO KEEP MY PURPOSE ON

Despite all these goings-on I did feel out of my element in this eccentric village. It was, after all, quite a distance from Westminster. When Stef, as I have said, maintained that our population consisted of people "who have died and gone to heaven," I felt I didn't know about heaven, but they certainly weren't of my world. Jo and Yvonne kept bringing back that world, and our second spring at The Getaway they took us with them to Kansas for a visit to the "new America" of Ernest W. Marland.

In the middle of the bare windy plains of Kansas we found his Ponca City, the town he had created from scratch. This millionaire had risen from a ten-dollar-a-week employee to become master of a fortune, it was said, of three hundred million dollars; and he had taken a cowboy settlement with hitching posts in the pavement and boosted it into this model town with hospital, library, school, recreation center, clubs.

Marland was square-jawed, of medium height, with hard blue eyes and a clean-shaven, American face. Ponca City was more grotesque than I had imagined, like a Western-movie city. It had a few asphalt streets, with boulders to tether horses to, but instead of horses, Indians rode in sleek limousines—Indians on whose lands Marland had found oil. They did not know what to do with their money, "except to buy cars and clothes," as he told us. They parked at the curb by those old hitching posts in front of the new shops, the five and ten, the A. & P., or the Esso gas station.

Marland's home was a palatial mansion with painted ceilings and paneled walls, set in grounds that embodied three European models, borrowing from St. Germain-en-Laye, Versailles, and the Petit Trianon. Every tree, shrub, and bush had been imported, as had the avenues of cypresses, the lawns, ornamental gardens, the artificial lakes and their Japanese ducks. A hundred Japanese gardeners tended the domain. Down one wide alley of Italian cypresses ran a line of giant statuary—life-size bronzes of Marland, his son, and niece-wife, Lydie, and several forty-foot models of the "Pioneer Woman," produced by sculptors competing for the hundred-thousand-dollar prize Marland had offered.

Touring the place with our host, we found in the kitchen six giant refrigerators with practically a whole slaughtered animal hanging in each. Six cooks prepared meals for Marland, his bride, his son, and servants, but what we had for lunch, incurring Yvonne's gastronomic outrage, was tinned sardines.

Stef and I were sitting in our room talking over what we had seen, when we heard the strains of a tinny phonograph. Since Pete liked music, I went with him in search of it, and at an open bedroom door down the long corridor met a strange sight. A chest stood with its drawers half open and lingerie dripping from it— exquisite underwear in all colors, dozens of pairs of stockings thrown higgledy-piggledy. In a corner of the room Lydie, Marland's young wife, sat with her broad face and sensuous lips puckered, ready to weep. When Pete started right in to dance to the record, she smiled instead.

"Oh, I'm so glad you came," she cried. "I'm trying to decide what to wear and I can't. Please stay here," and she danced a few steps with the little boy.

Yvonne had told me of a shopping expedition with Lydie in New York, when the girl had been unable to choose between two pairs of gloves, and Yvonne had laughed and said, "You can afford both, can't you?" Lydie was actually Marland's niece, whom Marland had adopted; but when he fell in love with her, he disadopted and married her. She had told Yvonne about her desire to be a dancer. "It's my only ambition, but E. W. won't permit it, so I can't do anything," she had commented sadly. The tinny gramophone went on grinding out its little tune.

Marland's grand paternalism was not despotic. He built education centers for his employees and for the town, churches, clinics, orphans' homes, a golf course; he had encouraged night classes. "At one time I had eighteen thousand employees enrolled in our night classes, and no one had to go who didn't want to," he boasted. His riches were fabulous. His oil holdings spilled over

into Mexico, Canada, England; he owned a plantation in Mississippi and a two-thousand-acre game refuge in Oklahoma. He
traveled in a private railroad car or in his own yacht, and he was
putting together a million-dollar art collection. He had imported
hundreds of ponies for his polo games, in addition to red hunting
coats, foxes, hounds, and the very woods for the hunt. And in the
hall hung a larger-than-life portrait of Lydie in her hunting
coat and stock, with a whip, on horseback. At a studio party Marland
gave for us, he introduced one tall, beautiful young man after
another to me, always with the same phrase: "I made him his first
million." Stef was enchanted. "If novelists would pay attention
to this Marland story," he said, "it would change the very content
of American fiction. This is the equivalent of the love story in
modern American life."

The later part of the "novel" of E. W. Marland turned into a
semitragedy. Bankers lured him, with offers of credit at low rates,
to expand, and he borrowed large sums. Then they called in their
loans and cleaned him out. Marland had to sell every last shred
to pay his debts, and went bankrupt. The palace folded, and the
forest, and the park. For a time he lived in the studio, then that
was closed. The gardens lay neglected. The wind blew through
the yellow grasses of the treeless Kansas steppe and through the
weed-overgrown mansion grounds. The embittered victim swore
vengeance. He became a Congressman—this man who had boasted
to me: "Why should I be a Senator? I *own* six Senators." He could
not do much in Washington, so he got himself elected Governor of
Oklahoma and served two terms. But they had killed his spirit, and
shortly after that he died.

I had now seen something of that "new America" Jo had been
so excited about, and I was not exactly overwhelmed. We went
back to our art colony. There were the "arty" again, parading up
and down Ocean Avenue in their pants of purple toweling, or
watching John Bovingdon dance nude in the rafters of somebody's
cottage. The latest modern musician was explaining psycho-physical
tonality; a poet published his theories in a slim volume called
*Seed Ideas,* printed by hand and bound in purple by one of his
devotees. And there was Mrs. Dickinson introducing a lecture by
a swami from Los Angeles, with the warning, "Mr. X will now
explain to us what we do not know in a language we do not understand."

This was the Carmel to which I felt I did not belong. Then

something unexpected would happen; someone would come with a new philosophy, or an old one refurbished, or a lecture on avant-garde art. There would be debates, recitals, chamber-music concerts, visits from Charles Lindbergh, the Sinclair Lewises, George Antheil, Gertrude Stein, and I would share in the village interest and excitement, as I did when we started *The Carmelite*.

Its beginnings were inauspicious. About forty people had crowded into a stuffy little room and were sitting cross-legged on the floor, or squeezed together on window sills. Pauline sat behind a desk tossing her head like a horse. Her laugh was a little like the neighing of a horse, too, and her front teeth had a gap between them. She was the divorced wife of an Austrian architect in Los Angeles she always called Aramess—later I discovered they were his initials, R. M. S.—and she was in many ways the moving spirit of the village. She had come defiantly up our garden path when I first arrived. "Your son is one of the world's twenty geniuses," she had started right in, "mine is another. Those of us entrusted with genius must see it flower; you and I must start a superlative school."

"I never particularly thought of Pete as a genius," I answered mildly, watering my stocks and phlox. "He's just a nice little boy—and I've found in Monterey just the person to run a nursery school, I think."

Pauline had to be "modern" about everything, but in her undifferentiating enthusiasms she sometimes saw further than the rest of us. When her friend Galka Scheyer came in 1928, with pictures by Paul Klee and the Blue Four that people laughed at and wouldn't have thought of buying, Pauline said Klee could be understood in either poetry or music. She was the first to introduce us to Dada, surrealism, Schönberg. Yet she could go overboard so easily. When she took Mark, her five-year-old, to the nursery school, run by our sensible, down-to-earth Julia Breinig in her family's hundred-year-old adobe, Pauline said to him, "Oh, Mark, don't you feel you could put the age of this place into a little dance?" This "crazy nut," as we thought of her, kept everything at a boil, the sensible and the ridiculous all mixed up.

"But she's crazy only in the best sense," Harry Dickinson maintained; and it must be said that Pauline achieved a good deal. She started our art gallery to show the work of local painters and exceptional photographers, Edward Weston, Edward Hagemayer, Ansel Adams; helped set up a music society that became celebrated, with international artists stopping on their way from Los Angeles to San Francisco to perform in Carmel; and it was Pauline the flibbertigibbet who sparked off our weekly, *The Carmelite.*

The paper ran for several years and helped reconcile me to our odd life in these distant sticks. We handled everything, world news and woodcuts by the latest abstractionist, poems and art criticism, village news and gossip, a children's column, and editorials on every subject under the sun. Pauline wrote on "Is the Superlative Good Enough?," Stef on mass production, Mr. Dickinson on Sacco and Vanzetti and the Majesty of the Law. I worked passionately in every department, from fillers to reporting, columns to book reviewing and interviews with visiting firemen, and was even seduced to ads—which gave me some heartburn when I ran up against the art complexes of our editor.

"This is not the ad I gave you," the moneylender in Monterey stormed, "my rates are 4¾ per cent and you have printed 4 per cent." Pauline smiled indulgently. "But he doesn't understand, ¾ doesn't make a good design and I cannot have any ugliness in this paper. What does it matter, 4, 4½, 5?" I suggested she leave the make-up of the ads to me.

The whole village was drawn into *The Carmelite*'s orbit. At studio parties they didn't discuss psychoanalytical plurality or "the inevitable polarity of thought," but the paper, its style and vocabulary, its make-up, illustrations, circulation. Stef thought up witty copy, we made up ads at parties like a parlor game, and people asked their favorite stores to advertise. The San Francisco papers began quoting us.

One of our contributors was Caroline Blackman, who painted and wrote, and later married the poet Orrick Johns. She lived alone in a small cottage under dense pines, "trying to achieve absolute poverty," as she claimed. She wrote mostly for her "bottom drawer," she insisted, but I did manage to extract a couple of verses for our paper, which in a funny way expressed me in Carmel to me.

> Other people's lives look tidy,
> Mine is such a mess.
> Yet I go to parties too
> In a party dress.
>
> Who's to tell the button
> Of my plan's undone?
> Or the safety pin I wear
> To keep my purpose on?

Often I was maddened by Pauline's reporting. "Human beings are caught within the flood tide of a great initiating," she would write of an exhibit. She opposed the machine age, mass production, factories, commerce. One morning, as I was struggling with bills, mostly unpaid, she floated into the office. "Peter, is the universe conscious?" she asked earnestly. "Harold and I were up all night arguing it."

But we did have sensible journalism. I was so much the opposite of Pauline, and others had their feet on the ground, too. Stef enjoyed writing comments, epigrams, and editorials. Hearst had asked him to do a syndicated column for a large sum and a circulation of twenty-four million, but Steffens refused. "I'd rather say what I want to for nothing and a circulation of three hundred," he maintained.

I became absorbed in the job. I was a journalist at last. It began to take all my time; when Pauline was away, I did all her jobs. Stef wrote to my mother: "I have no wife any more, I sleep next to the editor of *The Carmelite*."

The *Autobiography* was coming along. Stef worked steadily, but now he was writing and rewriting paragraphs again. Before he started work in the morning he would write personal letters—they seemed to free his thoughts for his book. (But he never addressed them, or put them in envelopes or posted them. This was my daily job.) Every few days he sent field reports to my mother on the growth of her grandson, sometimes written as from Pete himself, telling of some new discovery or observation. One little ditty-refrain he taught Pete to chant with him as they walked the garden together, which got under my skin on occasion, ran, "Pete and Papa won'erful, Mama and Anna are ab-surd." Mother appreciated the letters and had long given up trying to advise on upbringing.

The father could in fact never spend enough time with his son, and watched and commented on every step of his growth. And Pete returned the affection. I was driving a group of nursery-school children to Monterey one morning, when they started boasting about their fathers: "My daddy's an actor," "My daddy's a carpenter." Pete listened awhile in competitive silence and then announced, *"My* daddy's called Papa."

"I want to prevent Pete developing feelings of inferiority." This was one of Stef's chief desires. "Too many kids suffer from that."

To this end everything was to be looked at positively and constructively. When Pete broke his leg and was laid up, unable to play with the others, his father made it an achievement: "Pete's the only boy in Carmel who has a broken leg." He was not ordered peremptorily to bed in the middle of some unfinished game, but while helping him put away his things, his father would discuss the next morning's delights: "The sun'll get up and the sun'll say to Pete through the window, 'Aren't you up yet, who've I got to play with?' " until all disappointment had melted away. When Pete broke a vase, he wasn't scolded; instead, "That piece of china isn't as precious as the little boy's feelings." Steffens said he wanted to develop Pete's will power, so he enticed him to disobey; he would draw a line in the path and forbid him to cross it and, after Pete had scanned his father's face, decided it was "fun," and put his foot across, would warmly congratulate him. I was sometimes troubled by it all, but I felt Stef must carry through his theories and experiments as he wished.

I very much wanted another child, but the father would not hear of it.

"I don't want an institution, a nursery, I want Pete. I'd be jealous for Pete. Besides, if you have one, you'll want two, and if you have two you'll want three, so let's stop at one." I couldn't answer that argument. "You can have other children after I'm gone, you'll marry again—if one was happily married once, one marries again," he would say more seriously. I did contemplate facing him with the fact of pregnancy, but didn't think that quite fair; a matter as important as this must be agreed upon.

What I thought I did understand was Stef's "anarchist" dislike of binding "chains," of "institutions." Hadn't I had the same feeling in my earlier H. G. Wells days? Was he also afraid that if I turned to someone else we might not remain friends? He had seen too many unhappy divorces, with the child the football. He hoped we would be together "only because we wanted to, not because of any legal ties." Companionate marriage was in the air, so was anarchism. Emma Goldman still made fiery talks on the glories of free love. Stef believed we could have a secret divorce, that no one but ourselves would know. He mentioned it half in jest to lawyer friends from time to time, and one of his old associates promised that "one day" he would get us such a secret separation, "in poor

man's court in New York, where no reporters would go for a story."
Sometimes I thought Stef had a need to "get back at," to take some
kind of revenge on, a social system he could not respect, by some
such secret defiance of its rules. And I also felt I should perhaps
help him do what he wanted without considering my own feelings.
There was no question of a real change in our intimate relationship: our marriage lacked nothing; we had a marriage in its truest
sense; in every sense, the fabric of our lives was intermeshed, in-
extricably bound together.

I was becoming homesick for the outside world. Carmel was
beautiful, quiet, sunny, calm, good for Stef's work, but life was
rushing along and I was not "doing anything." Even *The Carmelite*
did not fulfill the hopes of my LSE and Fabian days. And my
mother wanted very much to see her grandson again. Rudi had
come through Carmel on his way to a mining job in Australia and
told me how much she missed us.

"Why don't I go to England this summer?" I asked Stef, and he
agreed. And when one day he came back idly to the idea that we
might try Mexico for that secret divorce, I responded almost in
mockery: "Since I'm going away for the summer, why not use this
opportunity?"

"Okay, we'll try it," Stef said, chuckling, and so I went off, on
Harry Dickinson's advice, to a "friendly" lawyer he knew in Watsonville, all rather as a lark. I asked if we could make secret arrangements, so that no one would ever be the wiser; and my first
shock came when the lawyer, hardly looking up from his papers,
asked, "You really want this?"

"Of course not," I blazed.

Then he began to be difficult. "I need instances of mental
cruelty," he said—that was the ground for divorce in California.
I could not think of any and he tried to help me out. "Does he
ever reproach you?" "For what?" "For wanting to go out, to dance
perhaps, *I* don't know."

"But I thought you understood," I said.

"There has to be mental cruelty," the lawyer commented dryly.

So I suggested to Stef that we leave things as they were, that it
wasn't so simple, that we stay happily married though married;
but Stef said, "Now we've started, let's go through with it." And
so one fine day it came out in all the papers: "May and December
Wedding Ended."

I was struck cold with anguish. A private joke had suddenly become a social fact, which I hastened to deny in the face of universal disbelief. Stef laughed; he was used to attacks and disagreeable publicity and having the world on his tail, but it was my first dose and I shrank from it in hurt consternation. Carmel buzzed; I did not go out, but Anna told me of the comments.

"Do they . . . ?" "Are they . . . ?" "When is she leaving?" "Does she get the house?" And when we both seemed still to be living at the same address: "Do they talk to one another?" A hardier spirit went further: "Do they . . . er . . . share the same room?" And one woman, some unknown friend of mine: "Fancy being cruel to that lovely girl!" The "mental cruelty" charge had stuck: people do believe "what they read in the papers."

Stef mocked them all. "You tell everybody," he instructed Anna, "that we have built a stone wall down the middle of the studio and that she lives on one side of it and I on the other." And to people who asked him direct questions on the street he gave differing answers, a new one each time.

"I never give the same reason twice," Stef announced, "so when my friends get together to compare notes, each has a different version and they can't make head or tail. . . ." And he enjoyed as always the tweaking of everybody's sensibilities about conventions.

But when I left for England I was depressed, and as I met old friends across the country and found that they had accepted the reports without an inkling of the truth, I grew resentful and exasperated—and more and more miserable. My attempted explanations met incredulity: this was not something one played with. It wasn't, either, I concluded wryly, and I cherished the sympathetic remark of one good friend, Garet Garrett, who had been living in Carmel: "Only God and Freud can understand this Steffens business."

# 13

## IMPOSSIBILITIES UNLIMITED

I was unhappy all the way east, reading the newspaper clippings about my "divorce," and on the boat to England I spoke to no one. I watched the sea and entertained Pete, who now, at five, enjoyed the trip. I wrote to Stef:

My darling,
Pete was first off the boat and dashed right down into "grandma's" arms. She took the divorce thing very well, though doesn't see your psychology and thought there must have been someone else you were "setting me free" for. No one sees why we do it. Mother had got clippings about it.

I went to the first Malvern Festival dedicated to the performance of Bernard Shaw's works, and had a long interview with him. Shaw said, "People in general do not like anyone to be first-class, they prefer mediocrity." His waggish white beard and ironic, Irish voice gave the impression of great good humor. He listened to my stories of Marland and mass production in America, and commented that English people would not turn in old automobiles the way Americans did.

"People grow attached to their cars, and give them Christian names," he said, and in his mocking aggressive manner asserted that if my name was both Ella and Winter, it must really surely be Ella Winter Wilcox. He was delighted with the honor done him in this first festival of his plays.

I visited, with my old friend Ena, the progressive school run by Bertrand Russell and his then wife, Dora Black. The children, two small Russells among them, were sitting on a row of potties, a "progressive" innovation. There was no formal discipline; we watched a cooking lesson, with the children stirring the cake in turn, clockwise or counterclockwise, fast or slow.

"Shouldn't it be stirred always in the same direction?" we asked.

"We give the children freedom" was the slightly haughty reply. "Every child follows his own inclination."

"Doesn't the cake have a point of view?" Ena ventured a little maliciously. There was no reply. Despite Russell's many new and challenging educational ideas, the school later failed.

A trip to Paris to visit the Davidsons made me aware of my homesickness, and by October I could stay away no longer. How unthinkable it would be not to have Stef to come back to. So much for our "divorce."

Pete and I arrived in New York on October 29, to be greeted by the stock-market crash. I had no realization then of all that it would mean, and the next winter was almost the happiest I had spent in Carmel. We still had our quota of surrealist musicians and slender little volumes of poems called *Loving Leaves* or *Frozen Fires,* and "authentic" parties, after which Mrs. Dickinson would sigh, "Oh dear, why does everything have to be significant?" But we also had our sensible friends, and even more visitors than before. They came in flocks to talk to Steffens, for something incomprehensible had taken place in booming America: the depression had come upon us. And as we were to learn from now on, it altered the American response to almost all political ideas.

We didn't know how long the economic depression would last or how serious it would be, but in those early months it exhilarated Steffens: events were proving the theory that capitalists must overproduce—and couldn't stop. "They've got their feet in the trough," he remarked, "and they can't take them out."

He wrote articles and editorials, one for Hearst, called "This Depression of Ours is Chock-Full of Good News," and he "watched American business not learn its lesson." This was the third great slump Steffens had witnessed, and he kept pointing to their resemblances.

"Questions are becoming more fundamental as the crisis grows," he recorded. "They're worried now, but wait awhile." He enjoyed the questioning, the confusion and bewilderment, and wrote mocking little articles for our *Carmelite,* commenting on events, delighted to prick and tease. But he was tired of the long haul of his book and impatient to get it done.

Alfred Harcourt was impatient, too. He had announced the *Auto-biography* every season for several years. "I've lived too long," Stef would complain again and again. "There's too much to tell, and how do I know anyone will be interested?"

There were also occasional personal depressions; Stef developed what he called "black moods," when for several days he felt "at the bottom of a pit" and could not "come up to talk" or communicate. I would feel I had done something wrong, possibly offended or hurt him in some way, for his silences were like the "not speaking" of a quarrel. Though he assured me it had nothing to do with me, I would be affected.

Jo Davidson came in the spring of 1930, and we had much to talk about, with the depression making everybody think anew. He suggested our spending the summer at Bêcheron and we jumped at the idea. Pete would benefit from hearing the language again— he was forgetting his first French phrases; and one final sprint might finish the *Autobiography* for Steffens. So off we went, leaving Anna behind to guard the house and carry on a romance with our Chilean gardener.

Crossing the street in New York, I ran into Albert Rhys Williams, who had settled in Carmel with his wife, Lucita, a movie writer who had followed him to Russia to marry him. Rhys was working on a comprehensive book of answers to American questions on Russia. He had gone through the early days of the Revolution and known its leaders, and was full of stories of those years. He told me about the coming of the early tractors to the villages: "They were first called 'anti-Christ,' then, when it was seen what work they could do, garlanded with wreaths and hailed as "Little Brothers of Jesus.'"

I had heard so much about Russia that I wanted more than ever to see it for myself, especially in view of the American depression, but Stef did not want to go again. When I ran into Rhys, he said quite casually, "Sherwood Eddy is traveling to Russia with a group in a week or two. Why don't you go with them? I'm joining them later to take three Senators through the Donbas region."

"Why not, Peter?" Stef said, to my surprise. Could it be as simple as that? Still hardly believing, I called on Sherwood Eddy in a tiny office high on Fifth Avenue. There was one place left; I took it. Eddy was kind, chatty, very liberal, a little religious, I thought, in a way I was shy of, a little too much a "do-gooder," but he was enthusiastic. He was taking thirty or forty people—teachers, students, clergymen, clubwomen, two rabbis, mostly older people but a few younger ones, and the three Senators.

It was a joy to get back to Bêcheron, to Yvonne and the boys and the engaging life of the French countryside. Yvonne was enthusiastic about my trip and promised to keep an eye on everyone. I took the train to Berlin, where I ran into Freddy Kuh again, and met Egon Erwin Kisch, the "frenzied" reporter who was an epitome of the bohemian Germany of the twenties. Kisch was a Czech, whose first book, *Der Rasende Reporter,* took Central Europe by storm. He was an explosive, powerfully built, square, thick-set man, with bushy hair and an intensity offset by a crackling sense of humor. He had been to Hollywood, and told me a story about Charlie Chaplin. "We became friends and one day met a beautiful girl. At the end of our evening together she had to choose which of us to accompany home, she had no idea who we were. And that girl will never know," Kisch bubbled, "whom she relinquished when she chose me." He was a fervent, devout rebel against everything. He propositioned me in the first ten minutes. "There isn't much time, every girl goes to bed with me, you're the girl, here's the divan." "Right now?" "Yes, right now, why not?" It was so much a part of the times—urgent, crazy, frenetic, live for the moment before the deluge—that I laughed, fenced, and was glad when Kuh turned up for supper. In the Romanisches Café, Kisch told us that the American Governor Alvan T. Fuller, of Massachusetts, was at the Adlon Hotel.

"A newspaperman's job isn't merely to report the news," he preached earnestly, "he must make it; now, for instance, this Governor of Massachusetts is in Berlin. We must show the world that Berlin will not tolerate here, not even for one night, the man who let Sacco and Vanzetti go to their doom." And he arranged for a bunch of young boys to shout insults outside Fuller's hotel, and Kuh put out the story on the United Press, and next day we read that Berlin "had not tolerated the Governor of Massachusetts; he had been scared away by an outraged populace outside his hotel and had fled to Vienna." He had, too.

I was exhausted as well as exhilarated when I finally joined my tour at the station in Berlin. The two days in the train were full of high jinks, especially with the Senators; the only staid one

Frieda and Adolphe Winter

Ella, Rosa, and Rudi Winter

Rudi Winter, 1917. His parents are
in the background

*Ansel E. Adams*

Sara Bard Field and Charles Erskine Scott Wood

Lincoln Steffens, Ella Winter, and Sinclair Lewis at San Remo, Italy, 1925

Ella Winter, Steffens, and their son, Pete, on his first birthday, at Alassio, Italy, November 21, 1925

Steffens and Pete

Yvonne Davidson

Jo Davidson in Carmel beside
his statue made in Paris of Pete
at twenty-two months

Jack Black, Fremont Older,
and Steffens at the Older
ranch, 1927

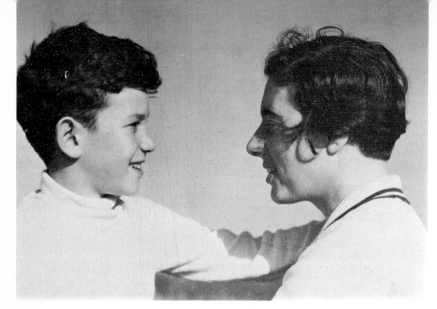

Ella Winter and Pete at Carmel

*Edward Weston*

Robinson Jeffers, 1929

Una Jeffers with Donnan and
Garth Jeffers, 1929

*Edward Weston*

Pete aged seven, 1931

Ella Winter in her study at Carmel

*Edward Weston*

Steffens and Pete

Jo Davidson, H. G. Wells, and Steffens at Bêcheron, 1930

Robert Benchley and Donald Ogden Stewart at play, Hollywood, 1936

Pete in 1936

Ella Winter with Donald Ogden Stewart and Donald Stewart, Jr., in Wiltshire, 1953

*Gerda Goedhart*

Bertolt Brecht

Oona and Charles Chaplin at home in Switzerland

*Newnes & Pearsons*

Ella Winter and Donald Ogden Stewart in the garden of their home in London, 1957

Ella Winter with her interpreter in China, 1958

FOUR HOMES: Villa Montagu, Alassio, Italy, 1925-1926

The Getaway, Carmel, California, 1927–1936

49 Mabery Road, Santa Monica, California, 1943–1950

*A. V. Swaebe*

103 Frognal, London, 1954–

was Bronson Cutting, of New Mexico. The other two, Burton Wheeler, of Montana, and Alben Barkley, of Kentucky, later Speaker and Vice-President, were like boys out of school, away from their responsibilities. One night the Southern Senator, in long woolen underwear, asked to be tucked into his railway bunk and given a good-night kiss. All through my first trip into Soviet Russia, in the great Kremlin Hall or a cathedral, hospital, or *kolkhoz,* he would make off-color Southern jokes in an undertone to me. The sharp-voiced lady club members did not approve of our frivolity, but many occasions were saved by our more serious members, like Robert A. Taft and Francis Sayre, Woodrow Wilson's son-in-law.

The three decades that have passed since that first Soviet visit have seen changes that make it in some respects now seem like another world, but I remember vividly how it struck me then. Enthusiasm does not prevent objectivity. I tried to transmit the essence of what I was seeing in letters to Stef, to a receptive person who had been there, even though so much earlier, who would want to hear the details and the outcome of his predictions.

The trip was a revelation. However much I had heard, I had not pictured the reality. These were still in many ways the early revolutionary days, with the fire and excitement, the hope and enthusiasm of the new young world. People were poor, certainly, poorly dressed, living in a single room, short of many things, with the shop windows exhibiting cardboard pictures of meat, vegetables, and eggs rather than the real thing. Yet millions of children, workers' children who before had had nothing and could hope for nothing, were eating, singing, dancing, holding hands in the new nursery schools, freed from squalor and disease and neglect. Health and education, literacy and knowledge were replacing the results of centuries of poverty and ignorance. Every conceivable method was utilized to spread knowledge of everything people must know, the elements of hygiene, biology, medicine, agriculture, how to handle babies or polluted water or the new plumbing or electric lights. Public trials taught people their rights. Everyone was learning and teaching everything—knowledge about syphilis, infection from germs, simple economics, reading and writing, languages, art, the rights of women.

These latter were especially stressed, and interested me particularly. "Marriage" was unnecessary. Two people could go to Zaks

—the marriage bureau—and signify their desire to live together by registering their names; and that was marriage. Divorce was free and took twenty minutes, abortions were legal, women could work outside the home and were paid the same as men. Household chores were deputed, whenever possible, to communal effort. Most domestic problems I had been up against could be handled by communal efforts. Birth was free. So was attendance at clinics for prospective mothers—and for nine months after birth—and a working woman could put her children in the factory crèche or kindergarten to be looked after and nursed there. I saw tots handed naked through what looked like a ticket window to a parent returning from work; to prevent infection, crèche clothes were kept inside and the parent dressed the child outside in his own clothes. It was surprising to see attention paid to such details—and for the poorest workers. That was what I kept saying to myself, "the very poorest" —this was the great difference with my world.

I wrote to Stef in August 1930:

The chief trouble with some Americans is that they bring their own economic ideas and judge Russia by them. The farmers won't be called *kulak* or *moujik* any more—*moujik* stands for stupid, illiterate, and rude—they have to be called *christianin*—farmers. . . . I'm beginning to see that economic laws are dependent on time and place, too, and are relative, not absolute. . . . Eddy fetches me whenever he gets hold of anyone interesting, "because I want to put you next to all the good things." (It's usually the three Senators, Francis Sayre, who is professor of international law at Harvard, Taft, and me.) After our drive we had another two-hour interview with Tiemkin, head of Moscow District Collective Farms. He was informative and humorous. It requires energy to unbutton your mind, take everything out and listen to—Tiemkin.

The town is torn up, new paving being hurried through before winter. Everywhere new buildings—it's like New York. These new buildings are modern—of the sort that excited us so in Los Angeles; even the blocks of workmen's dwellings. We can't see Lenin's tomb or Jack's [Reed]: they are building a great red marble mausoleum for Lenin to replace the old one, so it's all encased in wooden walls.

My room [at the Grand Hotel] is on the Square and the trams are noisy. Wheeler says there were practically no trams in 1923—and you should just see the numbers of automobiles.

We were in a continual rush, overwhelmed with people, facts, interviews that overturned all conceptions. I found the Senators perceptive, in particular Barkley, who, having been in office all his life, understood administrative problems. We became friends; I could interpret for him a little and helped him get a shave and haircut, after which he grunted: "Yo' gettin' mo' and mo' indispensable to me."

In another letter, I wrote Stef:

Our unbelief in Russia is a measure of the cynicism of the Western world. We went to a movie—the second talkie made in Russia, showing new machinery on the land. A crammed movie house gazed spellbound at wheat elevators, cement factories, McCormick-Deering reapers-and-binders. Through their eyes we could see it as "passionately inspiring," too. Imagine an American audience sitting for two hours through a movie showing only machines and grain elevators, as Senator Wheeler commented.

Everything I'd heard about Russia came back to me, and I could fill it with new meaning. The inefficiency, waste, slowness, and lack of skill were appalling. I liked someone's *bon mot:* "America is the land of unlimited possibilities, Russia that of unlimited impossibilities." But they were tackling them all the same.

I had one experience that symbolized some dim feeling I was developing. Mrs. Kisch at lunch put a box of cigarettes between us on the table, a popular brand hard to obtain. The waiter reached over and helped himself to a few, with a "Thank you, tovarish." We both looked startled, offended, then laughed. The waiter was not being brash, he had merely assumed the right to help himself as if we were truly equals. Any friend of ours would have done it. In his view we were quite simply the comrade guests, I felt, he the comrade waiter; there was no class gulf between us. It gave me an extraordinary sense of liberation, almost of freedom from guilt. No one is "beneath" me any more, I thought. Supposing it were one day like that all over the world?

Just before I left I ran into an old acquaintance, E. F. Wise, an English civil servant, whom I had met in Paris and danced with at the Majestic, before I even met Stef. He was the representative in England of the Centrosoyus (Central Trade Union) and a leading left-wing Labour M.P. He said that trade with Russia was growing, might become the economic saviour of the capitalist countries—if they could sink political prejudices—and that the possibilities of trade with Siberia, Russia, China were unlimited.

He also told me, "The left wing in Britain is going to do things; they're working for economic solutions." Then he added, "Please don't stay out of British politics for good."

I came out of Soviet Russia (those were the phrases we used then, "into" and "out of") almost in a trance; another world had indeed opened, I thought then. Perhaps I was overeager, or too optimistic or uncynical—some called it naïve and "wearing rose-colored spectacles"—but my passionate interest helped me to see with imagination a poverty-stricken, downtrodden, oppressed people given greater welfare and some dignity and self-respect and opportunity. Later developments might revise some opinions and put others in question, but what I saw on this first trip—and on later visits—gave me a basic understanding no future crimes or evils could eradicate, and a firmer belief in human possibilities that I have never lost. I could not be one to throw out the baby with the bathwater.

I went with Jo and Stef, who met me in Paris, straight to Bêcheron. They had had a visit of several days from H. G. Wells, who had doubted some of what they read him from my letters. He was not enamored of Soviet society, but wanted to hear about it from me, and later in Paris kept coming back to my accounts, wanting to hear more. It was a less optimistic Wells than he had been when I had taken Clarence Darrow to see him in England. Then he had asked Darrow if he were optimistic, and had retorted to Darrow's pessimism: "Oh, I like to think of the world going on while I'm asleep."

At Bêcheron I did not stop talking for days. Pete was delighted to have Mama back, Stef had worked well, and everyone listening to me was happy that "the future" of Stef's celebrated remark of 1919, "I have seen the future—and it still works," was still carrying on.

While visiting Jo we went over to the Château de Candé for lunch. Charles E. Bedaux, a Frenchman who started as a sandhog in America at ten dollars a week, had, like Marland, made himself into a millionaire, and come home to create out of this decaying old gray castle in the château district a modern mansion. Bedaux had invented a unit measure of labor so unpopular with labor, since it could be used to cut piece rates, that when the Duke of Windsor, after his marriage to Wallis Simpson at the Château de Candé, five years later, planned to go to the United States under

Bedaux's auspices, American labor disapproved publicly of his visit. But at this time his system was selling everywhere, and we were now taken over house and grounds, baronial halls, and castle turrets till we ended for cocktails in a small underground stone room that had been the castle dungeon. Bedaux had invited fellow estate owners, minor decaying aristocracy from the surrounding district, who listened to my stories of Russia in outraged annoyance. Bedaux himself, a short, broad-shouldered man, with a cynical, mocking look on his shrewd French face, was achieving some kind of satisfaction from this gathering. Successful and sophisticated, he wanted to retaliate now for former slights perhaps. I had the impression his ambitions were far from satisfied. Jo had been trying unsuccessfully to get him to sit for one of his ten-thousand-dollar busts; it finally transpired that Bedaux had promised that commission to a young sculptress, unknown, but a friend of Hermann Goering.

Our little family took the boat back to America and we spent the next winter in the East so that Stef could be near his publisher. We chose Croton-on-Hudson, near New York, and sent Pete on ahead to its progressive school. One afternoon a call came to say Pete was upset, would we come right away? We took the next train to find that the little boy had thrown his new London suit out the window, urinated on the floor, stuffed beets into his trouser pockets, and flung away his toys. They didn't know what to do. But when Pete saw us, he ran to his father, buried his face in his waistcoat, and sobbed heartbrokenly. It was the first time the child had been separated from both parents, "and he could not stand it," the psychoanalytically trained teachers surmised, "so he threw away what he most treasured, his toys and his new clothes."

They asked me many personal questions because of the bedroom incident. "But it's classic," I protested. "Freud says an unhappy child will urinate on the floor." "Ah yes," a teacher agreed, "but only up to four years old; yours is five and a half." I didn't argue.

"We'll move straight up here," Stef announced, "and we'll not leave Pete again, ever, not both of us, not at the same time."

The *Autobiography* was launched in April 1931. It was an immediate success, and no one was more astounded than Steffens. There was an aura of excitement at Harcourt's office. Most of the staff knew us—we had been in so often in the final months of proofreading, illustrations, indexing, and the other details of book-making—and had a warm, smiling affection for the author.

Stef had to talk everywhere, at bookshops, lunches, meetings, and autograph copies even for the salesgirls in bookstores. "Reports have come in from all over the country showing the book has 'caught on,' " Harcourt crowed. It was a startling and exciting culmination to the years of work, writing and rewriting in the little studios in Alassio, Carmel, Gaviota, Bêcheron, Croton.

"I guess I'm a success!" Stef said to me, unbelievingly. "I guess I'll go down in history now." The attacks on him after the McNamara trial, the way he had been "forgotten," discarded, had eaten deep. As the book's success snowballed, Stef felt he had started a second life.

I couldn't help feeling proud. The six years' doubts, agonies, despairs had their reward. I felt Stef had done what he sought to do, showed in a wealth of anecdote and incident what he had learned and unlearned in the course of his life—he had wanted to call it *A Life of Unlearning*. He had told the stories he had been telling me for years and which had so opened my eyes. He had found the form he had sought so long to sum up his life's experience—as he said, he did not wish to "die with his boots on." He had summed up, he had drawn a map from which the eager and confused and perplexed might find a way to gain insight into their own experience. Later, President Roosevelt told me he thought this the book to teach people about the real America. Reviewers praised Stef's humorous, ironic, witty method of telling what he knew, and called him, to his delight, "America's greatest reporter."

When Filene arranged a surprise dinner for four hundred of the characters in the book—from Anne Morgan and Bainbridge Colby to the most fervent "Red" or anarchist of Steffens' time—and all the columnists, editors, and book reviewers, the dinner became a celebrated and well-remembered occasion.

It was the beginning of five years of activity and enjoyment for Stef that he never believed he would have again. And I of course gloried in it with him. It was a little my baby, too.

One afternoon I was sitting with Alfred Harcourt, basking in Stef's success, when he asked suddenly, "And what are *you* going to do next?" I was startled. We had been so immersed in Stef's triumph, I had not realized I was loath to return to Carmel. I thought about the great subject of Soviet Russia I had only tasted, the new human relations I had thought might be beginning there.

"Why don't I do a book on love in Soviet Russia?" I teased Harcourt. He jumped up and held out his hand.

"Done," he said. "When do you start?" And then and there he offered me an advance to cover a six months' trip. As usual, my wife-and-mother feelings came uppermost at first, but Stef and Anna would look after Pete, who was by now well established in school; I would suffer without them, but it was possible.

During the winter I had met Doctor H. W. Frink, author of *Morbid Fears and Compulsions*, a tall, lean, spare man with a cadaverous face, a favorite pupil of Freud and president of the New York Psychoanalytic Association. We had become good friends, and I stayed in his boardinghouse in Hillside, Connecticut, while waiting for my boat; he even considered going to Russia with me. But one day, while in a department store trying to buy a pair of shoes, I found myself quite unable to decide between two pairs.

"I'm not coming with you to Russia," Frink said as we drove home. "I saw in that store what a state of conflict you're in, I suppose between your family and writing this book, and if that's how you're going abroad, you'd be no fun to travel with—no fun at all." And he could not be moved.

He told me many of his analytic experiences and confessed that he thought he had helped people most "over the dinner table." Having listened to me talk during this month, he said, "I can detect a pattern in you that explains your lifelong difficulty in making decisions. The moment you've determined on one course of action, all the factors against it come up, and if you decide on the other course, the factors against that will become paramount, so you'll always be torn." But I was not to suffer altogether in outer darkness. "I can't change your pattern," he said, "but if you know that this is what's going to happen every time you have a decision to make, if you're conscious of this mechanism, you might suffer just a little less."

Whether or not that was entirely the answer, I did find that the moment the boat for Europe had moved and my act was irrevocable, I felt relieved. I no longer wanted to be "rescued." In fact, I was exhilarated and looked forward with anticipation to the adventure ahead.

# 14

## RED VIRTUE

Before going into Soviet Russia again, I spent a month in Munich trying to find out about a new political phenomenon, Nazism. Little was known abroad of the National Socialist party and its fanatical leaders. Germany at this time was a confusing mixture of new experiments in art, culture, architecture, movies, and quite old-fashioned political corruption and decadence. Newspapers devoted space to workers' interests: sports-fields, clubs, swimming pools, housing developments; well-known restaurants belonged to and were patronized by the trade unions. A whole new section of the population was becoming "enfranchised," making itself felt in social life. And there were millions of jobless.

Berlin led a fevered night life; cabarets and brothels catered to every taste and need. Wealth was displayed and squandered, as in old Rome, I thought. Illustrated magazines specialized in every perversion and were sold openly on the bookstands. One fortnightly, *Moral und Mensch,* gave examples from literature—with illustrations, classic and otherwise, and a pseudo-scientific text—of sexual deviations throughout the ages. At the same time, original and daring scientific steps were being taken to help sexual deviationists. Magnus Hirschfeld, a physician of learning and experience, conducted an Institut für Sexualwissenschaft (Institute of Sexual Science), in which he tried to help homosexuals as well as train doctors and psychiatrists to have greater understanding, and tried to influence the police to a more humane and enlightened attitude. When I interviewed him, I found a bearded, kindly, portly individual of utmost gentleness. In many ways Germany was very enlightened. Brecht's *Three-Penny Opera* was playing to packed houses at this time.

The tolerance in social life was offset by violent political intolerance, anti-Semitism, antirationalism, antisocialism: radicalism and reaction were running a neck-and-neck race. People asked, "Might Germany be the second great country to try socialism?" And, at the same time, the Nazi party was mushrooming.

Many people simply shrugged their shoulders; it was none of their concern. Others were jumping on the Nazi bandwagon. Sherwood Eddy took us to Hjalmar Schacht, then Finance Minister, an almost Georg Grosz caricature of *"die herrschende Klasse"*—"the ruling caste"—with a coarse, round, bullet head, a face full of *Schmisse* or duelling scars, a long neck in an arrogantly high starched collar, and a ramrod back. A small Turkish boy brought black coffee and walked out of the Presence backward. Schacht agreed that the main problem was to increase consumption, but when I asked, "Then why all the talk of lowering wages?," he almost flew into a tantrum. "The workingman gets too much already, he's pampered beyond endurance—free baths in palaces, ultraviolet rays —what will he demand next?" Everywhere in Berlin the talk was of the need for a dictator; *"Es muss anders werden"* was the gist of all argument, "it can't go on like this." Rhenish coal owners were heavily subsidizing the Nazi party, or the other conservative parties, and newspapers. All were afraid of "the workers" and talked in Marxist terms of class war and class-consciousness. If the workers weren't class-conscious, powerful owners and employers in Germany at this time certainly were, we decided.

I ransacked bookshops for material on this new Nazi party, and obtained the books of their philosophical and political leaders— Karl May, the novelist, Alfred Rosenberg, Ludendorff's wife, Mathilde. Much of the stuff sounded like lunatic ravings, yet their incredible newspaper, the *Völkischer Beobachter,* sold widely and had extraordinary influence.

I heard that General Erich Ludendorff was living in Tutzing, a small town on Lake Titisee near Munich. I wrote and asked for an interview from this World War I military leader who had become one of Hitler's staunch supporters. When I arrived and found the garden gate securely locked, I rang a bell for about ten minutes. Finally a tall butler in *Lederhosen* came conspiratorially on tiptoe, opened the gate a tiny crack, his finger at his lips. When I told him of my invitation to come, he looked around fearfully, mo-

tioned me again to silence, then widened the crack enough to let
me in.

Still on tiptoe, he led me to a rustic arbor, where I sat another
fifteen minutes, when an imposing figure, also in Tyrolean pants,
arrived. He was tall, white-haired, with a stiff, military face. I
recognized the general, who sat down without a word. I told
him who I was and that I wanted to know something of the new
National Socialist party. "I've been reading your wife Mathilde's
books," I said.

"Ah," he said. "Then you know that Schiller was murdered."
I thought I had misheard.

He asked what magazine I was writing for, and when I mentioned
two New York periodicals—*Harper's* and *Scribner's,* as I remember—he again looked cunning.

"In the hands of Freemasons," he hissed, "both of them; of course
you know that," and wagged his head solemnly.

I asked what was coming next in Germany.

"*They* are trying to rule the world," he said. His fanatical tone
startled me.

"Who are?"

"The Freemasons, Bolsheviks, the world international finan-
ciers," he said.

"Why?" I asked. I mustn't sound hostile.

"They want to control," he said, still the conspirator. "They and
the Jews."

I had not heard such talk outside a mental hospital and did not
know how to proceed with a supposedly rational political interview.
But it didn't matter. Ludendorff warmed up and went on in the
same vein, told of other great figures of German literature who
were murderers or had been murdered, sometimes by "the unknown
hand," by "Jews," by some traitor. Two hours later the butler
reappeared, hushed me with his hand to his lips once more, and
led me on tiptoe, in silence, to the garden gate. I had met Nazism
plain.

Before leaving for Moscow I went to a public clinic for typhoid
and cholera shots, and horrified the doctor.

"You, a young woman, going to Russia alone—what will you
do when a Bolshevik rapes you?" His nurse added, "All the young
people there have syphilis," and both agreed that "all Europe's

postwar evils are due to Russia; they're all Jews there, Reds and criminals," while an assistant happily related lurid stories of what was done to women, "all of whom are nationalized property." These warnings were not a very promising omen for a book I considered calling *Red Virtue* (even though the "virtue" of the title was not meant in its strictly moral sense), but luckily they bore little relation to what I found when I looked, for the second time and more closely, at this "enigma" of a country.

The Five-Year Plan was now the essence of Soviet life. Everyone was discussing planning, in every field. Committees argued "the socialist way of life" for houses, cities, clubs, factories, parks. Doctors planned state medical care, teachers' education; nursery schools, the family, marriage, divorce, leisure, women's work, mother love—all were being planned, along with, naturally, culture, music, art, theater. "I guess sturgeon are thinking about how much caviar to deliver," someone quipped.

As on my earlier visit, I was particularly concerned with the changes in the status of women, one of the most underprivileged sections of the old society. I found that part of the new Russian plan was the determined drive to get women out of the kitchen and into public life, the farm, industry, the professions (the exact opposite of the pressure to have them slaves to the three K's, as in the Nazi world). Soviet women were judges, doctors, engineers, editors, bricklayers, and were learning to utilize their new independence. The cook who had "learned to govern Russia" could no longer be treated as a servant. Not that there weren't women who were leery of this new freedom; "If my husband no longer beats me, he no longer loves me," some complained, or, "Women's place is not in the furrows." But the majority approved without reservation. Domestic chores undertaken communally, as I had seen on my first trip, freed women from the home, and they accepted the Soviet argument that only by working outside could they become functioning members of "the new society." I felt that in this field the USSR was dealing with very real feminine problems in our world, too. The Soviets no longer considered feminism the answer to women's need to function in a wider field, a thing my energetic mother would certainly have appreciated in her less enlightened generation.

For a time I lived in a Russian apartment, cared for by a square, squat, illiterate little peasant girl called Motja, whom I tried vainly to lead into paths of equality. She insisted on walking behind me in the street to show she knew her "place"—and later she brought her boy friend to the apartment, who stole my camera.

As on my first visit, I found myself bewildered and intrigued by new Russian attitudes to some matters not seriously questioned in our world. Our viewpoints in many matters were so divergent; our treatment of criminals or juvenile delinquents seemed almost medieval. We tended to look at things from the individual's profit-making standpoint—"how will this benefit me, how much can I make out of it?"

"But here they don't," I wrote Stef. "The new collective human being, as they call him, is their ideal, and they are planning him consciously. Nursery-school children are trained to say 'our' instead of 'my,' and I heard one little girl introduce her mother to her schoolmates with the words 'This is our mother.'" At a pioneer camp, a crippled boy was put at the head of the line so that his comrades might learn consideration for others. Children were encouraged in surprising ways to feel themselves part of society: I found a "wall newspaper" an eleven-year-old girl and her six-year-old brother had hung in their home, with drawings criticizing their mother for hanging the washing in the kitchen, as "the old way of life," scolding Papa for spilling ashes on the living-room floor, and castigating the plumber for not mending the leak in the W.C.

Toys and games and children's books were newly directed to social purposes, and children absorbed politics with their porridge. A seven-year-old girl brought home to me the drama of the forcible collectivization. "My *izvozchik*'s [cabby driver's] horse is going to have a baby," she said in dismay, "and then he'll have two horses and be a *kulak!*" The changing ethics were responsible for some amusing anecdotes. An arithmetic class was asked, "If I buy apples at twenty-five rubles and sell them at fifty rubles, what do I get?," and the children chorused as one, "Three years in jail." A cartoon showed two four-year-olds admonishing a smaller, younger brother howling on the floor: "You can't play with us, you're technically backward." And the young people's newspaper, the *Komsomolskaya Pravda*, ran a scorching editorial inveighing against "bourgeois toys"—"toys that teach bourgeois habits, such as individual doll kitchens, absurd, silly, useless dolls. Why aren't we making toy tractors, toy model *kolkhozes*, radios?" At the Institute of Mother and Child a comprehensive exhibition taught parents and teachers what toys were "correct" for children for each year for the first ten years.

I came to know well several writers of children's books: Samuel Marshak with his broad pockmarked face and simple charm; his brother Ilin, author of *A Hundred Thousand Whys;* and Kornei Chukovsky, best known for his universally popular *Krokodil.* Leading artists illustrated these books. I found "old" bright-painted dolls that represented the minor nationalities, and "new" toy pioneers, Red Army soldiers, workers on conveyor belts. I went to Obraztsov's Puppet Theater, which was doing *Mowgli* and the *Jungle Books,* and attended children's readings where Marshak tried his latest works on child audiences and, asking for their views, was told, "We are of the opinion that this may be printed." I heard small voices criticize any and everything with large self-assurance. "I may be a circus performer or a violinist, I have not decided yet; I am gifted in both directions," a boy of ten remarked to me. I saw a *besprizornik* movie dramatizing the saving of those wild, homeless young boys, "the wild boys of the road," left stranded by the civil war. The movie said, "And now a new, original method was tried"; the boys were taught a trade with pay, given outlets for their energies in community life, without guards, walls, barbed wire, or punishments. (It was the famous Bolshevo, which I later visited, one of the humane and enlightened experiments in treatment of juvenile delinquency.) WILL THEY RUN AWAY? was flashed on the screen in great dramatic letters as the decisive moment came, and the audience sat forward on their chairs, breathless. P.S. They didn't.

I worked hard at my job. I visited prisons and mental homes, vocational-guidance institutions and the theatrical workshops of the Bolshoi, dancing and circus schools, clinics and prophylactoria. Here prostitutes in black cotton stockings were gathered in dull rows, learning to knit instead of living what I, with my admiration for *Sinister Street,* imagined might have been their alluring former lives. When I asked, "What happens to the ones who absolutely refuse to reform?," they answered ruefully, "We have to give some up as incorrigible."

A psychiatrist told me that "inferiority complexes have more or less vanished," since everyone could get somewhere, be singled out for something, win an "order" if only for faster work; or be made a member of a shock brigade, a city Soviet, the editorial board of a wall newspaper. "No one feels 'I can't succeed at anything, so what's the use of going on?'" he said, which might have been an exaggeration, but I saw enough to bear it out. It was brought home to me when, in one of our innumerable discussions of the new incentives, an engineer was asked what he got for discovering oil in the Black Sea. "I got the oil," he said. "Yes, but you yourself, you personally, what do you get for yourself?" He thought awhile and then replied slowly, "Well, everyone kind o' knows it's I who found the oil."

"You should see this again during this Five-Year Plan," I wrote Stef. "They're trying desperately to achieve some of the ideals you heard them talk about, and they're still so misinterpreted in our world. Roy Howard [head of United Press] commented here the other day, 'Russia has more news than any other country and is the least accurately reported.' The hardest-boiled engineers and businessmen respond to this belief of people in what they can now achieve." "The Soviet leaders do admit their mistakes," I wrote him another day, "as you said Lenin did. When they prohibited alcohol and found it didn't work, they made vodka legal but propaganda'ed against it by every means: lectures, posters, films, public trials, and loudspeakers even outside the vodka shop— to the discomfiture of the poor drunk as he stumbles out sodden." Of course all this could sound priggish and pedantic, all this propaganda, and sometimes quite primitive, like the notices put up in factory dining rooms to "wash the hands before eating, see the dishes are clean, and don't put boots on the table." But it was part of a poverty-ridden nation's attempt to pull itself up by its bootstraps, and, as such, it seemed to me, one could not condemn it.

I stumbled on one treasure for the book I was to write—a periodical I had never seen mentioned, devoted to personal relationships. *Toward a Healthy Way of Life* could be had only by subscription, and that only by the Red Army or selected factory committees; but I pulled strings and obtained a complete file. The paper dealt in detail with the creation of the new sexual morality and discussed marriage, free love, prostitution, promiscuity, deviations, sex diseases, teen-age problems, the problems of middle-aged women whose husbands strayed in younger directions—every thinkable and unthinkable sexual attitude. (But rather different from *Moral und Mensch.*)

I found an Institute for the Study of Crimes, which told of the methods at the "reform" school of Bolshevo and went on to talk of psychiatry, which I also found operated on a different basis from ours. I took the questions Doctor Frink had suggested to me to the chief psychiatrist in Moscow, Doctor Leo Rosenstein, and in fifteen minutes, as I wrote Stef again, "the questions fell away. Not one arose as a problem over here; they were taken care of by the new social attitude, as you found with those questions you wrote down beforehand on the Bullitt Mission: you didn't need to ask them."

I remembered Doctor Frankwood Williams telling me in New York of his own experience in Russia when he asked to see a mental hygiene clinic.

"With pleasure," they answered, "but first let us show you a factory." Doctor Williams investigated the factory. "Very interesting," he said, "and I thank you, and now I should like to see a mental hygiene clinic." "Of course," they assured him pleasantly, "but first please accompany us to a *kolkhoz*," and then to a kindergarten, a rest home, the Institute of Mother and Child, the Park of Culture and Rest. And he must see the puppet theater, watch a dance group, see the Dnieper power station, a middle school, a publishing house, a library where a writer was trying out his latest children's book on a group of children. Always and again Williams requested a visit to a psychiatric hospital or a mental hygiene clinic. Why were they keeping him from one? Finally they confessed to him that there weren't separate mental hygiene clinics: they didn't even really know what such a clinic was.

"And I grew to understand," Doctor Williams had reported, "that they didn't need separate mental hygiene clinics. They have set out to create a society that would produce an integrated, 'adjusted' individual. What they were trying to tell me was that their whole country is a mental hygiene clinic."

So I also found that individuals could be adjusted to society not by subjective, individual psychoanalysis but by adapting or accommodating them to the new social institutions, which did not seem to create our Western conflict between individual and social ethics and behavior.

I thought I saw a reflection of this new ethic even in American engineers who had come to help build the new Russia. Colonel Hugh Cooper was taking immense pride in constructing the new

Dneprostroi dam "for the benefit of everyone," not under the stimulus only of a profit to himself. An engineer called Austin, from Cleveland, was building great new Ford works in the old twelfth-century market town of Nijni Novgorod and boasted to me: "I'm building the first socialist city in the world—it's for fifty thousand people and they're carving it out of the bare steppes." I met a construction man called Bartholomew who responded with unconcealed pleasure to the feeling that he was working for love of the job. This burly Midwesterner, after trying haltingly to describe to me the stimulus that was different from any he had felt in private industry, launched into glowing appreciation when he spoke of the hospitality of a father who offered to "send his daughter to me in the stone outhouse to give me an old-fashioned Russian bath, pouring hot and cold water alternately as she birched my bare back—both of us naked. And it was her father, mind you, who sent her. I doubt I'll ever be the same man again."

But in the midst of the new and visionary I found an inefficiency that could drive one to desperation. "I suppose it's because they've had to be so hurriedly trained," I wrote to Stef, "and have no experience, and centuries of apathy to overcome, and perhaps just because they can get jobs whether they're good or not. But it takes days to get anything done. They never make an appointment, they tell you to come and then they'll arrange when you must telephone again to ask for an appointment. Lifts are always out of order; a current anecdote has a 'lift factory' entirely devoted to manufacture of the notices LIFT OUT OF ORDER. And the service in hotels! You can wait two hours and not get your meal. . . . I tried to iron a frock with a big, awkward iron full of coals, whose fumes nearly choked me. . . . Think what electric irons will mean, and they must come, Moscow already has electricity in every room."

I was struck by the strange mixture of attitudes toward the law as well as to ethics and morals. "They're partly law-abiding and puritanical, but also there is cynicism and a lot of petty pull. The old sad intelligentsia must try and obtain bare necessities by pull, since they are so discriminated against. Workers and peasants don't have to. . . . Will it get better or worse, or vanish, the way tipping has been abolished?"

One saw shocking individual tragedies, mostly of those "former" people—as the intellectuals and professionals were called. Shabby and down-at-heel, the least regarded of the new order, they sought out foreigners to complain of shortages ("eggs and butter and other vestiges of the old regime," as they wisecracked), inadequate clothes and shelter, and inequalities and discrimination practiced even against their children. Workers' children were given the first places in universities. Anti-Semitism was punishable by law. A sentence of three years could be imposed even for an anti-Semitic joke; yet one found plenty of prejudice still, despite the encouragement of Jewish (Yiddish) culture along with that of all other "minor nationalities"—some eighty or so. And despite the widespread attack on illiteracy and ignorance, it was not all gone yet, and it occasionally created diverting situations. When I moved to a private room, the janitor of the building, an old, shawled peasant woman, asked my birthplace.

"Australia," I said.

"Where is that? In which continent, Europe or Asia?" Nothing I said could budge her—every country must be in one of those two continents.

I heard Maxim Gorki lecture on literature to students. He was like a stringy poplar, tall and thin and frail, his face, with its big walrus mustache, paper yellow like old parchment. He looked as if he might topple over. But he talked for an hour, about writing and literary problems, and held his audience; some inner strength seemed to support him.

When a much-heralded party came from London—Bernard Shaw, Lady Astor, and Lord Lothian (the Philip Kerr who had been Lloyd George's secretary in Paris), my friend Charmion von Wiegand asked me to replace her as correspondent for the Hearst papers. The welcoming crowd at the station swarmed around G. B. S., taking no notice of the rest of the party—to Lady Astor's annoyance; what counted to Russians were writers and artists, not "mere" aristocrats.

Shaw remembered me from Malvern. "What on earth are you doing here?" he asked. Lady Astor, greatly to my embarrassment, handed me a food parcel from my anxious mother, but her irritation was caused not by the fact that "I've lugged a food parcel half across Europe for you" but that I was "Miss" Winter when I was a "married woman with a child." I asked Lord Lothian on Stef's behalf about the note from Lloyd George for Lenin at the time of the Bullitt Mission in 1919, and he confirmed that Lloyd

George had suggested the questions himself—an intriguing footnote to history. Lothian was pessimistic about the future of capitalism. "Capitalist countries are not achieving social aims, are not giving the security and full employment one sees here," he ruminated, commenting on the red banner stretched across the station platform: COMRADES! KEEP YOUR COST ACCOUNTING ACCURATE.

"At home, we'd have had 'Have you used Pears Soap?'" he commented a little grimly.

I went on a five-day trip down the Volga with my translator, a bright student who taught me Russian. When I wore a Russian blouse, she reproached me earnestly.

"You mustn't wear a Russian shirt like that," she said, "that's a man's shirt."

"What of it? We wear men's slacks, why not a man's shirt?"

"You don't get me," the girl said, worried. "Our women wore those blouses when they were fighting for equality with men. Now we have equality, so for you to wear a blouse like that is . . . is . . . historically inaccurate!"

We visited Stalingrad, which I found a flourishing new town dotted with workers' barracks-like new apartment buildings and the "green belt" that the Russians so prized for industrial cities. Trees sprouted along the wide boulevards, hiding some of the ugliness of a new town in construction. On the train trip, traveling hard on wooden benches, I found everyone friendly, talkative, and full of questions, particularly when they discovered I was an *Amerikanka*. They wanted to know about our technical paradise, which their slogans told them they must "overtake and surpass." They themselves had astonishing interests and bits of knowledge, and one student asked me, "Can you tell us the number of unemployed during the silk strike in Patterson, New Jersey, in 1911?"

On every train trip—to Dneprostroi, Stalingrad, Nijni Novgorod —Russian travelers talked, asked questions, wanted to expound on everything. At home I would not have thought of going to see how a library was organized and what foreign books it had; nor had I ever investigated a factory, trade union, farm, hospital, steel mill. Here every institution was something to study: you must learn its history, its present status and former "role," its methods, ideals. In a clinic we were filled in on the number of patients, their illnesses, treatment, prognosis. After I had seen the showers, the dining room, new installations, and surgical instruments, an enthusiastic woman doctor ripped a chart from a patient's bed. "Look!" she cried in rapturous excitement, "the temperature has fallen down!"

I went to Leningrad's Putilov Works, where Lenin had addressed a few workers before the Revolution, and found more than a fresh attitude to factory work. Workers were contributing ideas for improved methods and "struggling against illiteracy" and superstition; but they were also attempting to create their own culture, for the first time.

Back in Moscow, I ran into Egon Kisch, just returned from his trip to Tadzhikistan, Uzbekistan, and Kirgiz in Siberia. "Arabian Nights seasoned with Communism," he called it, and told how the Tadzhik peasants, who feared the new machinery, shot and killed the driver of the first automobile, and shot its headlights "to blind it." "Now they bring food and wine to the tractors," and he told of "centuries traversed in a day. The primitive peasants think the Communists invented all machinery, that the Emir fled on a horse and Lenin went chasing after him. They call electric lamps 'little Ilyitch lamps,' after Lenin's first name. At first they shot wives who dared unveil in public, but now the wives study to be engineers, doctors, scientists. The camel side by side with the airplane," Kisch wound up, wonder mixing with his appreciative amusement.

Before I left I made two good Russian friends—Lida, a tall Georgian girl with great black lustrous eyes and a sensuous mouth, and Vitya, a twenty-two-year-old blond boy with high cheek bones, who had latterly been teaching me Russian. They were close companions, always together, and I assumed might be more to each other, though they never admitted it. Lida had a husband in Georgia, but worked in a Moscow publishing house; Vitya in the housing ministry. I liked both of them a great deal and taught Vitya English, which he found difficult. We went to plays, discussed interminably all facets of "the new life," and wandered into all kinds of new institutions.

Both my friends were devoted party members. I asked for their definition of a good Communist. "A Bolshevik must be hard, steady, responsible, willing to sacrifice his own interests for the good of the whole, not care too much about the good things, stick it out whatever the difficulties." This was their answer. "You feel on the inside," Lida explained, " 'us' rather than 'they,' you don't have to keep worrying about yourself or be aggressive. You belong."

When I objected to the narrowness and intolerance of many Bolsheviks, the bigoted outlook or mechanically pattered slogans, she replied, "One can do a great deal of one's own thinking in the party, but it is like wartime; commands must be obeyed, though we do try to have people understand."

Vitya and Lida could remember Lenin; they had been adolescents when he died.

"For Lenin, action was what counted," Vitya said, and I remembered that Emil Ludwig had written exactly that. ("Act," Lenin said, "that's more important than ten Resolutions that 'resolve to act.' If mistakes are made, they must be acknowledged and corrected.") This phrase had made that lasting impression on Stef. I asked them about the Terror, about which Stef had asked Lenin himself, and Vitya quoted Gorki: "I know a pair of eyes that have been forever numbed by the burning sorrow of the Terror."

I kept putting off my return; I had still so much to find out, and besides, I had made these firm friendships. I couldn't tear myself away from Vitya and Lida; the last night, when I had given up my room, I stayed with them, all of us taking turns to sleep on the floor.

Very early in the morning Vitya slid down and crept under my rug. "It's your turn in the bed," he said. I looked at him. I didn't know whether Lida was asleep, whether she would waken. He was a charming young man; he knew I liked him. We had to get to Red Square early to find a place, for it was the November 7 celebrations, and it was my last day. His girl was probably asleep . . . yet I was a foreigner, bourgeois, even if nice; he certainly knew Lenin's "glass of water" admonition (against "a drink here, a drink there") and he had all his country's puritan, revolutionary ideals. Still and all, I was going away. I couldn't think of any Russian phrase to fit this moment. I had packed my dictionary. I felt his hand, the rough floor was pleasant (who needed a bed?), and then unexpectedly, loudly, a band blared the opening bars of the *Internationale* and Lida stirred.

"It's begun," I heard her mutter, "our glorious . . ."

"Arise, ye wretched of the earth," I hissed, and flung the rug back and got up. Vitya looked—was it disappointment, or relief that he had preserved his true ideals?

"We mustn't be late," I jeered. It was cold and foggy outside, and, shivering and silent, we dressed and stole on tiptoe out of the room. He tucked his arm in mine as we stumbled through the mist —regretful, rueful, remorseful? Gradually we fell in step and joined the procession marching to the strains of "A better world's in birth" till we reached the reviewing stand.

Lida and Vitya took me to my train and waved me sadly away. My beautiful six months were ended, my job, my excursion into another world. I could not have been more heavyhearted had I known the truth, that I would never see either of them again— and that the land they cherished so proudly would, a decade later, be a ravaged waste.

# 15

# THE THIRTIES—ACUTELY

Arrived in New York, I found an increasingly depression-riddled, worried country. I took the train home. I was eager to get at my book, but on Alfred Harcourt's advice, I lectured on the way to find out what questions about Russia Americans were specifically interested in. I found surprising ignorance and a still-widespread acceptance of the early myths about nationalized women, children taken from mothers at birth, families broken up, no incentives to work. There was much puzzlement because of the widely varying reports. Will Durant had published in *The Saturday Evening Post* a denunciation of everything Russian; Maurice Hindus, on the other hand, had written about a new world with hope and confidence, in *Humanity Uprooted* and *Red Bread*.

In Minneapolis I spoke to an audience of twelve hundred and was asked questions for two hours—about freedom of religion, freedom of voting, freedom of opportunity, choice of jobs, wages, incentives, the right to strike, marriage and divorce, the system of law, the system of medicine. When I finally sat down, quite exhausted, a little man jumped up at the back of the hall.

"Miss Winter," he called out enthusiastically, "could you please tell us how we can find out the truth about Russia?"

There was much going on at The Getaway. Anna was married now to an Irish electrician, Leslie McCarthy, and had a baby girl, Betty Ann. Pete was full of his friends and activities, Stef was lecturing to teachers, students, businessmen, who were all reading his book. Letters were coming to him daily from all over the country. I rented a small studio in the woods, where I could work undisturbed.

One day a headline hit my eye in Older's *Call-Bulletin:* JACK
BLACK IS DEAD. He had disappeared in New York, Older wrote, and
all search for him had been in vain; there was no trace, till they
found in a pawnshop one of Jack's treasured few possessions, the
watch given him by newspaper colleagues on the *Call.* Older
"knew," he wrote, that Jack must have carried out his determination never to be a burden on anyone he loved, so, Older concluded,
"he did what he always prophesied he would when the time came
—threw himself in the river with weights on his feet." It brought
back to me with remorse my last meeting with Jack in New York,
on my way home from Russia. He had come to see me, had told me
sadly of his illness and coughing, the dank little room he occupied,
the ending of his book royalties, though "I have my return ticket to
California by bus." In return I told him buoyantly of my enthusiastic new discoveries. I did not give the sympathy I might have
to a broken, finished man. He listened to my animated talk without making me aware of his despondency, and I was too zealously
absorbed in the world of the future to observe it. Now my chance
was gone. I hoped for one reprieve. "How can you be *sure?*" I
wrote Older in my painful self-reproach. "I know, Peter," Older
replied, and it was the kind of reply Jack Black would have made.

This same zeal and ardor, as well as my fervent absorption in my
task, led me to commit another sin, this time against my own
small son, which has remained a deep regret all my life. Pete had
been given a job by one of his teachers, who had the agency for
national magazines; the children could earn a small commission by
selling them and they looked forward keenly to this earned pocket
money, discussing at length what they would buy with it. Pete
followed his route conscientiously every Saturday on his bicycle,
when he might have been playing baseball, his satchel full of
*Collier's, The Saturday Evening Post,* the *Ladies' Home Journal.*
The *Post* was carrying the Will Durant articles attacking the Soviets,
and while I did not like to have my son peddling it, I did not
think I had the right to interfere. We were for children's independence. Stef laughed at my quandary.

But at this time Pete was also going through what his father
called "every small boy's stealing stage." He would abstract a nickel
here, a dime there, once even a dollar bill from a girl across the
way who adored him. I, with my English upbringing, was much
more disturbed than Stef and thought it should be stopped, even

punished if necessary. Then one day, when I was emptying Pete's blue jeans to send them to the wash, a cache fell out, the ill-gotten gains, I thought, of a practiced burglar—three dollars and seventy-five cents!

"No, no," Pete cried. "Oh no, that's for selling the *Post*. Miss Lockwood paid us today."

"Nonsense," I cried savagely, my pent-up restraint bursting forth, "I don't want to be lied to into the bargain."

"But Mama, it's true!" His face was crimson. "It *is* true, it is my own, what I've made from selling the papers. Please ask Miss Lockwood."

I was adamant, granite. He couldn't have made that much; it was the result of some awful theft to which he wouldn't even own up. I was a wall of self-righteous indignation, till tears sprang to the eyes of my small tortured victim. I kept the money and refused to go to Miss Lockwood. How could I explain to her my political resentment or give away Pete's stealing? I would not believe him and I would not check his story.

"Anyhow," I preached, "I've never wanted you to sell the *Post*, the paper that tells those lies about Russia. I've been there and I know—why should I stand for my son spreading lies?"

I can still see that desperate little seven-year-old face, the pleading sobs. Six months' work gone for nothing. I have asked Pete's forgiveness and been granted it, yet thirty years later I am still harrowed and cannot forgive myself.

I soon learned a new political lesson, that the current America would stand for almost any kind of horror, murder, rape, sadism, but not radical activity. One day in San Francisco, when I was about to go on a lecture platform, I overheard my Christian name spoken by a group of burly men I didn't know. When I asked my chairman who the strangers were and why they were looking at me so peculiarly, he laughed a hearty laugh. "The FBI," he said.

"But why should the FBI be here?" "You've committed an act," he said. "But I haven't done a thing!" "Oh yes, you're writing a book, that's a very dangerous act."

Carmel was interested, as always, in "a new idea." Mrs. Blackman's God Circle gave way to the newest "seed idea," politics. Lita Bathen wondered about coal miners' wages; Mr. and Mrs.

Dickinson and the Flavins discussed the unemployed. The question "Is the universe conscious?" gave way to "Can we make our social system work?" Mrs. Blackman, however, failed to bridge completely the gap between the two worlds. At the end of a long evening's political discussion, she sighed. "I want to go gently insane."

It was good clean fun for a while, then our rival local paper, the *Pine Cone,* raised a tiny threat: "We don't mind their propaganda unless they reach into the schools." There was a world depression, America had sixteen million unemployed, Hoover's promise of those chickens in every pot had not exactly materialized, and we had asked only whether children might not also know a little of what was going on. When I had first come back, the school principal had asked me to talk to the pupils about Russia; I told about Russian children, their games, toys, books, the clothes they wore, the food they ate, their schools and holidays. At the end of my half-hour talk I heard one little girl say to another, as they trotted downstairs, "Well, anyway, we've missed arithmetic." So I had hardly corrupted them for all time. Yet this talk was later used to accuse me of spreading "poisoned propaganda."

Steffens enjoyed his lecturing, too, particularly to students. He kept saying that he would like to write a book for children, telling them about the world. "I have been practicing on school children and college students," he would relate. "At a high school I cut out all entertainment and gave them what I called 'straight goods'; I told no stories, not an anecdote; for an hour I described things as they are, politics, business, education, science, and art, without relief. As at Stanford, I saw those kids come up to the edge of their seats, open their funny mouths and their eager eyes, and eat it all up. One boy rose to ask why the teachers did not tell it to them that way, and when I answered that the parents and 'the machine' would not let teachers teach the truth, the teachers themselves clapped and nodded approval. Things are happening," he would reflect, "everybody is listening, and the world aware of Russia, acutely."

This was the thirties, "acutely."


I finished *Red Virtue,* sent off the manuscript, and received a wire from Alfred Harcourt: "My hat off to you and anything else you wish."

Jubilant, I went off to New York to see the book through the press. I intended to stay a few weeks, but they stretched to three months. For, while I was east, living at the Hotel Winthrop correcting my galleys and page proofs, Hitler burned the Reichstag, and the Nazi terror was released against an unsuspecting world. And with that, I found a cause for action, something to fight against, something that I had seen at close hand, of which I had rather more knowledge than most. I eagerly plunged into the fight.

I spoke everywhere—I now enjoyed speaking; I wrote articles and worked with committees. Joe Freeman and I organized a Committee against Hitler. Joe was better informed about culture on the Left than anyone I had met, with a brilliant, incisive mind. He was passionate about his beliefs and could make a fascinating panorama of world events. He was also a poet, and editor of the *New Masses*.

Liberals wanted to do something about Hitler, and we met in my hotel room to discuss what. Among our first anti-Nazis were Senators Wheeler and Barkley, Emily Balch, Hendrik Van Loon, Norman Thomas, Doctor Ernst Boas, Professor Alexander Meiklejohn, Amos Pinchot, Roger Baldwin of the American Civil Liberties Union, Jo Barnes, later foreign editor of the New York *Herald Tribune,* Doctor A. A. Brill, the psychoanalyst, Doctor Abraham Flexner, and several other Jewish leaders. Our committee was to support all victims, not only Jews. I asked everyone to join—clubwomen, Quakers, heads of universities, clergymen and newspapermen and doctors. We soon had five hundred members.

What we had to do was explain to the American people what had happened, for it had come so suddenly. Recent visitors to Germany had been favorably impressed and must be counteracted. We published pamphlets by doctors and scientists—Nazis against medicine, Nazis against culture, against science, against women. We made a short anti-Nazi film with Professor Franz Boas, Van Loon, Norman Thomas, Roger Baldwin, and me. We sold, for ten dollars a copy, the ten-cent Reklam editions of the German classics, which contained not Schiller, Goethe, or Heine, but the *Brown Book of the Hitler Terror*. Wealthy Jews thrilled to even this small contact with the anti-Nazi underground.

A few speakers came, now and later, from Europe with firsthand information. Lord Marley gave us graphic pictures of great Jewish surgeons cleaning latrines, kicked and clubbed by the SS, of Jews forbidden to sit on park benches, their children to visit playgrounds or swimming pools, like Negroes in the segregated South. I saw photographs of those storm troopers, with no corners to their mouths, brutal and bayoneting, standing at the doors of stores to forbid people to enter. We tried hard to tell of the persecutions in those years, but it was difficult for people to take in. What I myself recoiled from most were the accounts of people forced to crawl through the mud to kiss the swastika.

The viewpoint that saw "two sides to every question" was hard to swallow now; Nazi and anti-Nazi were not simply "sides" in an intellectual debate; yet later Lord Marley was forbidden the University of California campus for an address, as "showing partiality," while a Hitler supporter, because he was a history lecturer, gave eleven lectures. I was glad, when Karl Billinger (Paul Massing) wrote the first full account of the beatings and tortures of a radical in jail, under the title *Fatherland*, that Stef was asked to write the foreword.

I also, with a young friend, indulged in some direct action we thought justified. We set out to break up Nazi meetings by shouting first from one part of the hall, then another, giving the impression, we hoped, that the place was full of angry opposition. In face of the violently intemperate language of the Nazi speakers, some of them German, we felt one must create a counter-demonstration. The audiences must have had the impression there were dozens of us.

In April my book came out and made quite a splurge; it was very well reviewed, everyone was complimentary, and I tasted for a short moment the delights of a fêted author. The Chicago *Tribune* wrote that "the book becomes a presentation of the Russian Communist as a stumbling human being, as anxious as the next person to solve the urgent problem of human happiness," and spoke of its "warmth" and "penetration"; it was an "admirable study of . . . people actually trying to change the processes of human nature, and who think they have." Other critics called the book "vivid," "sincere," "successful in grasping many of the ideas and aspirations of present-day Russia." *The New Yorker* characterized it as "a Moscow *Middletown,* remarkably illuminating," adding "the author maintains a degree of objective detachment that would do credit to the most austere sociologist." *Scribner's Magazine* dubbed it "the completest and most informative book on the subject," and most reviewers commented on the fact that it was the first "comprehensive, intelligible, extensive, clarifying" inquiry into human relationships in the USSR, where "human beings are constructing the new order but the new order is also forming human beings." The book was understood. I had achieved what I had set out to do, and I was very happy.

I was now, like Stef in 1931, "in demand," at private houses and public meetings. I was asked for articles, was interviewed in the press and on the radio. I found people eagerly interested and full of curiosity. I noticed, however, that many asked quite intimate questions relating to their own sex lives, even elderly married couples. My Soviet facts made them feel I must be some sort of authority on sex generally. This intrigued me, but I was a little taken aback when a university student asked me to lend him my hotel room for the weekend. "My girl lives with her uncle, so we have no place to go," he pleaded.

One night at dinner at Sherwood Anderson's, I met a towering, broad-shouldered man, who nevertheless seemed somehow childish, Thomas Wolfe. An argument developed about anti-Semitism with Max Eastman, Eastman accusing Wolfe of it and Wofe replying in violent self-defense. He took me home after, and we walked the twenty or so blocks in the mild spring air. He was deeply disturbed by Max's charge and tried to justify himself. By the time we reached my hotel, he asked if I could introduce him to "some Jews." I suggested Joe Freeman and Mike Gold, and he declared himself eager to meet them.

That evening was the beginning of a singular, ships-that-pass-in-the-night relationship. Wolfe took me out almost every night to dinner and talked compulsively. He was then breaking with Max Perkins, his close friend and editor at Scribners, and he minded that intensely. One night in a restaurant he hurriedly changed tables when he caught sight of Perkins; he apparently could not bear to talk to him as yet. Another evening he complained of his family and the bad time he had had when he went back to North Carolina after his German trip. Reminded of my own troubles with my mother, I laughed and said, "Don't you know you can't go home again?" Wolfe stopped dead. "Say that again!" he commanded. I did, surprised.

Then, in great excitement, he asked, "Can I have that? For the title of an article?" "I don't own it." I laughed. "I merely made a remark based on my own experience."

The next few days he kept telephoning me, more and more tense —could he have the phrase for a brief *New Masses* article, for a much longer article for *Harper's,* and finally, "Oh, please—may I have it for the title of a book? I have a million words in grocery boxes in my hotel—and that's what I'd like to call it." I graciously gave him permission for one million words—but no more.

Before leaving New York I rediscovered an amusing acquaintance. I was invited to dinner and the opera by Charles E. Bedaux, the château owner whom I had met while visiting Jo and Yvonne at Bêcheron.

I was unused to luxury among my recent political friends, whose notion of lavish entertainment was supper at a cafeteria on Sixth Avenue. I was stimulated by the thought of getting to know better, and on my own, the fabulously wealthy and somewhat mysterious French industrialist.

The door of the Park Avenue apartment was opened by an impressive butler from the French château. The apartment was exquisite, the smell of flowers overpowering; great bowls of spring flowers stood in every available spot. My host came with both hands outstretched, as though I were a dear and valued friend. "I heard from Jo that you were in town; I remembered you well and wanted so much to see you again." I was flattered into a sense of well-being that increased when Bedaux recollected details of my Russian trip and wanted to hear all about my second journey and my further views on Russia.

Other guests arrived, among them Maurice Hindus, whom I knew from Moscow, beautiful Clare Boothe from *Vanity Fair,* and Donald Freeman, another editor of that same magazine, who, I learned later, was in love with Miss Boothe and who not long after killed himself, it was said, out of despair for her. Dinner was served, with the same tall butlers behind each chair. Bedaux made me quite markedly the guest of the evening and called on me to tell them all about the USSR. After dinner he took me into his study and pulled something out of a locked drawer. "I'm writing a book on the devil," he said, with his slightly accented voice, "a character I find truly *passionant*—the only worthwhile character in literature."

"I didn't know you were a writer, too," I complimented him.

"Oh, I do a great many things," Bedaux replied vaguely.

The party climbed into his limousine and drove to the opera, where I was seated next to the host again, and after it to the Abbé de Thelem, a fashionable night club. When the other guests left, our host told me, "Wait, I will see you home," and en route he suddenly asked, "Would you care to see a rather remarkable place?" He sent his chauffeur home, hailed a taxi, got out at Thirty-third Street, and went ahead of me up some winding stairs. I felt a little uneasy. Was I letting myself in for something?

He opened a door into a brightly lit apartment, furnished completely in Chinese style with bamboo walls, black and gold dragons, polished teak screens with jade carvings, and a wide divan covered in red and gold embroidered silk. From above hung painted Chinese lanterns, lighting ceiling paintings of lions with jade eyes. Incense was burning, and its scent flooded the room. My host proudly watched my surprise.

"Dee-lightful?" he asked. "You like eet?" I liked it, but I must be going.

"Let me just show you one more thing, then we will go." He opened a hidden door and stood in a kind of alcove. "Look through here," he invited, showing the frosted glass of the hidden door, and then, "You understand, you can see everything inside the room?" He paused, still anxious to impress, I thought, rather like a child. "Now go out and look in." I went out and tried, but could see nothing. My host was quite charmed.

"Do you know anyone you could bring here?" he asked.

"Bring here? To show the flat you mean, you want to rent it?"

"Do you know anyone who might like to be here, together, man or woman, I do not mind, anytime I could come. They would not know I was there, you see." I could have laughed. Should I suggest, say, Calvin Coolidge, Elsa Maxwell?

"I have seen wonderful things," Bedaux mused on, almost to himself. "Once I drove from Poland to Cannes in a single night for two hours only."

"Was it worth it?" I could not help asking, curiosity overcoming propriety.

"It was," he said, and got up. "You will think of someone, yes?" Downstairs he hailed a late taxi and deposited me at my hotel door in silence.

It occurred to me, of course, should I have permitted this? But I was always more curious, more interested in what goes on, than in what anyone might think of me. And did this odd gentleman want to use me for something else? I soon found out when he telephoned me a few days later, and after a few compliments, said, "I would like you to introduce me to the head of Amtorg that handles trade relations between this country and Soviet Russia. I wish to speak about business with him."

"But you are an important businessman—you can simply telephone for an interview yourself!"

"I prefer to do it through you, yes? You are, I think, *persona grata* just now, you have written a book, it is highly praised, it might be more acceptable if I came through you." What he wanted, this big industrialist told me, was to sell his labor-measuring unit in all the Russias. "Their industry can do with it. They are not yet efficient, and I increase efficiency. Italy has my unit, I have revolutionized the Fiat works, Germany has introduced it, and this country of course very widely. I have made a fortune here."

"But with so many countries, does the USSR matter?" I asked, somewhat naïvely.

"I wish to be in every country," Monsieur B. responded. "I could help rationalize their industry. It would aid them, and it is a limitless market. I would make very great profit."

My curiosity about his idiosyncrasies did not extend to his profits. The later history of Monsieur Bedaux was less intriguing. During the war this author of a book on the devil was arrested for dealings with the Nazis in North Africa, something about an orange crop and manipulations of Sahara oil. The trial never took place. He hid a sleeping pill every night and, when he had enough, took them all in one draught. The case was closed.

# 16

# "THE MEN ARE STORED IN JAILS"

Myrtokleia—that was her full name, but she was known as Myrto—was a long, gangling girl with helpless Zazu Pitts hands and a vaguely lost expression in her large soft grieved brown eyes. Her dark hair hung untidily loose, but her eyes were what struck you, great, hurt, questioning eyes, puzzling as to how you could help humanity. She lived on odd jobs, and she had typed my book on Russia. Anyone who could cut through the jungle of my corrections, excisions, insertions, and arrows leading all over the margins and to every scrap of space on the page was bound to become my enemy or my friend, and Myrto had learned to handle it. This had endeared her to me forever.

Myrto had had a colorful career. She had run a tavern in San Francisco for bohemians, out-of-work artists, disintegrating young men, girls who were semiprostitutes. She would help any underdog with a free meal, roof, and drink, and there were endless tales of the destitute of both sexes she had befriended. She was prosecuted for selling liquor without a license, accused of all the vices some of her protégés had indulged in; and while awaiting trial, all the belongings her protégés had not appropriated were attached. The young prostitutes in jail marveled at Myrto. "They would stare at me unbelieving, you mean you do it for *nothing?*"

When Myrto came to Carmel, she took a job as waitress, and protested for the underpaid kitchen help. And then she met some radical who told her things didn't have to be like that. She could hardly credit it, but she went along with this friend to help organize the unemployed, protect the evicted, and shelter the stranded and their children.

She put her heart into everything she did, got out leaflets, arranged meetings, organized demonstrations. She accompanied the jobless on hunger marches, demanded concessions from city councils and boards of supervisors. She had just returned from leading a hunger march in Sacramento when she came running into our living room, distressed and indignant. "Peter, you've got to help, you've got to come with me right away to Watsonville. They've got fourteen of our guys in jail who haven't even mattresses to sleep on, and we must find them bail."

I didn't know anything about bail. It was a dry word connected with law courts and petty thieves; I had no connection with it. And I didn't want to move again, after my strenuous lecture tours. For all that spring and summer of 1933 I had been speaking on Soviet Russia and Nazism, explaining, expounding, and collecting funds for the International (Barbusse) Committee for All Victims, not only Jews (a distinction many were still unwilling to make, it being political, with a definition of fascism not yet generally accepted). I wanted to rest, to "cultivate my garden," but I couldn't withstand Myrto's hurt, imploring eyes, and the next thing I knew I was in my little green roadster, whizzing with her along the concrete highroad to Watsonville.

"There's been a strike among the lettuce pickers," Myrto explained. "They get fifteen cents an hour and work ten hours a day and now they're asking for twenty cents. They pay a dollar a day for a wooden shack or a torn tent, and stoop over lettuces all day in this broiling sun. Did you know ninety per cent of all America's lettuce comes from the Salinas Valley? They call it 'The Valley of Green Gold.' You can imagine how much the packers and ranchers make."

"Where do the pickers come from?" I asked.

"They used to be Chinese or Japanese, because foreigners take lower wages than Americans; but when they asked for more, they were sent home. Now most come from Mexico or the Philippines. They follow the crops, and have to live all year on what they make picking in the summer."

Myrto gave me more details. "They'd planned the strike for months. It's hard to organize these traveling workers, but as soon as the men stopped picking, the cops arrested the leaders and now our best men are all in jail." We stopped at a red brick building, called Odd Fellows Hall, by a green park shaded by cypresses and pepper. "That's the park where I was hosed off my sugarbox," she said, laughing, and suddenly I was panic-stricken. Law courts, trials, jails, judges—what was I getting into? I was fighting Nazism in Germany. This wasn't my world.

The courtroom was filled with workers in their overalls, Filipino and white. In the back rows sat leathery-faced Americans with the square jaws one associated with cops or sheriffs. American Legion pins and deputies' badges decorated buttonholes. An alert young man was asking questions for the prosecution. The defense attorney was a big blond genial San Franciscan, hired by the workers' International Labor Defense. "George Andersen," Myrto whispered, "he's showing what the setup is between the workers and ranchers."

"What were they arrested for?" I asked Myrto.

"What d'you think? For being strike leaders of course."

"Did the police say that?"

Myrto stared at me. "Oh Peter, where have you been? Of course they never *say* that. The men are charged with vagrancy, or violence, or assault, or whatever suits them, though it's the police who do the assaulting, like when they trained that fire hose on us the other night. I had to wring out my dress."

"But won't it be easy to show they aren't vagrants?"

Myrto merely made one of those helpless gestures, and I turned to the actors in the drama. The wizened old judge was chewing tobacco and spat a glistening brown stream across the room, then gabbled the list of prospective jurors; twelve people took their seats in the jury box. A grocery clerk with a toothbrush mustache was the first to be questioned.

"Is it all right to strike, in your opinion?"

"If a man does it the right way, without causing any trouble."

A real-estate agent, a store manager, a narrow-faced ranch foreman, a housewife gave similar answers. "I believe in organized labor, but not the way they do it" was the burden of all their replies.

One picturesque old man, with drooping white mustaches, leather boots, jacket, and red bandana pulled through a silver-embossed necktie ring, announced proudly, as his profession, *"Vaquero!"* and added for the judge, "Cowboy!" Now a red-faced policeman stepped to the witness stand.

"Officer Thomas, what do you know of Defendant Remsen?"

Thomas cleared his throat.

"He never worked—"

"How do you know?"

"I never *seen* him work."

"Do you go to the ranches to see whether men are working?"

"No, *sir.*"

"How did you know the men were vagrants?"

"They was roamin' from place to place, up to no good."

"How did you know they were 'up to no good'?"

"Well, they was standin' outside that place, 'the workers' center,' they calls it, jabberin' back and forth."

"Is there any harm in 'jabbering back and forth'?" George Andersen asked.

Police Officer Thomas clinched his evidence: "I couldn't understand what they was sayin', they wasn't speakin' English."

Gaetano, a neat, small-boned, brown little Filipino, in gray pants and blue sweater, took the stand.

"How much were you getting in the lettuce fields?" Andersen asked.

"Fifteen cents," said the Filipino.

"And how much did you strike for?"

The prosecutor quickly intervened. "Irrelevant, immaterial, nothing to do with the case."

"Ah, but my client's whole case is that they were being underpaid, what they considered . . ."

"We are not considering the rights or wrongs of laborers, we are trying the accused on a charge of vagrancy," the prosecutor snapped.

It was very hot and tempers were getting short. Whenever the strike was mentioned or the conditions of lettuce pickers—their pay, their tents, their children or the hated system of the middleman contractor—the prosecution interrupted: "Irrelevant, immaterial, nothing to do with the case," and the evidence was ruled out. Andersen tried in vain to get "vagrant" defined.

"I am a vagrant, you are a vagrant when you lie in your patio and take a sunbath!" he cried at last in exasperation.

"Irrelevant, immaterial, nothing to do with the case." I wished the assistant D.A. would get a phonograph.

While we waited for the jury's decision, Myrto introduced me to some of the prisoners and we gave them cigarettes. "Of course they can't convict you," I said, trying to reassure them—sure myself it would be impossible on that absurd evidence. Then we all filed back, tamping out our cigarettes. I looked at my watch: the jury had been out eight minutes.

Judge Brewer removed a wad of tobacco from his mouth and addressed the foreman. "Have you reached a verdict?"

"We have, your Honor."

"Do you find defendants guilty or not guilty?"

"Guilty, your Honor."

So I learned my first lesson, brought home to me over and over all that burning, radiant summer: strike leaders were arrested not for wanting more than a few cents an hour for fruit-picking but for "vagrancy," "disturbing the peace," "rioting," "resisting officers," "use of obscene language"—and were imprisoned for the duration of the harvesting season. They became "agitators" and thereafter could get no jobs. After this lettuce strike in the Salinas Valley the workers' club remained wrecked and deserted, and the men were too frightened to meet elsewhere. The editor of the local paper said, in answer to my query, "But they were only Filipinos, weren't they? They have no right in this country anyway."

All that season I continued my practical education in sunshine-drenched orchards, on cherry and pear and apricot and cotton ranches. My next firing line came with a banner headline one morning: TWENTY-FOUR ARRESTED IN CHERRY STRIKE. "Fade in," I thought in movie terms, "on a big juicy bunch of red cherries." The paper carried the same invective about "Reds" and "agitators." The pickers had been in the cherry trees when sudden whistles blew, and police dropped from trees and lobbed long-range shells into the orchard. As pickers ran screaming in confusion, police arrested the twenty-four.

Again Myrto loped in. "If you're interested, I got this from the San Jose jail," she muttered. I could just decipher a faint pencil scrawl on a soiled scrap of paper.

County Jail
San Jose

Dear Comrade Myrto,

Johnnie Dennett was beat up and put in solitary because he wouldn't give his father's address. George Lonigan's been took to hospital, he couldn't eat for three days with his broken jaw, they threatened five Mexican comrades with deportation if they didn't plead guilty so they did. The rest of us insisted on jury trials. A Mexican priest is trying to bribe the other Mexes with suspended sentences if they'll plead guilty.

Despite the fact that I wanted to get on with my own writing, that I did not want to leave my home or my garden or my family, and resented getting involved again in concerns that were not of my making, one could not resist Myrto, and I found myself once more whizzing north along the familiar California coast.

In the spring the Santa Clara Valley is a lake of white. Prune and pear blossoms hang from their trees like bridal veils. Heat haze billows up from the asphalt roads between geometric rows of pear and plum, almond, apricot, apple, with trunks painted white set in brown earth crisscrossed by irrigation channels. When the blossoms turn to fruit, the boughs hang so heavy that stakes must support them. And in the summer men, women, and small girls and boys under broad, broken-brimmed straw hats swarm up ladders to gather the fruit. Peaches, plums, apples, berries are dropped into buckets, loaded into crates, packed in boxes, and trucked away to be stoned, cut, dried, canned. The trees we passed dripped red, gold, and purple fruit, and the scent was overpowering.

They were at work, the brown-faced Mexican fruit tramps, or white folk off the ranges from Texas, Arizona, and New Mexico, who had come on foot or hitchhiked or ridden the freights. Whole families had trundled in swaying jalopies full of pots and pans and children, with tents and mattresses hitched to the cars. They pitched torn and dirty tents on roadsides in dry arroyos or river bottoms, or in the orchards where they picked, at fifteen or twenty cents an hour. (The lettuce strike had raised some wages.)

I drove past tawny hills like mountain lions, with wild scrub trees crawling up them. The road curved through dark-green live oaks and gaunt gray Australian eucalyptus, to the coast towns with wide boulevards flanked by signs: JESUS SAVES * BURMA SHAVE * FISHBURGERS * IN GOD WE TRUST ALL OTHERS PAY CASH.

In San Jose I stopped before a white frame house with palms, pepper, and cypress rising from its lawn. Standing at her gate was Alice Park, an ex-suffragette, a dumpy little lady of fifty in white Chinese silk, flushed, hot, and nervous. She had asked me to help her form a group of liberals who would know the real facts. She greeted me with "They wouldn't go till you came. I'm so glad you got here, come right in."

I unstuck my hat, and Mrs. Park said to her crowded roomful, "We are here this hot afternoon because we care about the rights of American citizens and workers. We must know what happens in a fruit strike. Miss Winter will tell us about her experiences."

I looked around the shaded living room. Two clergymen sat on the sofa, one thin and intense, with a high forehead, the other moonfaced, with an apologetic smile. Some pale young men in glasses, three middle-aged women, a local reporter, and a fat woman in blue silk completed the group. I told, as quickly as I could, what I had learned in Watsonville.

"It's all from your point of view," the reporter burst out when I had finished. "Aren't there two sides to every question?"

"And aren't there . . . er . . . *agitators?*" the moonfaced clergyman asked.

I noticed a small blond-haired, delicately boned girl on a footstool, who dropped a quiet remark, or gave some needed information, once in a while. Miss Park whispered, "That's Caroline Decker, the secretary of the Agricultural Union." She had a pink and white skin and very fair straight hair that fell to her shoulders, and tiny white hands that she used as she talked. She looked like a dancer, but she talked like an economics instructor as she told what the workers earned, the market price for cherries, the relations of the banks to big and little ranchers, and how agriculture was financed. We kept coming back to Rancher Tracey, the largest orchard owner, who, one of the group said, was burdened by a mortgage of ninety thousand dollars.

"A number of the smaller ranchers said they would be willing to pay thirty cents," Caroline said, "but Tracey won't let them, and they don't dare go against him."

"Dare?" The room was shocked.

"Rancher Tracey is also a banker and would refuse them loans or call their mortgages if they did," the little union organizer finished evenly, and the meeting was over.

The next day some of us visited the jail, presided over by a short fat man with fleshy jaws and a bunch of rattling keys. The male cherry pickers were in the big tank, he said, the girls upstairs. He was friendly enough: most prisoners were his "boys," but as for the cherry strikers—"if they'd only be reg'lar," he protested, "those agitators." Caroline had told us that the girls, in jail six weeks now, had been out of doors once, had had one bath, slept seven in a cell built for two, and one had t.b.

"Oh no," Mr. Buffington rattled his keys, "you can't see the

women, not without the matron. But I can't understan' how nice
people like you—you seem all right, but you're all wrong—how
can you . . . ?" He kept unlocking and locking iron doors with
thick iron bars. "This jail is too old, we want a new jail, we tell
everyone, see this paint, it's peelin', it ought to be repainted, but
they threw out the whole bond issue."

At the door he turned to me confidentially. "I sometimes wonder
if I should have taken up this work, I haven't made a thing out've
it—an' they've just cut my salary. I was tellin' the wife the other
day, I wonder if I wouldn't be further along if I'd agone into a
bank."

I clucked my sympathy.

"Now, I could get on with a person like you," he said. "We
understan' each other, you just wanna change a few ideas, you
wanna see it right. . . ."

I had some time to fill in and strolled over to the courthouse,
where a trial was in progress. I went in; the court was crowded,
a murder case.

A young man with a thin, delicately carved face and high cheek-
bones stood nervously in the dock; he was being questioned about
a gun in his car. His gun? Yes. Had he shot it? Yes. His lips were
dry, his ashen face strained, a beautifully molded face, I thought,
half-Indian.

". . . and then a light was flashed into the window, it was a
gun and I got scared, I thought someone was threatening to kill
me," he was almost whispering. "It was quite dark, I had a revolver
and I shot." The crowd sighed. It was bad luck, the policeman
died.

I felt very mixed up. Here were cherry strikers in jail who should
be picking cherries and a girl with t.b. who should be in hospital
and a boy on trial who looked lost and friendless but who had shot
a policeman and become "a murderer." A colored man, a bum
out of work didn't have a chance.

Next day we asked to visit the strikers again.

"Aw, now," Mr. Buffington protested, "leave 'em alone, but here,
you can see a murderer, wanna see a murderer? I've got him in
the little tank." I couldn't see very well, but gradually a face came
out of the gloom, a sensitive face, half-Indian, dead-white.

"Is his trial over?" I cried. "Is he . . . have they . . . ?"

"The works," Buffington said. "Here, Joe, you c'n come out a minute." He grated his key in the lock, and the boy came slowly out. He did not smile; Buffington pulled his arm, not unkindly.

"C'mon, Joe, stand here, I won't hurt you. This fellow don't look like a murderer, does he? You're a writer, ain't you, well, ask him questions, here, Joe, answer the lady's questions, she's a writer, you'll get in the papers some more." The boy stood silent.

"Talk to her," the jailer appealed. "Don't look like a murderer, does he? C'mon, Joe, tell the lady, they like to write stories about murderers."

Joe looked at me.

"He won't hurt you," Buffington reassured me. "How old are you, Joe, nineteen?" I could not think of anything to say.

"Well, you won't be here much longer, Joe—tell her."

Joe lowered his eyes.

"I came to see the cherry pickers," I started desperately, and saw Buffington's disapproval. "I only wanted . . . I'd like to tell you . . ." I tried again, then choked and turned and almost ran out of the jail. There was nothing I could say. There was nothing I could do for Joe.

But I could possibly do something about the cherry pickers, and Jerry Warwick gave me an opportunity. I had met Jerry, a good-looking boy with green eyes and a scholar's face, in Caroline's union office in San Jose.

"I'm one of the cherry pickers out on bail, and I want to raise bail for the rest," he said. "Can you help? We can't leave them to rot in prison."

"You don't look like a workingman." I gazed at his clean white hands, clean shirt sleeves rolled up neatly above the elbow, his well-shaven face.

"I was a student," he said, "but now the judges think I'm a bum like the others. But you, now, they can see you belong. Judge Cress has refused to accept bail for Juanita, the girl with t.b., from her own doctor." Jerry explained the details of bail raising. They needed twenty-one thousand.

"But that's impossible!" I was jolted.

"Not with you. We'll get them out with you helping."

So—there I was driving the good-looking young student cherry picker from county to county, calling on doctors, social workers, prosperous liberals, while Jerry told me about himself. "I was working on a thesis on social change, but I was troubled about the conflict between the rights of the individual and loyalty to the community. I didn't know that I agreed with the college radicals—they're awfully sure of themselves."

We called on the Santa Clara judge, an irritable man with staring eyes and a pout. He glared at us especially when I said, "Judge, we want the papers you need to bail people out with."

"Who do you want to bail out?"

"The cherry pickers in San Jose, eighteen of them."

Now he stared at me quite unashamedly, then pulled some forms reluctantly out of a drawer; there weren't eighteen. "Why d'you have to give that newspaper story that said I refused bail to a sick t.b. girl?" he threw at Jerry.

"Didn't you?" Jerry asked.

"I didn't refuse, they came at four fifty-five, I have to go home at five, so it was too late." He lived above his office.

We drove to San Jose to find bail people, discovered two, and had to take them before a San Jose judge for papers; then we drove back to Judge Cress. We spent the day chasing from one to the other, driving back and forth, miles each way, the heat waves sizzling on the asphalt, where, I quoted to Jerry,

> "The snake is fried in the desert
> And the flea no longer plays."

Late in the afternoon, exhausted by the heat and effort, we bearded Judge Cress with enough money and property to bail out seven prisoners, and he refused to accept it.

"This signature has to be in ink," he said.

"Really?" I said, and then I collected all my strength. "Judge," I said, "it's late, it's getting later, and I'm bushed. We've been up to Palo Alto and back three times, sixty miles altogether. The forms are signed correctly, we've got the bail, and we're going to get this job done, tonight. I'm not going back up there." I warmed to my indignation. "If I were Mr. Herbert Fleishhacker, you would sign these papers without any fuss." I drew myself up and enunciated, "Well, I am Mrs. Lincoln Steffens and—"

He held out his hand for those papers, and in five minutes we were out of that office with freedom for seven prisoners in our possession.

# 17

# "DEATH GOES ROUND THIS CIRCLE"

In Carmel, they listened to my accounts with excited interest. Strikes were something most people knew very little about, something connected with railroads, steel mills, coal mines—damp, dark, dreary factories or places underground—not with sun and scented trees and bright fields. But because of our fragrant valleys, the human element in our stories of these strikes, and all the talk there had been about them, there gradually grew up a small nucleus of public-spirited Californians who became increasingly anxious to help in the struggle of the underprivileged workers in the California fields: Noel Sullivan, a gentle, courteous millionaire with a Catholic conscience; Langston Hughes, the Negro poet; Francis, the blacksmith; Dan, from Yale; and others who had sympathy and understanding. A few joined us from San Francisco, including Marie de L. Welch, my poet friend, and Emily Joseph, the shrewd, hardhitting wife of a wealthy businessman who happened to have a "social conscience."

Stef kept telling the journalism students from Stanford and Berkeley, "Don't take it from me, don't accept what I say, look for yourselves. Go to the strikes and watch the trials yourselves." No teacher had sent them into the field like that, and they went back to their colleges and asked questions; they had seen a new side of their world picture and there were heated debates. Some of them were the sons of bankers and shipowners and ranchers, and the questions could grow uncomfortable; I sometimes feared some irate parents' appearance in Carmel with a cup of hemlock.

Stef did things with a humor that was hard to oppose—for instance, in the matter of the Caroline Decker Typewriter Fund. The police or the American Legion were always, as he termed it, carrying out "some righteous raid" on private or union offices, and in one of these they smashed Caroline's typewriter. The union had no money, so Stef started a fund to buy her a new one and sent his appeals—listing himself as chairman, treasurer, and secretary—to the big businessmen who were in general sympathy with, if not the instigators of, these raids. Louis Oneal, a "boss" in San Jose, sent an indignantly amused letter with his reluctant ten dollars—and the money came in, even a surplus "for paper, carbons, and new ribbons," as Stef wrote his contributors. How could they fight that?

I don't remember how I came to know Sam Darcy, the California Communist leader. Perhaps on a platform, but I had a sense of him before I knew him. Occasionally he drove to Carmel, for Stef also appreciated finding out directly what was going on—he was still the newspaperman wanting authoritative news from the people making it, and liked to feel "in" things. Darcy was never in the foreground. He was not a "gray eminence," either, but he had much to do with those strikes, since the new little agricultural union was "Communist-led." When I saw him very occasionally in his stuffy little office combined with the *Western Worker* in San Francisco, I was rather intimidated by his preoccupied, slightly impatient air. Gradually I came to know him as a rare mixture of theorist and practical politician, intelligent, farsighted, and uncompromising, a martinet to minions and colleagues. "Very strict disciplinarian," Caroline observed, "blows up at the least inefficiency. I have big fights with him." He was strongly built, with blond hair and blue-gray eyes in a large face; he had started life as a carpenter. He told me once—he rarely talked about himself— that as a child he had seen his father carried on a stretcher from a cop's night-stick attack on a picket line, and from then on "I was a Communist." As district organizer, he had made of a decrepit California party an active and effective instrument for their purposes; for me, who liked to understand my world, Darcy's clear analyses from the local to the international situation linked things up to make an understandable picture of the whole.

The San Joaquin Valley was planted to cotton for hundreds of square miles. In October the bolls ripen and must be picked or they go to seed and the cotton harvest is ruined. Migratory workers— from Mexico, the Philippines, or blighted areas in America—

picked the cotton on thousands of acres on the big ranches, some of them vast consolidations leased to tenants or run by farm managers. Utilities, railroads, packing and ginning companies, banks and city industries also owned cotton ranches, though their owners never saw a boll of cotton.

Mexicans had picked cotton for several years, but the depression had lowered wages to a catastrophic forty cents a hundred pounds, and a man could pick at most two to three hundred pounds a day. By 1933 "Okies" and "Arkies" had begun to arrive, driven from the Dust Bowl by the drought in Oklahoma, Arkansas, Texas. They trekked west in old jalopies and dilapidated trailers (so movingly described in John Steinbeck's *The Grapes of Wrath*) and swelled the "regular" force of migrants who came year after year to the overcrowded shack towns and trailer camps. We saw these in the ditches of rich orchards, tents of sacking, boxboard, and bits of canvas, the squalid lean-tos attached to a rattling trailer. There might be one room, but without floor or window; or a dugout in a dry river bottom. The Mexican "Jimtowns"—pieces of tin and galvanized iron—housed whole families, who cooked and ate and slept in one small space, with nowhere to dispose of their refuse. Water was carried long distances from rusty pitcher pumps, and flies from the vermin-infested refuse and the pit toilets brought disease to this rich, bursting, sun-drenched land.

These conglomerations of hovels were the "homes" of two hundred thousand traveling pickers, who picked cotton for a few months and lived on relief or starved the rest of the year. It was these pickers that Caroline and her friends now started organizing in an attempt to better their lives in the cotton valley. The little agricultural union entered that valley of cotton and "raised the demand" for "a dollar a hundred," and then they struck. Caravans of workers drove slowly along the highways and called to the pickers from the hedgeless roads to join the strike. They brought leaflets to the shack towns, threw them into the fields, held meetings in the townships—Pottersville, Red Bank, Wasco, Farmersville. They journeyed from township to township, telling the workers a strike could help them. Pat Chambers, a small dark Irishman, called the pickers to a meeting in Pixley that set off a big battle: ranchers, furious at the unaccustomed defiance, handed out guns, pickax handles, and clubs, and ordered deputies to "Circle round 'em, boys, circle round 'em, keep your guns on 'em, and when's the proper time, let 'em have it." So—they had it. Two workers were killed at Pixley and another at Arvin—a Mexican who had acted as deputy consul when he had not been picking. The valley seethed.

We could not stay in Carmel and merely read about it. Our little bunch gathered one early dawn and traveled to the valley in three automobiles, led by Noel Sullivan in his Cadillac. In Tulare, the heart of the strike area, we met a small, worried relief worker, Miss Throckmorton, who was glad to be able at last to talk to her own kind.

"We've had a lot of trouble," she started in at once. "The pickers are suspicious of us, they won't give us their car numbers or their nationality, but we have to have these, because most of them have no address and how otherwise can we check on who gets relief?"

"Why do they object?" we asked.

"That's just what you can't make out. They say they will be 'discriminated against' if their license number is known, that the ranchers won't give work to strikers, and they're afraid we want to know their nationality to report them for deportation. There is some law that a person who has once had county relief is deportable, but of course we have no such intention!" She wiped her pince-nez; she was thin, hot and exasperated, and strands of damp brown hair hung down. She was here to give government relief, and the starving migrants wouldn't take it.

"The farmers resent relief because the pickers can go on striking, and the strikers say that our relief can break their strike. Some grocers have told men that if they take relief, they must go back to work or face deportation, but of course they had no right to say that. We make no conditions.

"What can we do? With a hundred and fifty miles to cover and one assistant, we never get the right address. These people never direct you right, they tell you, 'There's a camp six miles past the house with the red roof, three turns after Green Ranch,' and we see no red roof and don't know where Green Ranch is and there's no one on the road to tell us. They're all out *picketing*. It takes us half a day to find one family!" We expressed our sympathy. "How can we make them take relief?" echoed after us. Miss Throckmorton had buttonholed a local reporter and started in again on her distressful tale.

I went to "Strike Headquarters," a small room with bare floor and one bench. A quiet-spoken boy in a turtle-neck blue sweater pecked at a typewriter, and some Mexican women, their hair in matted plaits, sat around suckling their babies. Bits of paper tacked on a soiled board had ill-spelled messages in English and Spanish, and a list of names was printed in uneven letters on a gray cardboard from a Uneeda soda-cracker box. There were flies and a smell of sweat.

I don't know what I had expected. A smart office, the bustle of a political campaign? These straggling women and children did not represent my picture of a "big, organized strike," nor could I imagine orders for fourteen thousand people pounded out on that rickety machine. Then we all started off for Camp Corcoran, the encampment of four thousand cotton strikers, but stopped off first at the office of the district attorney.

"We've come to see you about the strikers in jail," Emily Joseph said. "We consider their bail excessive and you've just raised Pat Chambers' from two thousand to ten thousand dollars." The D.A. was affable, a little indulgent, like a doctor toward a patient suffering from fantasies. "Criminal syndicalism is a very serious charge," he said—to which Emily briskly responded, "But you can charge anyone with it, it's a portmanteau act covering anything." She had done her homework. The man stared.

Noel spoke up now in his hesitating, courteous voice. "We think you should disarm the growers. It is dangerous the way they are going around with guns, since they have already killed three workers."

"I would have no right," the D.A. said, recovering himself, "it is for the sheriff to see the peace is kept."

"He can disarm the farmers, then?"

"He has to see the peace is kept."

"Don't you consider," Noel prompted again, in his ingratiating, gentlemanly tones, "don't you consider one might say the peace has not been kept when three men have been killed and only the ranchers carry guns?"

"The Grand Jury dismissed those charges." The district attorney was beginning not to smile.

"Yet if men have been murdered, you might say the peace has been disturbed?" Marie Welch, from a well-to-do, sheltered home, blushed as she trod this unfamiliar ground.

"It's the sheriff's job to see to all that," the D.A. almost barked now, "why don't you go to him?" So we did.

The sheriff admonished us: "I mean exactly what I say, folks. I can't take the guns from them farmers, they go hunting and they have hunting licenses."

"Does that mean," Emily barked back, "that we should refer the murder of those workers to the fish and game commission?"

"Now, now, lady, it's very easy for you eddicated people—what do you say you are, the League for Political Pensioners?—to come here and be high-hat. I said the farmers had hunting licenses, so they could carry guns."

"Can the workers carry guns?" I had to say something.

"They couldn't have a gun a minute in their hands without shootin'. They means harm and vi'lence, them workers."

"But they haven't harmed anyone?" Marie and I burst out together.

"How long you bin in this town? One afternoon? What could you find out in one afternoon? I bin here all the time and I see what them agitators do, nothin' but a bunch o' troublemakers—the more trouble, the better pleased. But not here in my county, *no*, sar."

"Don't they pick cotton?" we chorused together.

"Them aren't real pickers, they never come here to pick cotton, most never seen a boll of cotton in their lives. They bin sent in here." He paused for emphasis. "And I'm tellin' you, ladies, you'd be shocked if you heard some of the things they say in them street meetin's they're continually holdin', it's surprisin' it's allowed."

"It isn't as far as we can see," Marie suggested.

"Now miss—or madam is it?—what you want to go sayin' a thing like that for? No street meetin's bin interfered with by my office so long as they don't go attackin' the Constitootion of this country or usin' bad language or pointin' guns."

"Will you disarm the growers?" Emily reiterated, quite sharply now.

"Only the district attorney can do that." He was offended.

"That's funny, the D.A. said only you could." Then Emily made a misstep; she mentioned "scabs."

"What's that word you used?"

"Scabs," Emily repeated, "that's what workers call men who go on picking when a strike's been called."

"What do *you* call them, sheriff?" Noel asked.

"Never heard that word before," the sheriff said. "Glad to have learned it. Sure you city folks know things."

"You're here to interpret United States law," Emily fought on stubbornly, and the harassed sheriff lost his temper.

"I don't care about the Constitootion of the United States," he said. "I am the law of Tulare and I say in Tulare County while I am sheriff—"

But he never finished the sentence. "Death goes round this circle," Marie murmured, and we marched out of that hot, stuffy, insufferable room.

It was dark when the car slowed up at Camp Corcoran—the tent city the size of a block in which those thousands of cotton pickers squatted to sit out their strike. A few people stood about a makeshift gate. Was this the entrance? Someone came around to our car.

"I think you better walk from here," a quiet voice said, and led us through the murky gloom. We stumbled along in almost pitch-darkness among tents, people, burning oilstoves, refuse, wretched and smelly as in the shack towns, smells of greasy cooking, stale fish, damp clothes, and sewage. An occasional dim lantern lit up the mud we struggled through; there were small muffled sounds that gave the feeling of a crowded city, though we could not see the crowds. A sick baby wailed—and I had a sense, in that darkness, of people waiting, waiting.

We came upon Caroline Decker.

"The big thing is to keep this camp going," the little blonde strike leader said. "They're doing everything to break us up. They don't want these people here; it keeps up strike morale to have us all together. They've made us put in toilets, and a crude open-water system—it has cost hundreds of dollars—and now they're threatening again, if we don't improve it, to evict us."

"Can't you close them?" Emily asked.

"There's no money. We haven't a cent, we've hardly enough for gas and oil for the pickets, and we have to feed these starving kids."

"The relief worker told us they're feeding the strikers," Emily went on.

"With so many strings attached that the union has advised the men not to take it," Caroline retorted. People kept coming up to her in the blackness, asking a question, delivering a message in a low voice, melting away again into the sound-filled silence.

*"Viva la huelga!"* ("Long live the strike!") came a cry out of the blackness. We stopped outside a dirty evil-smelling tent.

"Light," called Caroline, and a figure brought a swaying lantern, by whose murky yellow beam we could just make out a bunch of bedding, a broken chair, some gaping children. A frowsy woman came out with a bundle, a tiny wizened baby whose face was almost black—black as I had seen them in Vienna; his tiny eyes gazed unseeing.

"I've never seen anything like it," Emily exploded, and in a whisper added, "The baby's dead!" Mexicans stood around unmoving, wondering, I supposed, who these strange people were, commiserating all of a sudden with a wretchedness they had always lived in.

"This camp is cleaner than most of the Mexican camps," said Doctor Burton, a camp doctor who had appeared out of nowhere. "I've been in this region a long time and they rarely have toilets, just pits, rarely running water as close as this, and never a nurse or doctor. Their babies die like this every year—it's nothing new to them."

"Do people *know* about it?" someone asked in a choked voice.

We wandered about, peering as well as we could into lightless tents, at piles of cans, rusty stoves, broken-down Fords that served as bed and roof. Children lay asleep, huddled on the muddy ground.

"How much would it cost to put in the piping system?" Noel asked.

"Two hundred and fifty the way they want it, but our men say they can fix it well enough to fit the requirements for about fifty-seven dollars, if they do it themselves and we get the piping wholesale." Caroline's voice sounded close to despair.

"Where will four thousand people go if the camp is closed?"

"On the road," she replied, "and they'll create the same health menace there. The police will probably chase them along to 'break up the crowd,' as they call it—and break up our solidarity, too. That's what they're after." I had never heard her like this.

We walked back to the store. Policemen's cars and motorcycles had gathered, and the cops turned and looked us over. As we stood by our car, I saw Noel write something and hand it to Caroline. "For the pipes." He hesitated. "I hope that will be enough." It was a check, and it was enough.

\* \* \*

There had never been a strike in these fields like this one, they said, so well organized, so "solid," and so efficiently led; and yet how slender the strikers' resources were, how few and "amateur" their leaders, we had discovered with astonishment.

So when one day, back in Carmel, I received a telegram asking urgently for money, any sum we could raise, I ran around to friends, collected nineteen dollars, and wired it to Caroline. I learned later that on that day they were so broke, so without funds for gas or oil to send the pickets out, that the whole resistance could have ended then, and the strike been broken. But when I later talked to John Francis Neylan, the Hearst attorney in San Francisco, he was bitter about "the power of those agitators with all their money."

"Where do they get all that money?" he wanted to know.

"What money?" I was quite dumfounded.

"The money they spend, on lectures and articles and organizing and fund raising and public relations. It would cost us thousands of dollars." He would not believe that "all that" could be done out of a sense of pity, or outrage, or humanity, or just plain justice, for nothing.

A farm manager who visited Stef and me to discuss the summer's agricultural strikes did admit that the pickers did not live exactly sumptuously. "But do you know what they'd do with a dollar a day if they got it?" he hissed, then lowered his voice. "They'd *spend* it! Just spend it!"

As the facts of the strike began to be known, there was considerable talk, and an official investigation became necessary. Governor James Rolph, Jr., appointed a fact-finding committee consisting of Archbishop Hanna, George Creel, and a professor from the University of California; people flocked to the hearings. Norman Thomas flew from New York and listened in open-mouthed astonishment as the ragged procession of men and women described the details of their lives. It was the first time that these migratory workers themselves could describe, before an official body, their lives and their indignities, and it came from them in a flood. Blonde little Caroline cross-examined, and she knew what to ask. For three days this strange procession of normally silent "underdogs" had their day in court. And it had its effect. Wages were raised from thirty to fifty cents a day, and national attention had been called to the migrants' story, to their wretched existence, their miserable shack towns. Yet the leaders were still in jail, and the next year and the next the same struggle must take place. The fundamental problem was not solved. Progress can be mighty slow, I reflected—not for the first time.

Marie Welch wrote poems about these strikers, one on Camp Corcoran, and another, "Harvests," which I especially liked:

> Now among good harvests
> The human harvest fails;
> The fruit and grain lie on the ground,
> The men are stored in jails.
>
> The stem is rotten on the root
> And the seed on the stem.
> Store away the meagre yield
> Of men with life in them.
>
> Store them fearfully away,
> The fellows who maintain
> The right to live as honestly
> As fruit and grain.
>
> Lock and wall may have their hour
> But the new crop will be grown
> From the seed that's hoarded now
> In the barns of stone.

# 18

# "VERY STUPID—OR VERY CLEVER"

During this time, in the fall of 1933, Filene had asked Steffens to stay with him in Boston. He wanted his biography written and asked Stef to pick the writer. This was an important offer to Steffens, apart from his interest in his friend, for his small income—some left him by his father as stock in the Sacramento bank —had been cut in half by the bank crash and he owed the government the full amount of the stock. Filene wanted his friend alone.

Stef had also had several requests to lecture, one from Harvard. His talks were highly successful, particularly the one to the Harvard students, in which, he wrote, he had been "in fine form." But he was besieged day and night with requests for interviews, speeches, articles; his many friends made demands on him; and there was no me to protect him. After an address to the Rotary Club in Chicago, which also made a hit, he wrote me, ". . . my left leg has developed an alarming tendency to turn left." He seemed scared, especially when the next day it grew worse.

Doctor Kocher and I met him at the train and Stef was put to bed. He had had a coronary thrombosis. I tried now to make a life around his bedside, providing the activity he liked best—talking to the young people who still flocked to the house, writing his triumphant little paragraphs for our local papers, seeing his old friends.

It was almost three years before Stef's strength failed. They were three full, rich years, among the best of all the thirteen years of our brimming life together. There were no doubts about "us," and I was thankful I need no longer try and think about breaking a relationship that had worked out to something so fulfilling, so satisfying, so rich with love.

Unexpectedly, just as Stef was settled, I got a wire from the *New Masses*. Would I report the San Francisco waterfront strike for them? The country was full of strikes and this was one of the most momentous. I was pleased to be doing something I considered important, and for a paper for which I would have to pull no punches.

In San Francisco I went first to the longshoremen's headquarters on the Embarcadero and found Harry Bridges, the voluble and tough union leader, a wire spring of a man with a narrow, sharp-featured, expressive face, popping eyes, and strong Australian accent. He heartily greeted a fellow Australian, a "limey," as he dubbed me, though I was a little taken aback at my first real taste of a worker's "intemperate" language—stevedore slang. And Bridges' talk was quite unrestrained. But I felt I was getting "straight goods."

While we talked, men kept coming in and out, giving Bridges terse information, picking up picketing instructions and leaflets and copies from a big pile of mimeographed sheets of a *Waterfront Worker*. An ink-stained desk held a typewriter at which longshoremen sat down from time to time and pecked out something with one finger.

Two former strikes some years ago, I learned, had been crushed and a company union set up. It had been impossible to organize a real union. Then came this Australian. Originally destined for the priesthood, he had turned to the sea instead, shipped out from Melbourne, and, incensed by waterfront conditions in prosperous California, had stayed on to arouse and help the stevedores. He was a good worker himself, and soon a favorite with "gang bosses."

"The seamen couldn't get together because they were divided into so many crafts," Bridges explained forcefully, "machinists, cooks, stewards, ships' scalers, painters, boilermakers, the warehousemen on the docks, and the teamsters who hauled the goods. The 'bosses' want to keep it that way so they can make separate contracts for each craft and in each port, which weakens our bargaining position. We're asking for one coastwise contract, from Portland to San Pedro, for the whole industry, and a raise too, but the most important thing we want is a hiring hall under the men's control."

This became the crux of the strike, the focus of the struggle, as it was the sorest point. The men hated the method by which they were hired. Jobs were given to favorite longshoremen—to the "safe" men, who "played the game"—but even these had to "kick back" part of their wages to the foreman who gave them the job. Every morning longshoremen had to line up on the dock and wait to see if they would be chosen, and if there was not enough work to go around, they went home empty-handed to their wives. There was no security of income, however small, and the indignity in addition incensed as well as humiliated them. Exasperated hatred and competitiveness replaced what should have been the comradeship of work and the "solidarity" of workingmen fighting together for their common interests. "That's the only weapon we have," one or another would comment as they listened to Bridges tell me, "standing together."

This strike became the biggest in American maritime history, with fourteen thousand men idle. Stevedoring up and down the coast practically ceased; at the height of the battle, a hundred ships rode at anchor at their moorings in San Francisco Bay. The struggle lasted for months. As it continued week after week, shipowners grew as incensed as the Associated Farmers had been, and as violent. Strikers were clubbed, beaten, and gassed; every means was used to bring them to heel, including promises from officials, not quite honest offers from the Eastern union leader Joseph P. Ryan, who was then booed out of the city. The Red scare was brandished, until the simplest longshoreman could be accused of "treason," "conspiracy," "overthrow of the government," "attacks on constituted authority." "It isn't a strike at all" was the main contention of the Industrial Association. "Labor is seeking government control." Inflamed headlines kept the populace at fever point.

Talk grew of a general strike. There had been only one previously in United States history, in Seattle in 1926, and that had failed. Now, after an unsuccessful attempt to open one port, Portland, by force, troops were called out in San Francisco, and police staged a pitched battle, known as the "Battle of Rincon Hill." Workers were chased with clubs and guns, even machine guns, and two fleeing men were shot and killed. One, Howard Sperry, was a veteran, and Nicholas Bordoise, a Greek cook, was on his way home after cooking for the pickets on the Embarcadero. A doctor friend who attended the wounded in prison said it was "like an assault in wartime." And all day the police cars tore through the echoing streets, their sirens screaming.

This was the turning point of the struggle, and a general strike resulted. Fifty thousand San Franciscans marched in the funeral procession, stopping all traffic, jamming sidewalks. I stood on a street blocked solid with silent people, no police in sight, because they had been told to "keep out of the way and out of sight on this day when labor is burying its dead." Instead, longshoremen policed the procession and the town.

The life of San Francisco came to a standstill; the city was a ghost town. No streetcars ran, no trucks, no automobiles. No soldiers stirred from the waterfront. Shops were closed. Pickets alone stood on street corners. But I did overhear a group of businessmen discussing where to lunch. The strikers had permitted only nineteen restaurants to remain open, and the city men were enraged. "Telling us where we may eat!" they exclaimed.

"They'll tell us next where we may buy our clothes." "Or take our holidays." "Or buy gas." "Or if we may buy gas!" "And whether we may make a living." They were very angry and their onslaught ended with the well-worn question "Why don't they go back where they come from?"

A short time previously a Hollywood personality had spent a night at our house and, on parting, had given me a hundred and fifty dollars. "Use it any way you want," he had said, "for any purpose, I never want to know." It had burned a hole in my pocket, and on impulse I had brought it with me on this trip. I wondered what had become of Sam Darcy. Was he lying somewhere with a broken head, or in jail, or beaten up? A girl gave me a telephone number. Someone answered, "Hold on," then came back and said, "I can't talk. Go to the corner of X and L streets and wait," and hung up. I walked trembling down the ghost street amid the screeching sirens and stood on that street corner. I was afraid. I did not know what to expect, and when a car pulled up I froze.

"Get in," a voice ordered, and repeated fast, "Get in, quick." Fear made me fumble the door handle and there was an impatient exclamation. I obeyed, and there, in the driver's seat, large as life, sat Sam Darcy, hatless, smiling at me but his eyes searching the road. He drove fast, along the coast road out of the city, till we got to a deserted spot beyond the Cliff House. I hadn't been able to say a word, and now Sam was laughing at me openly.

"What's the matter with you?"

"But you . . . you . . ." I sputtered, "how can you at this moment be driving like this, in this city, with the whole police out after you?"

"Oh, it's not that bad," he mocked, quite happily.

"But . . ." I dared not even say his name.

"Well, I *am* in hiding," he apologized. "I don't much like it, but the comrades insisted at a meeting last night." A meeting—in this town they had held a *meeting!* "They decided I had better lie low for a day or two; I don't like lying low." A police car zoomed by, and I bent my head so they would not see me driving with Sam Darcy.

"You call this lying low?" I protested out of my fear, and reached in my purse for a handkerchief to blow my nose and hide my face and unexpectedly came in contact with the creased ball of notes, which on a sudden impulse, because I was afraid and ashamed, and he was braving it out, I grabbed from my purse and gave him.

"Gee, nothing could have come in handier," Sam said, pleased and grateful, "we've got to get out a leaflet. . . ."

May the movie luminary, now a pillar of society and the Republican party, never know where his money went.

And what were to be the results of all this turmoil? Despite the comments of a leading banker that "labor is through in California for a generation," public opinion was won over as never before. The democratic nomination for governor went to Upton Sinclair; left-wing leaders were elected to union offices; a liberal judge set free many of the arrested strikers; and eight thousand new workers joined unions. Longshore pay was increased, but, above all, the longshoremen won their hiring hall, the hated "shape-up" was abolished, and an understanding was gained of what economic action could accomplish when everybody pulled together.

And then the "Cagney affair" blew up. James Cagney was one of a number of Hollywood people who had read Steffens and enjoyed coming up to Carmel to talk. Some had contributed funds for the strikers. One morning the Hearst newspapers carried banner headlines: James Cagney had been "sending funds." My heart stopped. I had been so protective of all the Hollywood people who had helped. What could have happened? Soon it came out— a police raid on Caroline's office had turned up a note referring to "Jimmy's money."

I felt physically ill. I saw myself as having ruined Cagney, ending his four-thousand-dollar-a-week salary. I expected him to be justly furious, to break off relations, never again to visit. The telephone rang. I managed to pick up the receiver. It was Cagney.

"Hullo darling." I heard his cheery Irish voice, with its peculiar pronunciation of the *r*. "How are you? I'm all right." I wept with relief.

By this time, with all the publicity, I had become so "notorious" that unexpected people wanted to "meet me," among them Paul Smith, the boyish, redheaded young editor of the San Francisco *Chronicle*. On one of my trips to San Francisco he came for a "quick drink"—and stayed talking for three hours.

"So you're the famous Ella Winter," he began, in surprise. He had expected, he said, "some rip-roaring, hate-filled, hideous termagant, and instead I meet a nicely dressed, scientific-minded economist." Could others of his friends meet me? Then, could he come to Carmel? He had long wanted to know Steffens.

The result of this was that Paul and Stef developed a friendship that both enjoyed and treasured. The freckled redhead at twenty-six, running a big city newspaper, represented to Stef, I think, his own newspaper beginnings. He saw in Paul a successor as well as devoted disciple.

Paul was delicately built but strong, with the white skin that goes with red hair. He was not tall, but his grace and his lively green eyes made him seem agile and always on tiptoe. Sometimes he looked like the all-American boy, fresh, eager, full of life, who wouldn't take anything from anybody. He came often, and grew to be almost one of the family. He would go off with Pete to bathe or play on the beach, and on one occasion, when the treacherous undertow had carried Pete beyond his depth and for a terrifying moment the child struggled helplessly, Paul rescued him. After that they were inseparable.

Paul would bring his problems and Stef would tell him what he had done under similar circumstances. Once I heard Stef tell how he always used to try for some humorous paragraph or filler at the bottom of a page, so that "the reader would turn the page smiling." Stef's most important advice to Smith was about Bridges. After the strike the longshoremen's leader had become such anathema to shipowners and businessmen that he could be mentioned only with contumely. When Paul asked Stef about an interpretation of some longshore policy, Stef told him, "In my day, when we wanted to report labor, we interviewed the union fellows."

"But Bridges! We're not allowed to talk to him, we're forbidden to interview him."

"What kind of newspaper talks only to one side?" Stef teased. Without waiting to say good-by, Paul was in his car, whizzing back to his office. He met Bridges, for the first time, and printed the first interview the *Chronicle* had ever had with "the militant labor leader." Paul was "called in" by the banker backers of his paper—Paul, their favorite, their white hope. They were giving him all this power and responsibility at his young age, and look what he had done with it.

"My dear Paul," the leading banker remonstrated, " 'militant' is a *good* word!"

And after the general strike, Carmel also was no longer an amiable, easygoing, unself-conscious little village. Upton Sinclair was running on a ticket to "End poverty in California," and Carmelites passed you in silent hostility on the street if you wore a Sinclair button, or they crossed ostentatiously to the other side. Stef kept up an ironic teasing to his friends, even remarking once or twice that "the good people who can't go over into the kingdom of heaven will have to be shot."

At a picnic for Dorothy Thompson, Sinclair Lewis, and Charles Lindbergh, I sat next to the wife of a painter, Paula Dougherty. Why did she suddenly seem so unfriendly? "Not just once," she kept saying, "you haven't said it just once, I've heard of it three times, and that's no joke any more." "But what, Paula?" "You and Stef are heard saying you have a list of people to be shot," she responded darkly.

Sometimes it hit too near home for comfort, as when the daughter of a close friend of mine was to marry into a rather conservative business family. I had bought a new frock. But my friend came to me, the morning of the wedding, very distressed.

"My husband doesn't want you to come to the wedding," she cried. "Oh, I can't tell you how awful I feel." I was rather taken aback, since I would not really have stood out among four hundred guests; but it was hardly an occasion for organized protest. When later I met the husband, I asked what harm he thought could have come to his daughter from my presence.

"They might have had to talk about the class struggle on their honeymoon," he answered, quite seriously.

We became a favorite target of attacks in the newspapers, especially small local sheets. Apparently the combination of Stef, with his long radical history, and my possibly too-vocal partisanship, was too much. One calumny I rather appreciated placed me squarely with the great courtesans. I had "slept with twenty-nine Negroes." Stef's comment pleased our friends: "Why not thirty?"

The *Pacific Rural Press,* a paper devoted to the interests of farmers and ranchers, and normally concerned with prices, marketing conditions, and pest control, stepped into the political arena and wrote a blistering editorial charging us with failure to bring up our son in a "civilized" manner. He was supposed to have urinated in the school playground. Our local *Pine Cone* embroidered on it, adding its quota of jeers and abuse of the child.

I watched Stef as he read the article. He remained thoughtfully quiet for a time, and then said slowly, and with a dismay at himself that I could hardly bear, "Every man has his price, I learned that long ago, Peter, and they're reaching mine. My price is Pete." This made me so indignant at our detractors that I took a heavy howitzer to that editorial and enlisted all our friends to protest and stop their subscriptions. Martin Flavin wrote to the editor:

Political differences of opinion have always served in this country as an excuse for editorial license. . . . Violations of good taste are traditional and too common to inspire protest. Still, I do not recall that I have hitherto encountered an attack on an adversary which undertook to score by—slapping a child.

However, one had become fair game and not only for the lunatic fringe. The next assault was a telephone call from a drunken Legionnaire advising of the intention to burn our house that evening. And the business of the license plates never stopped—local Legionnaires taking down the numbers of automobiles seen outside lectures on any kind of current event, or suspect private houses such as ours.

But the culmination came with the dispatch of a spy to Carmel, a real, live spy, who rented a beach house and stayed four months. Someone had sold San Francisco industrialists on the idea that "all the money"—for the waterfront troubles, the maritime strike of thirty-five thousand, the general strike, the "agitation" in the agricultural fields for higher wages—came from Moscow, that the Soviet Consul brought it to Carmel, and Stef gave it to Harry Bridges.

A mysterious Hungarian who said he was the former world heavyweight boxing champion, Sharkey, settled in this Carmel house, "to write his memoirs and a scenario about his life," as he said. In Carmel he could find leisure and some young writer to help him with the work.

We wondered about the "Sharkey." Was he Tom Sharkey? Jack Sharkey? When had he fought last? His Hungarian name was Baczsy, he did tell us, and he would as soon be called that. Since he seemed a little punch-drunk anyway, and could have been a boxer, with his broad muscular build and broken nose, it didn't make much difference whether he was *the* Sharkey or just any Sharkey. Anyway, he installed himself in this big house, with three little girls he said were his, hired a nurse (our Anna's sister-in-law), and gave large parties to which he invited anyone who would come. For months he held open house, and was openhanded with food and alcohol.

Stef was interested in prize fighters—he had written a study of the Carpentier-Siki fight—and was pleased to see any new person at his bedside; and this Sharkey came with copies of the *Autobiography* and *Red Virtue* to be autographed. At first we rather enjoyed our singular friend; he had good parties and he was quite amusing. He gave picnics and suppers on the beach as well. He talked like a radical, and idealistic Rhys Williams thought it "significant" that this inarticulate ex-boxer was so interested in our grapes of wrath. You could never tell whom history would affect, Rhys rhapsodized.

I began to think, however, that the boxer was rather silly; once, a little drunk, he produced a sawed-off machine gun, which he asked me to hold. "I've never had a gun in my hand," I said as I refused, "and I don't want one now. There are too many cases of their going off accidentally." Sharkey was a little befuddled, in addition to his usual punch-drunkenness, and babbled: "Won't this be wonderful when the Revolution comes?" He persisted in trying to thrust the gun into my arms, but I grew irritated and left —luckily. For, after Baczsy departed, four months later, saying he must finish elsewhere the movie they were going to make of his life, I received a very perturbed letter from the quiet, older woman he had used in Carmel as his secretary; she begged me to come to San Francisco to see her.

And then the strange story came out. She had been hired, she said, to "uncover a nest of dangerous gangsters," to which end Sharkey-Baczsy had installed microphones in his house and her cottage with a cable to his house; she was to take down on her typewriter whatever she heard any of us say.

"When I met you all," she said, deeply distressed, "you seemed so pleasant and friendly, I couldn't believe you were dangerous gangsters. Especially the Reverend Rhys Williams."

"Did you write down a lot?" I asked, wondering if anyone had ever said anything silly.

"I have one very clear statement of yours," the woman answered. "It is 'What terrific muscles you have, Sharkey!'" I laughed, but she was almost hysterical with self-reproach or possibly relief at getting rid of her sense of guilt.

"After I was sure you were not gangsters, I turned the heating system on whenever he warned me you were expected," she said. "He had told me that would prevent anything coming over." This secretary also threw light on the machine-gun incident. Baczsy had grown a little desperate at not getting more "proof" to show his employers (and earn the eighteen thousand dollars they paid him) and decided he must get more action. He planted an automatic camera behind a screen and engineered a thrilling newspaper photograph. When he asked, "Won't this be wonderful when the Revolution comes?," the screen was to be pulled away, the camera would click as I held the gun, and my "subversive" answer would be recorded over the mike.

"He threatened if I gave him away he'd kill me." The girl, even now, was white with fear. "So I didn't dare tell any of you at the time. I think he may even kill me now."

One might have thought the instigators of this grotesque cloak-and-dagger fantasy would have been ashamed when confronted with this story; but no, they would admit nothing—they believed they had merely failed to get their "proof." They had spent their eighteen thousand on a plot that misfired—plus a hundred-dollar bonus for "getting close enough to obtain autographs" in our books! And they were certainly not going to admit they had been taken in.

It might have been more amusing had there not been the danger that someone might believe such nonsense. When I remonstrated with our local Monterey editor about something he had written intimating "secrecy" on our part, I asked him, "Why should I be secretive when what we want is to have conditions known? I speak and write, I've published a book—wouldn't it be very stupid of me to try and hide my ideas now?"

"Very stupid," he agreed, and then looked at me with a new cunning, "or *very* clever."

# 19

# STEF

There was between Stef and me the knowledge of his illness, though we did not mention it directly. Sometimes Stef would refer to it obliquely: "You'll marry again, Peter," he said more than once. "If a woman has had a happy marriage, she marries again." He asked of me one favor: "I don't like the thought of Pete calling another man Daddy."

"That I can promise you," I said quickly.

Once Stef made a remark of sad contentment, perhaps to prevent my grief later. "I've had my life," he said, "I'm ready to go. When people have fulfilled their lives, it's no tragedy." He felt that way about other people's lives and wrote about the death of friends even with triumph. Of Fremont Older, who had lived his life to the full, Stef wrote:

Fremont Older, big and powerful, gentle and seventy-eight, fell dead across the steering wheel of his car. Perfect. He had just been writing an editorial on Death, a subject he had thought much about latterly, an event he was quite prepared for. He felt, and sometimes said, that his fighting life had long been rounded out to a neat peaceful close, and he dropped like a flower, as he knew he would.

Stef sometimes got up, put on his dark-red Chinese dressing gown and ate lunch in the living room with us, or sat in the sun on the balcony. He still enjoyed discovering new—or very old—truths. He and Jo Davidson were talking in my little carpenter's study, catching up on a two-year separation, and Stef was telling Jo of his attempts to explain the depression, of "the eternal fact that people don't seem to learn." Suddenly the two men looked at each other in a joint recognition of something.

"You can't tell people anything," Stef said, expressing their simul-
taneous thought, "you can only remind them of things!" "We've
found a truth," Jo whooped, "a new truth—and it's just an old
platitude, 'You can't tell people anything.' "

But mostly Stef welcomed visitors from his bed, and he enjoyed
them as much as at any time in his life. And so many came: our
Carmel friends, students, people from Paris, from New York, Holly-
wood, London; Carl Sandburg, and Professor Meiklejohn, Kyle
Crichton; old newspaper colleagues like Lowell Mellett and Spike
Hunt; Witter Bynner, Professor George Counts, Carey McWilliams,
Max Eastman, Gertrude Stein and Alice Toklas.

Jo Davidson stayed five days on his last trip, and while he was
there I took the opportunity to go to San Francisco, but when I
returned Jo was upset. "Peter, never leave Stef again. He can't
stand it, his face looks like a piece of green cheese!" I could not
tell Jo that the impact of his own immense vitality was draining
Stef's strength. I did try to carry the burden of many conversations,
but Stef insisted on participating, on entertaining those he loved
so well.

I tried to keep to the doctor's "no longer than half an hour"
rule, but it was difficult when people came from afar, from the East
or London, as, for instance, Mother and my sister. Their world
now seemed very far away to me: You can't go home again.

Pete was solicitous of his father and took his arm to walk him
slowly down the steps and into the garden. They bathed together
still as they had always done, and had long discussions in the
bathtub. Pete went to the movies every Saturday and told his father
all about the film, and when he didn't quite understand the
ethics of a gangster movie, Daddy would explain. They discussed
religion, the making of the world, science. When Pete had asked
his father the very first time (at about three) how babies were
born, Stef had explained to him fully, using all the Latin words.
The child could not have understood, but he knew he had been
treated seriously and put his arms gratefully around his father's
neck. "Thank you, Daddy; now can I go out to play?" Their mutual
trust and understanding never waned.

John Steinbeck frequently dropped in from Pacific Grove, where
he lived in a shack on the coast. He was excessively shy, a red-faced,
blue-eyed giant. On one occasion he slouched into Stef's room,
sat down at his bedside, and began to complain.

"I don't know what to do about them, they won't get out of the way."

"Who?" said Stef.

"There's disaster rolling down the hill and they won't move."

"Who won't? Whom are you talking about?"

"I can't make them pay attention, they just stand there. . . ." Steinbeck sounded as if he might break into tears. "They won't heed me. . . ."

Stef was growing irritable. *"Who?"* he repeated. "What are you lamenting? Who won't move?"

"My characters!" Steinbeck exploded. He was writing *Of Mice and Men.*

Every morning I put his little old Corona typewriter on the bed table and, after he had read the newspaper, Stef tapped out a paragraph or two for his column. One morning I plopped down the little machine in irritation. Stef looked at me and I at him as I suddenly realized what I had done. He had always hoped he would not "be an invalid and make you into a sick nurse." No word passed between us, but I was ashamed.

His seventieth birthday came. Sam Darcy was in the Soviet Union and I had written asking him, among others, to send Stef a birthday note, which I knew he would appreciate. On that April 6 telegrams of greeting came from writers and artists, poets and musicians all over that world. Stef could not have been more pleased. There were messages from our own longshoremen, too.

The head of Stef's bed stood against the window, and he turned often to look into the garden. Beyond the cypress trees and the passion vine were the road and the sea, the Pacific in all its moods. John O'Shea, the Irish painter, the melancholy artist, said sadly, "You know why Stef turns to look out so much? He knows he may never go out there again, that he may be looking at it for the last time."

Doctor Kocher thought Stef was seeing too many people and suggested he go to the hospital, where he would get more rest, but Stef would not hear of it. "I'd rather die sooner than leave my own home," he said, and we did not broach the subject again. But Doctor Kocher confirmed to me that Stef could not recover. There was no known cure for arteriosclerosis. Stef dreaded another stroke that might paralyze him, perhaps lose him the power of speech or writing. He wrote, read, talked, teased, enjoyed his visitors till the last, happily reproaching those who could not "see" the future he believed in so steadfastly.

On the afternoon of August 9, 1936, Doctor Kocher came for his daily visit, and he and I sat with Stef. Stef said he did not feel well, then suddenly he raised both arms.

"No, no," he cried in evident pain. "I can't—" Doctor Kocher ran out to his car to get adrenalin. When he returned, Stef had fallen back. Kocher listened to his heart, then shook his head. "It's over," he said, and took me out of the room.

Later, when I was alone in the house, I went back in our room. Stef lay there and I could not believe that I would never talk to him again. But there was no breath. I felt suffocated, as if I had none.

Yvonne had said our marriage might last five years, but that we'd be lucky to have even those five years. It was thirteen years. I had had him thirteen years.

I stayed a long time with Stef alone in our room. Then I called the ranch, where Pete was staying. They said he was asleep, but they would drive up next day.

The next day Pete came back. "Can't I see Daddy? Won't I ever see Daddy again?" he cried to me. Janie had told him. In the morning his whole pillow was wet, she said.

With Stef's dislike of "institutions," I did not want any sort of ritual on his burial. His friends came, walked about the house and garden, then filled the living room. I asked Pete if he wanted to be there. "No, no," he said. I had dressed him in white, and at the last moment he slipped in by the far studio door and stood in a corner and listened.

Everyone spoke, the people Stef loved, his friends. Everyone said something—of what he had meant to them, to American life, to our community. They spoke simply, as they felt. I remember Una Jeffers with her bright, warm face and clear, firm voice saying almost defiantly, in the humorous railing tone in which she and Stef so often teased each other, "He loved his home, whatever he may have preached. He was a man most deeply attached to his wife and son, this home and this garden, the town in which he lived among us."

Then they all got up and walked about and talked to us. O'Shea said to Pete, "He was a great man, your Daddy, Pete."

"Yes," Pete said, with surprise, "I'm beginning to see that. I thought he was just my Daddy and wrote a book."

We drove to San Mateo, where Steffens' family vault held his father, his mother, and his sister Louise. In an open churchyard they had placed the coffin piled high with wreaths and flowers. We had no service, but amidst the flowers, Erskine Wood got up, with his broad flowing black bowtie and his gray beard, his gray hair flying, and spoke about his oldest friend. They had told me I should speak, too, but how could I? My voice would break, I would not be able to control myself.

Pete looked at the flower-laden coffin in sudden anguish. "Daddy isn't in that box?" he asked me in panic. It was not a moment in which I wanted to tell a lie, and I tried quickly to enter the thoughts of an eleven-year-old about death. Pete must be picturing "in that box" the father he knew: loving and tender, always there for him, ready to listen, to talk, to enter into his play. There was not time now, in this open field, with the many friends around, coming up to speak to me, or standing silent in sorrowing groups, to try and explain death to this child.

"No," I said, "no, Pete, Daddy isn't in that box, Daddy is with us, with you and me as he always was and as he wants to be always." The little boy seemed relieved and held my hand, and I knew that Steffy must stay in men's minds, where he would want to be, teaching, loving, making clearer, if he could, things that puzzled them—and then I knew what I would say to our friends. And I stood by the coffin and said just that.

# PART III

# WAR AND NO PEACE

# 20

## END OF AN ERA

The death of Steffens was not only the end of a period in my personal life, it also coincided with the end of an era. We did not see it so clearly in 1936, but history was moving rapidly and America joined Europe and the world. Stef had lived to see the beginnings of the Spanish Civil War. Indeed, the last paragraph I found in his little typewriter after his death was about Spain and how "the popular front there is fighting my war for me and for us. . . . Spain's is the first, the opening battle of man for man, perhaps . . . the most decisive." The defeat of Spain, which Steffens did not see, and Munich after it, when we had hoped Czechoslovakia might be able to resist, made the coming of the Second World War certain. It proved to be also the end of an epoch.

In these years we had supported the Roosevelt policies of encouragement of unionization and greater labor effectiveness in the affairs of the country. We had seen the classic resistance of both industry and landowners to the power of labor, but labor had fought, and captured a few positions. Abroad, fourteen million German socialists and Communists had caused her fearful industrialists to finance the "madman" Hitler.

I was not aware when I drove through the pear and cherry orchards and protested violence against the little pickers, or attended a lettuce strike trial, that I was taking part in a historical process—one rarely is aware at the time. But now that my personal life must radically change I became conscious that the life of the country, indeed of other countries, was being fundamentally altered. The struggle between fascism and some form of democracy was not only coming to a head in war, the conflict between these systems was making itself felt in all our personal lives.

Carmel became for me a place without a purpose. I had lived there because Stef loved it, and it was the place for him, and so for us, but now the savor went out of it. Our little paper could not hold together, and there was nothing else for me, nothing to keep me there. "Why does God make people if He's only going to take them away again?" Pete asked me—a question that I could not answer.

I dug the garden, but there was no one to enjoy it. I roamed the empty house. One day I came upon an old trunk that Laura had sent down when she gave up her house in San Francisco and that we had never opened. I unlocked it, and there tumbled out untold packets of letters tied with pink ribbon—hundreds upon hundreds of letters Steffens had written his mother, father, sisters, from the time he left college, all preserved intact. I had also kept all he had written to me, and it came to me then, with this hoard spread around me, that one way to bridge the gap in my life was to go through them all and edit them for publication. This I did over the next two years, obtaining additional material from all over the country.

The months went by; the long summer turned to autumn, and Pete was back in school. But despite our friends, I was lonelier than ever in Carmel. When California writers planned a congress in San Francisco dedicated to Steffens and asked me to speak, I went, though reluctantly. It was there that I first met Donald Ogden Stewart.

The congress advanced various schemes to keep alive our local weekly (*Pacific Weekly* now—*The Carmelite* had died), chief of them being that I should try to obtain funds in Hollywood. Lucita Williams had the prospect of a possible job there and said she would like to come with me. "I knew Don Stewart years ago," she said. "When I went to Russia to join Rhys, he was on the boat; in fact, I shared a cabin with his mother." We took a room at the Hollywood Plaza, and Lucita dropped Stewart a note to which I added a polite postscript.

A bouquet of yellow roses arrived at the hotel and Lucita was delighted. "So like old Don, look what he's sent me," she cried, then read the card and said in surprise, "Why, it's for you." Later, when I was alone, he telephoned and said he was speaking that night at an anti-Nazi meeting and could we meet afterward?

That night as we talked I realized how lonely I had been. We drove about the town. He was alone, too—his wife was with their two little boys in the East. Would I like to see Hollywood night life? He took me to various places, including the Clover Club, where he cheerfully lost fifty dollars gambling while I calculated what *Pacific Weekly* could have done with it.

I would not have imagined that someone "in movies" would become interested in me, for practically my only relationship to the profession had come from our few visitors to Carmel. But Hollywood was changing from the peculiar isolated colony where actors had wild parties and door handles of gold to a place more conscious of its role in the world. And in this new development Don Stewart was playing an important part.

I do not suppose I could have been drawn to anyone who did not share my larger concerns. Don had become newly aware in the past few years of social questions, and it was all still fresh and challenging to him. He was tall and slender and very graceful, with blond hair and blue eyes that very often held a puckish look like that of a wise and naughty child. Humorous and gentle, shy and warmhearted, Don was strangely untouched by the Hollywood he had lived and worked in for some years. He was a gifted and humorous writer and talker, and he loved gaiety, cheerful people —a "gala" atmosphere, as he called it. He had lately become passionately interested in what was happening politically in Europe, the United States, Germany, California; he read hungrily, and was fascinated by my experiences. Radicals at this time were frequently charged with "boring from within," and when eventually Don and I began seeing more of each other, our friends were gaily malicious at what they thought of as the double success of my efforts —one was supposed only to influence ideas, not the holder of them.

Don was born in Columbus, Ohio, and he had characteristic American traits, from an outward conformism to a consuming interest in the World Series. But he had a rare courage and independence of mind, and a stubborn, almost puritan, integrity, which withstood all blandishments. (I soon dubbed him John Knox.) When he believed in something, he felt he must act on his beliefs. He was making speeches for the Hollywood anti-Nazi movement in out-of-the-way halls or on the piers of Venice or Santa Monica, unostentatiously and with an unconcern for possible effects on his Hollywood position. As the movement grew in the film colony, he was called on more and more to chair meetings—his spontaneous humor made him a witty, popular speaker and toastmaster—and to sign an increasing number of protests and petitions. His sponsorship of so many committees and delegations gave rise to a satiric story: when President Roosevelt awoke in the morning, he would ring for his orange juice, his coffee, and "the first eleven telegrams from Donald Ogden Stewart."

When I first met Don in San Francisco, he was in the audience to which I suggested that the Hollywood writers—including at that time Dorothy Parker and Joel Sayre—could help the antifascist movement with their wit and humor to enrich the rather bedraggled jargon we then used. Don accepted the challenge, and when he found himself meeting Harry Bridges (at Paul Smith's), and next day, visiting Tom Mooney in San Quentin, he was the first to admit that he and other film writers missed, needed, and wanted just such contact with reality. One thing that especially drew him to me was my closer contact with that reality. The simplicity of Don's nature, or rather that childlike element that is in all creative people and that I particularly appreciated, occasionally took a quaint form. "Now that we're for the workers," he said to me, "how do we get to talk to them? Do we ask the plumber in to lunch?"

On that first Hollywood trip I was scheduled to give a talk for our *Pacific Weekly* to a gathering at the house of Dorothy Parker and Alan Campbell. The place was full; people drank, ate, sang, danced, in that order. I was weighed down by black depression and sat alone by a fireside. Sam Hoffenstein was singing loudly at the piano, and there was a constant going and coming of people at a slight angle, with glasses in their hands. No one really seemed to want to hear about our little California paper, although after my short talk some contributions were promised. Nevertheless, I felt so low-spirited, I wanted only to get away. I crept to the powder room and cried, and when I washed my face, a tall ungainly girl with rather coarse features was combing her hair before the mirror.

"Who are you?" she asked sympathetically, and when I returned the question, she responded casually, "Me? Oh, I'm Lionel Stander's sec'etary and mistress."

On the road back to Carmel I stopped at a wayside "café," a flyblown shack called Tony Taix Sandwiches, and heard on the radio, over my cup of coffee, an English king give up his throne for the woman he loved.

On later trips from Carmel to southern California I skirted the fringes of the Hollywood "movement." Don was president of the Anti-Nazi League, which a German called Breda had set up with a German prince and many big producers as sponsors. Another great excitement in Hollywood at this time was Spain: Hemingway and Joris Ivens, the Dutch documentary movie maker, British writer Ralph Bates and André Malraux spoke, showed films, raised funds for the Loyalists.

Don took me to a talk by André Malraux at the home of Salka Viertel, whom I had met briefly in Carmel with her Viennese poet husband, Berthold. Salka greeted each new group of guests with a warm, personal, interested welcome. She wore a long unadorned white gown, with gold belt and sandals, a beautiful contrast to her short wavy red hair and gray-green eyes; her warmth made everyone feel they mattered to her, as indeed they did. In a Hollywood in which I had already sensed that no one cared very much for other people, I felt immediately at home here, and Salka Viertel did become one of my few intimate friends in Hollywood—and remained so.

Malraux, whose *Man's Fate* we had all so intensely admired, came up, like Jeffers, to one's expectations. Lean and tall, with intense, melancholy gray eyes in a very pale face, and dark-brown silken hair brushed slantwise to show his high white forehead, he told dramatically, in exquisite French, his stories of Spain, of the children afraid to play with toy airplanes because they knew planes only as carriers of death. Malraux had himself led a flying squadron throughout the war, and he kept this eager audience spellbound as he brought the Spanish Civil War to Graustark.

Graustark was the country in which Don was currently working, and he took me on the set of *The Prisoner of Zenda,* where I watched Madeleine Carroll act the Princess Flavia to Ronald Colman's Rupert of Hentzau, and where, when her black velvet gown came undone in the absence of her dresser, she asked me to hook her up again. Never in my far-off Melbourne childhood, reading the Zenda books to Rudi as we lay on our stomachs on the schoolroom floor, could I have dreamed I would one day be adjusting the Princess Flavia's robe.

On one Sunday, I was invited for buffet supper by Clifford Odets and his new young Viennese actress wife, Luise Rainer, who had recently won an Oscar for her acting in *The Good Earth.* The guests were mostly European refugees, about forty writers and artists driven from their homeland. We sat around a long table while Luise, looking like a bright but insecure elf with her bright brown eyes and her small face fringed by black hair, waited on us. Odets sat at the far end, somber and sulky, talking to no one, while his wife clucked at him appeasingly as she kept disappearing behind a curtain to bring out more and more delicacies, from *Wiener Würstel* to *Sachertorte*.

Next day a distraught Luise called me. How had I liked the party? I told her how I had enjoyed those German writers, the whole atmosphere so different from Hollywood. "For me it was Europe, the Europe I miss," I said.

"Exactly," Luise cried. "And Cliff is furious at me because we did not have servants to bring in the food and wait on table. 'Even if it was their Sunday off, you should have hired others,' he said. I told him all theatrical people did it like this on Sunday nights in Vienna, but he said this wasn't Vienna, it was Hollywood and in Hollywood one had servants; otherwise, why come here?" This incident reflected for me some of the curious values of the movie colony.

Granville Hicks had agreed to help me edit the Steffens letters, so I went to stay at his home in Grafton, New York. When school was over, Pete came east, perfectly composed and untroubled by his first train trip alone. He had played his violin for the passengers. But he was lonely in New York and Grafton. He carried in his pocket a baseball game in which he played both sides, scoring—on whatever scraps of paper he had in his pocket—the play called for: "two-base hit," "flied out," "double play," "home run"—the game of a solitary child. I must find him company. Don's boys were at a camp in the Adirondacks; Pete liked it, he could swim and hike and live the outdoor life he loved; so he joined them and I drove up from Grafton every weekend to visit the three boys.

I met some of Hicks' friends, university men—Newton Arvin from Smith College, Robert Gorham Davis from Harvard, Robert Lamb from Williams College and his wife, Helen, who taught at Sarah Lawrence. They were stimulating people and we shared political beliefs. I was particularly drawn to the Lambs.

At the end of the summer I had a decision to make: I would need another year on the *Letters* and I could not reconcile myself to sending Pete to boarding school. We discussed living in New York, but he did not like it. "New York is all red and green traffic lights," he said. His cousin, Clinton Hollister, was interning at the Mayo Clinic in Rochester and had a house with his wife, Neila, and small boy. They wanted Pete, and Pete liked his Hollister cousins. So I took him to Rochester, saw him safely installed, and returned to my Winthrop Hotel in New York. And then in November, as I was leaving for the theater to see Odets' *Golden Boy,* I saw a newspaper item: "Donald Stewart run over by automobile, taken to hospital unconscious." I found the play the most tragic I had ever seen.

When he recovered, Don came to New York in January, but was called back soon after to write another picture—his friend Philip Barry's *Holiday,* as it happened—"to pay for hospital bills." He had been told he ought to recuperate for several months, but Hollywood medical men were in a financial hurry. In May his wife, who had met a Count Ilya Tolstoi in Florida, asked for a divorce.

That summer Pete went again to the camp near Lake Placid. I had finished reading proof and the *Letters* were on the press. One day in August Don suddenly arrived from his farm with a beaming face.

"I've got to go to Hollywood tomorrow, will you come with me?" He was always sudden like that. We could get there in time for Pete to start school in Beverly Hills. I said yes.

I rented a house in Westwood Village. Don worked with Scott Fitzgerald on *The Women,* and we spent evenings with him and his friend Sheilah Graham, a pretty English movie columnist, who told us of the violent alcoholic periods, after which Scott would be distressed and ashamed. He seemed to me then a broken man.

Don wanted to get married, but I had difficulty with the idea. Stef had said I would marry again, would have wished me to marry again, but I felt a great reluctance. To give Pete a sense that he had a voice in our common future, I asked how he regarded the idea and he rejoiced. He was very fond of "Uncle Don," loved and appreciated him—as he always has, and it was mutual. But I could not yet think of the past as past.

However, such hesitations come to be thrown aside, and in March 1939 we were married at City Hall in Ventura. Our friends were very happy, and so was Pete. But his first words were "Can I

call Uncle Don 'Daddy' now?" The one promise Steffy had asked
of me! In my mind I discussed it with him: he would want, above
all, wouldn't he, his child's happiness? And his son was seeking
that father-son relationship that had meant so much to both. And
Pete would now have two little brothers calling their father Dad.
So I was sure Stef would not hold me to that promise. And again
Pete himself provided a solution: he referred to Stef as "my other
daddy."

# 21

# DON'S NEW WIFE

Now I was taken up by the real Hollywood, the movies. There was curiosity about "Don's new wife." I was invited to dinner parties by the Goldwyns, Clark Gable and Carole Lombard, Adrian the dress designer and his wife, Janet Gaynor, the David Selznicks, the Lewis Milestones. Mrs. Sam Goldwyn asked me to lunch and quizzed me on politics. "Please explain Marxism to me," she said.

"Oh, not over this lovely steak," I protested. "Yes, yes," she insisted, "I want to know." Unwillingly, and as simply as possible over my salad, I trod warily, softly, making it sound, I hoped, fairly harmless and painless, and I avoided pointing any finger. But a little later I was told that Mrs. Goldwyn had remarked, "Very dangerous woman."

At dinner at his house, Sam Goldwyn seated me on his right and talked about Joannes Metaxas, the Greek dictator, and how he, Mr. Goldwyn, was helping the democratic Greeks. I listened in silence, and over the ice cream he complimented me. "D'you know, you are the most intelligent woman I've met since Lillian Hellman?" When the ladies went upstairs to the powder room, Mrs. Darryl Zanuck, Olivia de Havilland, and Mrs. Goldwyn exchanged information on their latest "little dressmaker," who "ran me up this little number for an absurdly low sum." Each told how little her gorgeous frock had cost, till I was alarmed lest they ask me and I appear as an extravagant wastrel, for mine had been a present from Don and had cost three times as much.

My evening with Clark Gable and Carole Lombard started unpropitiously. I was nervous at meeting two stars, and I had bought another new dress, this time a modest little black one. When they opened the door to us, Don said happily, "This is my wife, she was rather nervous, so she bought this new dress." They took us into the living room, and Clark patted the cushion next to him for me. I do not have to describe the tall man with the big features, the laughing face, nor Carole's boyish, friendly manner. She immediately talked of the scrapes she had gotten into, "climbing surreptitiously in and out of Clark's windows" before he was divorced. We sat long over cocktails, and I grew ravenous. The butler announced dinner, but Clark waved him away.

"Later," he said, "this is too good—and we haven't finished cocktails." I waited; the conversation was sparkling, lively, full of banter, but I felt it could be continued over food. The butler came back, was waved away, returned—in vain. The pheasant couldn't be "held over," he intimated, but Clark said they could go out and shoot a few more. Then the conversation turned to Doctor C., a well-known "top drawer" lady of pleasure whose services had been sought as far as New York, and by a mayor. I had often heard Don and his friend Robert Benchley jest about her, so I mentioned her name while Carole was speaking of several women on the set who were not strictly movie actresses. Carole's eyes suddenly sparkled.

"Oh, you know her? She's such fun. She's worked with me—she's studying singing."

"She has a miraculously scented ointment, I hear," I ventured.

"Come upstairs," Carole commanded, "I'll show you something," and she took me into her exquisite bathroom and opened a cupboard onto an Aladdin hoard of tubes, jars, pomades, unguents, and other paraphernalia, and for an hour expounded on their properties—I might say, one of the most intimate conversations I had ever had, and with a movie actress I hadn't known an hour. When we finally got downstairs again, it was truly time for dinner, and this time we were allowed in and at the pheasants.

After dinner, when the men had imbibed merrily, I sat next to Clark again on the sofa. We had been talking about Hitler and I had described some of the horrors. Clark put his arm around my shoulders protectively. What would a world of young girls not give for this, I thought. "Never mind, li'l girl, never mind," he whispered in my ear. "We'll see tha' Hitler doesn' get you, we'll look after you." I felt foolishly, gloriously protected.

Robert Benchley was the friend of Don's I cared for most. He had a marvelous voice and the gayest humor. He lived at the Garden of Allah, a cluster of cottages round a pool, and he mixed

drinks and told stories and laughed. He laughed so that you had
to laugh with him, even when the joke referred to times I had not
shared, or football or baseball games I had not seen. Benchley
was extremely fond of reminiscing with Don, yet he liked to talk
seriously, too, about politics or plays and books; one of our first
conversations was about a young writer's first book, *The Heart Is
a Lonely Hunter,* which he said enchanted him. He was then making his own short features, but hadn't much respect for movies:
he insisted, "I just need the money to educate my sons." Benchley
was sad about giving up his dramatic criticism in *The New Yorker,*
for he liked the job and he liked to be in New York in his gaudy,
overdecorated room at the Royalton, crowded with his friends and
with objects he had been given by all the jokesters over the years,
including an Eastern bead curtain and an iron deer.

We went to Carmel twice, back to The Getaway. Don was editing
a book on a recent congress of American writers, and our three
boys went to the local schools. To my joy, my brother, Rudi, and
his wife and little daughter came to Carmel to live. Rudi was very
happy: California suited him, he loved us, his little house, his wife,
Thea, and little Sylvia, who all took readily to the easy life of the
sunny village. I felt Rudi had at last some of the happiness he
deserved. He was the gentlest of creatures, amiable, goodhearted,
generous, and loving. Then, unexpectedly, he was taken ill from
an infection caught in Mexico, where he had gone for a few days
to get the immigration visa he needed to live in this new country.
His doctors could not diagnose it; there were operations, but he
could not throw it off, and at Carmel's Community Hospital, after
five days' delirium, Rudi died. It was shortly before the discovery
of penicillin, which could have saved his life.

I was glad only that my mother, who had died two years earlier,
had not lived to know it. It was terrible for Thea, in that little
house love had bought and furnished in the woods, with their
four-year-old who could not grasp what had befallen her. We took
them into our house.

Over a year later, when I was thinking of renting The Getaway,
a macabre incident took place. On one trip north to put it in order
for tenants, I was told that some children had found a package
in the desk downstairs and had played with it. It seemed like some
kind of urn.

That was just what it was. A few weeks after Rudi's cremation

I had been working in our house when there had been a knock at the big studio door. Impatient, I had ignored it till the maid said there was a parcel with thirty cents to pay, and the boy would not give it to her. "I thought I better give it to you personally," the messenger apologized. "The parcel is from the undertaker's." Thea had not wanted to know anything about Rudi's burial and had left it to me. I did not wish to bury him in Monterey, a town with which he had no connection, and not knowing what to do, I had put the urn in a box far back in Steffy's desk, in his study.

Now strange children had broken open the desk, and I must bury the urn. But where? The Getaway was in strangers' hands. But I still owned a tiny cottage I had once bought in the woods, to work in; the garden was untended and neglected, but the place was ours.

I asked Pete to come and help me dig a hole. We found a space and a fork, but the baked earth was like stone. We hacked and hammered, but could hardly make an impression. Pete asked what it was for, but I could not reply, my throat was dry as the earth. Nowhere in the little garden was there any soft ground. Pete grew tired and did not want to go on, but I could not trust my voice to explain, until finally I managed: "It's Uncle Rudi, Pete, we must make a deep hole; when he's buried, perhaps flowers will grow, and Rudi would like to know he was in our little home." Pete cried; we managed finally to dig the hole, put the urn in, and cover it over with the earth.

After Rudi's death the attraction went out of Carmel for us, and when Don was offered the screenplay of Philip Barry's *The Philadelphia Story*, he took the job. We rented a Spanish-type house in Beverly Hills, on the "wrong" side of the tracks, and I tried to make a home, with the aid of two cats, budgies, and a cocker-spaniel puppy that George Cukor, the director, had given me. Duck and Ames, my two new sons, whom I could not bear to call stepsons because of those early fairytales about wicked step-mothers, went to a progressive school in the Ojai Valley and came home weekends, while Pete went to the local high school. We carried on, as well as we could, our antifascist activities and went to an occasional Hollywood party.

I remember one such cocktail party at Cukor's house, when Joan Crawford, in a heavily flowered picture hat, grabbed me and begged, "Stay with me, I'm so scared, don't leave me." I knew her from *A Woman's Face* (Don's movie, featuring Conrad Veidt, the last movie made before that actor's sudden death), and I stayed in the doorway the whole afternoon, holding Joan Crawford's timid hand, among such golden girls as Loretta Young, Hedy Lamarr, Constance Bennett—who owned forty-seven fur coats and two hundred and eighty pairs of shoes—Ginger Rogers, Lana Turner; and resplendent men, all of whose faces grinned or frowned from a thousand advertising hoardings: Franchot Tone, James Stewart, Robert Taylor, Cary Grant, Charles Boyer.

The party I liked best was one we ourselves gave for Dorothy Parker and her husband, Adrian and his actress wife, Janet Gaynor, and Don's Eastern friend, Joan Payson, sister of John Hay Whitney. Artie Shaw said he'd bring a girl. He did, the singer Alice F., who was very silent until our clumsy old springer spaniel jumped in her lap, which seemed to make her ecstatically happy. She talked to him, patted and petted him; he seemed her lifesaver throughout the evening. When Artie called next day, he confided to me that she had asked what games we'd play, and when he told her, "Oh, they don't sing or play games," she was upset.

"What do they do, then?"

"Talk," Artie said.

"Talk! You don't mean they just talk a whole evening?"

"And," Artie laughed, "d'you know what she brought along to the party? A little pocket dictionary." Dear Hollywood!

I appreciated Adrian, who was interesting and amusing as conversationalist, as well as an accomplished dress designer. He had been to Carmel and shared my pleasure in Una Jeffers.

He was fond of human frailties. "I try to find out what people are good at," he said, "and talk to them about that, not about what they don't know. Now you, for instance," and he looked at the thick red plush curtains of our rented house and the imitation Canaletto on the imitation stucco wall, "to you I would not talk about interior decoration." That night I ripped the curtains down.

Yet, ironically enough, it was partly Adrian's animadversions that led me to start my collection of modern art, which has been one of the joys of our later life. A young friend from a small art gallery happened to comment on that bare expanse of stucco wall, and suggested we let him lend us some of the paintings stored in their gallery. He brought a Klee as his first offering, the first one I had seen since Pauline's friend, Galka Scheyer, had come to Carmel with the Blue Four. After a few weeks, when the art dealer came to reclaim his picture, I had so fallen in love with it that I could not part with it, and to his amusement asked if it were possible to own it. Don made of it my wedding present. Klee was at that time so comparatively unknown that I was able to acquire more; then I looked at other paintings, and if I liked one very much, bought it. I also bought work by young California artists, thinking it was our duty to help them. But I became such a devotee of European moderns that I soon had on our walls Kandinsky, Arp, Utrillo, Dufy, Chagall, Feininger, Miro, Picasso. It was before the great art boom sent prices rocketing and made a circus out of it. I continued my searches in New York, and one day Charmion von Wiegand, who had exchanged painting for reporting, said to me, "If you have any dough at the moment, there's a poor old man, a wonderful artist of seventy-two, who is ill and can't afford a doctor, I wish you'd come and see his things." So I spent an afternoon with Piet Mondrian, thin, austere, ascetic, who talked about the pictures hanging all around his white walls, the geometric paintings now world-famous. We had a fascinating talk, Mondrian telling me why he painted as he did, and then and there, to his delight, I bought two paintings. It had been such a stimulating afternoon, I promised myself another visit very soon; but before I could carry it out, he had died.

Some of Don's earlier socialite friends kept up their relationship with him despite his new political orientation, and our wedding breakfast had been given us by Joan Payson. She had been Don's closest friend in that society, and she later invited us to an annual ball she gave in July, where I met a great many people who had been for me only names. But I became quite depressed. They seemed to me to have so much power they could have been using for good, yet all the political conversation that came out of that party for me was one banker's remark: "That sonofabitch Hitler double-crossed us." However, on our New York and Washington trips I also met James V. Forrestal, whom I rather liked, probably because of his voice and the easy charm of his manner; and "Jock" Whitney, who dined us in Hollywood. Rosalind Russell, a fellow guest, attacked Harry Bridges for his failure to become naturalized. When I asked if, had she lived in Britain, she would have given up her American nationality, she stormed, "Of course not," and then looked at me in disbelief. "Is that it?" she asked, for Bridges' clinging to his Australian nationality had been made to seem some kind of subversive crime.

The peculiar Hollywood mixture of dinner-table politics never ceased to astonish me, as when Miriam Hopkins wore cotton stockings to boycott Japanese silk. Or when a dinner party in evening dress drove to San Diego in Cadillacs to join CIO longshoremen in picketing a boat bound for Japan with scrap iron. Or when Norma Shearer raised her glass at a very exclusive banquet of top movie "brass," with the women elegantly clad in sequined evening gowns, to toast "the glorious banners of the victorious Red Army." Actually Hollywood was split down the middle in its political sympathies, one producer giving money for anti-Nazi work while another tried to entertain Vittorio Mussolini. Writers even started to cut one another on movie lots, and one never knew at any party whether one would be conversing with a star who was in favor of Hitler's world or one who supported the underdog. It was the more complicated by the fact that stars must be hired and writers write and directors direct cheek by jowl with someone they might be cutting socially. Don played a large part in all this, in the revival of the Screen Writers' Guild, the boycotts and picketing, and anti-Nazi activity generally. In fact, the first week I knew him he gave me money toward an operation on Harry Bridges' ulcers.

Hollywood for me was a company town, with me not in the company. Everyone talked movies, thought movies, inhaled movies, and inevitably went to movie parties. After dinner, if there was a projection room at a producer's house, movies were shown. A few film people were good company, but, for me, not very many. I liked Harry Kurnitz's parties, because he had musical evenings, with concerts by string quartets, after which Frank Loesser or Abe Burrows or Larry Adler would play or sing. My Hollywood life was a mixture of a real and a dream world. Though political concerns were real enough, the way Hollywood did it was a contrast to my former experience. One threw cocktail parties, drank as much as possible (at a dollar a glass for the cause) so that ambulances, bandages, and drugs could reach the Spanish defenders, or protests be arranged against Nazism in Germany or violence against fruit tramps in Imperial Valley. The Hollywood inmate, it was supposed, preferred to be with his own kind, fellow agents or directors or actors, rather than mix with migrants or Negroes or other underdogs. I thought this mistaken; it might have been a shot in the arm, as with the Stanford students, to see for themselves. Still, the "progressive movement" in Hollywood, as the wider anti-fascist movement was known, while some laughed at its drolleries, was influential and important. It helped to re-elect Roosevelt, to keep America fighting Hitler, Franco, and the Japanese; it played a part in keeping America liberal and actively anti-Nazi during very crucial years.

Of course, part of the reason for movie people's liberal sympathies may well have been the gaping contrast between their often astronomical salaries and the miseries of other parts of the world. Another consideration I always thought held for writers was that few respected the work they did for these large sums. When I asked a celebrated novelist what he was working on, he always replied with the same formula: "Oh, a little Paramount B number," and I noticed that few writers would describe or even name their work. Artie Shaw told me wearily, "I make twenty-five thousand dollars a week with my dance band, but if I want to give it up, they say you're crazy." He liked us, he said, "because you make sense, you're not phony."

It was too easy to ridicule Hollywood support of progressive causes, and to mock when, later, film people asserted they had been "duped" or "deceived." Quite possibly, political implications were not always understood by them, but even the least aware could grasp what help meant for people in danger of their lives. The shadows of the concentration camps lay over Hollywood as over the rest of the world, and there was no disgrace in heeding the appeals; Hollywood's decent generosity was later misrepresented, often denounced, and the earlier sympathizers officially condemned. Men were blacklisted and disgraced for doing little more than helping the helpless through organizations set up to do so. "Why should a person with every comfort, safety, and money," one actor asked me, "have to be 'hoodwinked' or 'trapped' to give to less fortunate people?" As Jimmy Cagney put it, "I make four thousand a week, that adds up," and another time, "When down-and-outers come to me for a couple of bucks, I can't forget I was a little mick on the East Side, and tell myself, 'There but for the grace of God.' "

It was perhaps the world-wide publicity connected with the film industry that enabled it instantly to command world-wide attention, and because film stars had such influence, their acts and utterances stood out. "When Joan Crawford burps," as one actor put it, "it echoes from Bombay to Berchtesgaden." And when Fredric March or John Huston or Miriam Hopkins or Humphrey Bogart or John Garfield gave to Spain or supported the Red Army or boycotted silk stockings because of Japan or helped the campaign of Franklin Roosevelt, those actions stood out—and could later be attacked the more easily. It was ironic for the studios that had put millions into such publicity build-ups to see these reputations used for causes they could not countenance.

During the time the Japanese were invading China, and general opinion in America was anti-Japanese, we knew of China chiefly through Edgar Snow and his *Red Star Over China*. Now Nym Wales, Snow's wife, came to Hollywood with the story of the Industrial Co-operatives or Indusco, the form of self-help the Chinese peasants had evolved. Small, mobile workshops were to supply their own armies and civilian needs behind the lines. Americans could approve such self-help; it was "democracy in action." The workshops had been started by Snow and Rewi Alley, a New Zealander and confidential adviser to Madame Chiang Kai-shek, but they now urgently needed financial help because of war difficulties.

So Mrs. Edgar Snow came from China to raise funds, and I offered to help set up a Hollywood committee. I had already enlisted the interest of a number of people, when Mrs. Snow called a halt: Sam Goldwyn was interested—not only interested but enthusiastic. He had offered to send two publicity men east at once to start a national campaign—"a million-dollar drive like the March of Dimes; you mustn't be modest, this is great stuff. The President himself supports the Chinese people." Mrs. Snow was swept off her feet. "But," Mr. Goldwyn warned, "don't do anything with anyone else, don't work with unimportant people; this must be handled exclusively at the top. Don't set up any little Hollywood group. I'll attend to it all, it's a million-dollar operation, I tell you. Just wait till I get it organized."

So Mrs. Snow told us to call off our plans, and sat back and waited—and waited, as frantic cables from China burned up the wires. The need was immediate—and desperate. Finally Mr. Goldwyn called Mrs. Snow, with only one warning: "Before we begin I must make just one call," and he telephoned a leading banker

in New York. Nym Wales heard Mr. Goldwyn reply, "Oh, I see. . . .
Oh, you would. . . . Oh, you do. . . . There are—ah, considerations, yes, yes, of course, I see. Very well, as you say, W. W." He
hung up and said to Mrs. Snow: "This may not be . . . quite the
time, not just this moment perhaps, I'm advised that with China,
. . . China, I'm advised to wait. And I suggest that you wait.
Now, next thing my dear, I must call off the trip to New York of
those two publicity men. They might possibly go later, not now
—and I must ask you, my dear, to wait, too." Mrs. Snow never
heard from Mr. Goldwyn again, and after a while Indusco failed
through lack of funds. So I learned another lesson.

Besides helping campaigns of all kinds to further the antifascist
struggle, Hollywood writers wanted to express this in films. Chaplin pilloried the little dictator, Hitler, but met some opposition.
He told us, however, that if he were stopped from showing the
picture in movie theaters, "I'll put up my own circus tents all over
the country and charge ten cents." I met Chaplin when H. G. Wells
and Harold Laski stayed at his house. Wells was rather in despair;
his world had blown up. Laski had more elasticity. It was a different Wells from the one I had visited with Clarence Darrow, when
Wells had answered him with such optimism.

Chaplin was a fascinating person. Small, agile, black-haired, with
very light blue eyes, he had an extraordinarily mobile face and
hair-trigger humor. He would jump up and act out anything he
thought funny, seemed always on the jump, his small, electric,
graceful body springing up like a dancer's. He stood by the fire
with Harold Laski one evening, talking about *The Great Dictator*,
as he always talked of the film he was making. At his house, the
moment dinner was over, he would start reading a script aloud,
acting it out as he went along. Once when he was reading the
script of *Limelight* to us, I, having dined perhaps too well, fell
asleep—and awoke to see Charlie peering at me, unbelieving.

The victory of Franco in Spain was catastrophic to us. It had
never occurred to me that the Loyalists might be defeated—that
*we* might lose, that reaction could win. Whatever setbacks we had
encountered in the orchards and lettuce fields, we had never thought
it more than one battle not won. Now, suddenly, one had to face
the fact that the war also could be lost. But there followed the
shock of the Hitler-Stalin pacts. Could the whole USSR have sud-

denly turned anti-Semitic, antisocialist—in a word, fascist? Impossible. One looked for some acceptable explanation, but the second pact, reiterating "unshakable friendship" between those two unshakable enemies, left one dazed. The outbreak of war was almost anticlimactic.

When the Left refused to support the British during the period of "the phony war," I was out of sympathy. To me, there was a vast difference between Nazi Germany and "Imperial Britain," but to my amusement my arguments made me suspect to former friends. "As usual, the Briton at heart an imperialist," Granville Hicks, my coeditor on Steffens' *Letters,* mocked. Nevertheless, when Don's old friend Robert A. Lovett, then Under Secretary of the Navy, said to us in Hollywood that "a handful of British fliers are holding the fort for Western civilization," I fervently agreed.

After the fall of France we in Hollywood—various anti-Nazi bodies and the League of American Writers pooling their lists—sought to save Central European writers interned in French concentration camps. Affidavits had to be obtained from studios or individuals, and a bond of a thousand dollars put up for each refugee. We helped bring over Catholic and radical writers, Protestant and Jew, liberal and socialist and democrat. The refugee colony in Hollywood expanded rapidly. Don and I gave a Thanksgiving Dinner for several of them—Alfred Doeblin, the German essayist, Lisl and Alfred Polgar, and Leonhard Frank, the author of that moving best seller *Karl and Anna.* Our three boys and a small niece of Don's, still in a high chair, made up the party, but not even the "turkey and fixin's," the cranberry sauce and pumpkin pie, could reconcile the exiles or dispel their melancholy. Mrs. Polgar yearned over the little girl, but they emerged as the tragic, uprooted figures they were.

André Simon turned up, and Don and I discovered, to our amused surprise, that he and the "Breda" who had set up the Hollywood Anti-Nazi League in 1936, and a "movie writer" Otto Katz I had met in Moscow in 1931 were all the same person. "André Simon" had written the *Brown Book of the Hitler Terror,* which I had sold in covers of German classics to raise funds for Hitler victims. Normally expansive, enthusiastic, on top of everything, he was subdued now as he told us dreadful eyewitness stories from his courageous underground sorties into Hitler Germany. It was still hard to credit that that country I had known could be perpetrating such savageries.

Simon has been the butt of some colleagues' raillery for his methods and romancing, and he did carry on fantastic adventures in the Spanish Civil War, in France, in Mexico—on every antifascist front. But he lent his talents to the right causes. After the war he settled in his home town of Prague as a journalist, where I visited him several times. But the Stalin terror caught up with him, and he found himself in jail. After two years, mostly in solitary confinement, he made a last speech in court, as extravagant in self-blame as any exaggerated hazard in his life, was condemned on the charges then in vogue, and was hanged.

Among the refugees through whom we kept our contact with the European realities were Bertolt Brecht and his wife, "Helli," Helene Weigel. The Brechts lived in a modest house in Santa Monica, with a fig tree in the garden that Helli tended with care. Deprived of her natural expression, this fine actress devoted herself for her many years in the United States to domesticity. I collected old clothes with her for Nazi victims in hiding in Germany. She had a striking face, with carved, lined features, and was as forthright as her husband, though not with his quiet banter and raillery. Bert Brecht could be savagely ironic. He saw the satiric irony of our times, as well as their bitter tragedy. The wicked glint in those scoffing eyes behind his black steel-rimmed glasses, his quips and parodies, made every visit with him memorable.

He would recount some fantastic story he was making up, make sardonic comments on a play or movie he had seen, or poke fun at movie people. One exception was Charles Laughton, with whom he worked for a year on *Galileo*, finally produced in both Hollywood and New York. With the evil-smelling little cigar that Brecht would chew to the end, his bad teeth, and the short hair he brushed forward like a monk's, this wily, witty genius did not at all look the poet he was. He dressed with great simplicity, in gray flannel or corduroy shirt and trousers, never collar or cuffs, and he always wore the same little workman's cap. He thought himself ugly, but he fascinated many women, one of whom shared his life with his wife for over twenty years.

Brecht was at this time collecting material for what should have been his last great play, on Albert Einstein, but which he did not live to write. Once when we went to the little house, Brecht started: "Criminal, great criminal, with a guilty conscience, puts his little violin on his shoulders so, and while he plays tells the world how to make the bomb," suiting the action to his words in mocking satire on Albert Einstein, who had felt such terrible guilt. (Later, in Paris, Brecht said to me, "One can now of course no longer mock him.") We met Brecht often at Salka Viertel's, with the Thomas Manns, or the Aldous Huxleys, the Max Reinhardts, or the Chaplins. Brecht admired Heinrich Mann more than his brother, Thomas; Chaplin he adored.

Christopher Isherwood was living in the room above Salka's garage and walked by my study window on his way to the beach, when we would pass the time of day. He was quick-witted, with a chaffing sense of humor. Of medium height, with his straight blond hair brushed slantwise, there was something eternally boyish about him, face and laugh and manner. He was a pacifist and conscientious objector who had worked with the Quakers in the war and now helped the objectors in California jails. But he had lost his earlier interest in the politics that had taken him to Spain and led him to write the long verse plays with W. H. Auden—*The Descent of F. 6* and *The Dog Beneath the Skin.* He lived for a year at the Vedanta Temple in Hollywood, a monastery where the poet Gerald Heard preached, and developed a deeper interest in mysticism. I liked his self-deprecatory accounts of how studios "expect me, a writer, to betray my truths just because I need the dough."

"And do you betray them?" I asked.

"If I need the dough badly enough," he jeered. He lived a long time above Salka's garage, most of whose more or less singular tenants became our friends. In fact, we shared with Salka much of our life—friends, worries and joys about our three sons each, interest in Hollywood personalities, concern over politics, gardens, dogs. During the six months we spent almost every year "on the coast," we were able to create a kind of isolated bohemian life, especially after we made a home of our own out there on Mabery Road in Santa Monica.

All this time I was writing articles, including one, under a pseudonym, that made some stir, about contacts between American aircraft factories and Nazi ships that came into California ports. While we were in Carmel on a visit, the FBI telephoned from San Francisco, and Don answered a little unfelicitously, "Is it about that article? My wife didn't write it." The investigator gently insisted on coming down anyway. At first he hedged around: did I have any idea who might have written it, could I help them? I did not wish to lie to a government official and hoped he would not ask a direct question; I countered with why was he so anxious to know the author of the exposure rather than the facts exposed? (I still believed, perhaps naïvely, that "the enemy" was the enemy.) The official hemmed and hawed: "We always like to know the identity of such observers." Then he did ask the direct question.

I was in luck. At that moment there was a commotion and shouts in the roadway. I went out to the balcony, and there at the garden gate stood Steinbeck and a group of friends, clamoring for a drink. I called to my visitor: "Would you like to meet John Steinbeck?" He replied gratefully, "I would, very much," and joined us on the balcony, where the gang stayed until it was time for this Federal Bureau of Investigation investigator to take his train back to the city.

# 22

# DYNAMITE

Don had bought a farm in the Adirondacks, in upper New York State. Like many other writers, he wanted to get away from Hollywood and devote himself to more serious writing. He had started his career with six humorous books, several of them wildly popular in the wild twenties, had then been lured to Hollywood, and, with the advent of talkies, had written scripts for many of the leading stars, including his Oscar-winning *Philadelphia Story*. He still, however, wanted to continue as a playwright, especially after his early Broadway successes, *Rebound* and the musical *Fine and Dandy*. He liked the film medium and did not join in the popular fashion of denigrating film writing, but with more and more to say about these momentous times, he sought a freer and more independent form of self-expression. In pursuance of this aim he had acquired the beautiful Frazzle Top Farm, isolated in a small village near the Eastern Canadian border. To this he now took me.

I found an old complex of buildings dating back a hundred years: three wooden houses painted yellow set in two hundred and fifty acres of grassland and pine forest, approached by an old painted iron bridge, with a trout stream and many ancient trees. It was very much away from it all, a night's train journey from New York, and the nearest railroad station was thirty-five miles. Rockwell Kent had a farm nearby, and Louis Untermeyer the poet was within motoring distance, but the farm was remote enough for any writer's needs.

Among our visitors, Harry Bridges came, with his new fiancée, and Ludwig Bemelmans, the Austrian ex-waiter turned writer, who was making a musical out of his Hotel Splendide stories with Don. Bemelmans took a liking to Bridges and wrote a very complimentary article on our western "firebrand" friend for *The New Yorker,* to Harry's great amusement. Paul Smith came, too, and while he was with us telephoned his old friend Herbert Hoover—to "right the balance," as he put it a little too joyfully. "It'll at least confuse the telephone operator, if not the FBI," and he laughed.

In June, the invasion of Russia by Hitler ended major divisions of opinion in America: with all the horror in Europe, political confusion at home was over, and the undivided antifascist movement could now fight the anti-Nazi war. Or so I thought.

We spent a busy fall farming and writing, the older boys now in eastern boarding schools, the youngest, Duck, still with us, attending to comics and the village school. And then—Pearl Harbor. The news burst on us, as on so many millions, over the radio. Was it a beginning or an end?

When Don was offered a chance to make a truly antifascist film in Hollywood, *Keeper of the Flame,* he felt it could be a contribution to this war against Hitler. I must still find a way of making mine and it was not in chicken raising. Don disliked the idea of living in New York as being too close to the distractions he had sought to avoid, but both Upper Jay and Hollywood seemed now out of the question for me. Wondering how I might get into things, I had a vivid dream. I had been sentenced to death but was running away, with jail guards closing in on me. They had almost caught me when I escaped into a crowded department store, where I could hide among the customers. But the guards spied me, chased me again through crowded aisles, were gaining on me and on the verge of arresting me, when I looked down at my frock: to my amazement it had changed color. "I'm saved, the guards won't recognize me!" I gasped, marveling even in my dream. "I'm safe!" I was so impressed by the dream's vividness that I asked a psychiatrist friend to interpret it for me. "It's trying to show you that your salvation is in your own hands" was her interpretation. "You mean—it's up to me—to get away from the farm and find a place in New York and . . . ?" was my interpretation, and then and there I took a train, found an apartment in Greenwich Village and, to his delight, had it ready when Don came back. And now I must get into this anti-Nazi war.

I went with an introduction from Jo Barnes, foreign editor of the New York *Herald Tribune,* to Colonel "Wild Bill" Donovan, then head of the Office of War Information, and eagerly described my qualifications. He listened, then said I would hear from him. I did, and the answer was no. I couldn't believe it; what could be wrong? All my friends were in the OWI. Where had I failed? Jo Barnes laughed. "Want me to tell you what Donovan said?" he asked. "He said, 'That girl is dynamite; don't touch her.' "

So I still had to cast about for something to do to play my part. I did manage to raise funds for Allied War Relief by organizing an art show of paintings and sculptures owned by celebrated public figures, but it did not satisfy me. Rolling bandages and donating blood did not, either. I accompanied Don to Washington, where he contributed to a psychological-warfare radio series, and where we stayed with his old friends the Robert A. Lovetts. I met again William C. Bullitt, now a very different Bullitt from the brash young insurgent of Paris days.

In New York our flat on Eleventh Street became a center for those who still assumed the war was against fascism and "the enemy" clear—Robert Lamb, now of the La Follette Civil Liberties Committee, seamen, longshoremen, lawyers, even Washingtonians, economists, newspapermen. We struck up a close friendship with Charles Wertenbaker and his wife, Laël, both on *Time,* and Don became godfather of their first-born. Wertenbaker was a tall, charming, gentle man, a stimulating companion, with a long, slow, drawling Southern voice, and Laël a lively, warmhearted girl and first-class newspaperwoman. We loved them both.

Don's return from writing *Keeper of the Flame* led to an amusing occurrence. The stars were Tracy and Hepburn, and there had been acrimonious differences about the script. Now there was a brisk ring on the telephone, and when I answered, a peremptory voice demanded, "Ella?" It was that authoritative, thrilling voice of Katharine Hepburn. "Ella," it proceeded, "I hear Don *loath-es* me!"

"As a matter of fact, Miss Hepburn"—I started to prevaricate, but decided instead to match her bluntness—"Don *was* rather upset . . ."

"I thought so," she interrupted. "We must have it out. I'll come and see you." This is what I have always admired about Katharine Hepburn: she says it. Of course, Don forgave her. For me it had the reward of starting an enduring friendship.

Don now wished to put on his new war drama, *Emily Brady,* based on stories of Robert Lamb's about "fascist" practices in a certain large automobile plant. The play was original and un-compromising, but when Don took it to the most liberal producer on Broadway, he met opposition. "I'm scared," the producer said. "It's such a powerful play, and if you make it better, I'll be more scared." And Don had wanted to get out of the unrealities, the fantasies of Hollywood, to put the truth on the stage! The process of trying for other backers and producers was murderous for the sensitivities of an artist. Each had different objections, each con-sidering himself, apparently, an incipient playwright, though what lay behind their worries and suggestions seemed to be more the question "If I put up fifty thousand, will I be sure of making a profit?" I could do nothing to alleviate Don's distress, the blows to his pride, or the frustration.

On a hunch I asked the New York *Post* for a job, any kind of a job. A few days later, the editor, Ted Thackrey, telephoned me in considerable excitement. The *Post* had suddenly decided to open a foreign bureau in Moscow and "You are the obvious person to go. Will you be our Moscow correspondent for two years?" I couldn't believe it. I had so coveted the job of every foreign corre-spondent, especially those few who had managed to get into war-time Russia.

As usual, there was the family to consider, and then we had a stroke of luck. Billy Rose found in *Emily Brady* "exactly the play I would like to produce, and Orson Welles is the man to direct it, and he is in Hollywood." The long-distance wires sizzled with Welles' enthusiasm; he'd never thought to find any play so moving, so "just what I dreamed of directing." Meanwhile Don was asked to write another movie (*Without Love*) for Hepburn and Tracy—a fitting title for my absence, I thought—and he could discuss his play with its enthusiastic director-to-be in Hollywood. The younger boys would be at boarding school. I could not stay away two years, of course, but I would cross that bridge later. I must certainly not pass up this opportunity.

I had to wait some time for a visa and a boat, and then, just before I was to sail, the State Department asked me to sign a paper to say I agreed to travel on a freighter carrying dynamite. I was scared and not much consoled to learn that it was to have a convoy of a hundred ships.

I had a strange experience on the dock. My poet friend May Sarton had typed out, as a parting gift, a little selection of poems, classic and modern: Goethe, Hölderlin, Rilke, Schiller, some Shakespeare, John Donne, Jeffers, Muriel Rukeyser. From Muriel, my close friend, and from Don I had bundles of letters I was taking to reread. The other passengers, nine in all, women State Department officers, Army and health officers, were waiting for the tender, when two officials asked me to empty my duffelbag and started to examine all my papers. They leafed through May Sarton's selection of poems, and it was amazing, every poem had some suspicious word: "treason," "betrayal," "revolt," "treachery," "perfidy," "forswear," "enemy." The men looked me over with increasing suspicion. "B-b-b-but that's Goethe," I said, "a well-known poet, a famous . . ." The word "German" stuck in my throat—and Schiller was German, and Rilke, and Hölderlin.

Then they insisted on reading Muriel's and Don's letters.

"I'll throw them in the sea," I threatened. No, that would not do; "You are inside the territorial limits of the USA, you cannot do that." But while they were still poring over the intimate blasphemies in Don's letters, I went to an empty ash can, put Muriel's beautiful, poetic letters at the bottom and set them alight. The men came over. "We said you can't do that." "I know," I said, "but I did it," and they let me go.

Years later my oculist asked me if two FBI men had interrogated me on that occasion, and I told him the story. "That's right," he said. "I happened to have one of them as a patient, and when I mentioned you as another, he told me rather shamefacedly about it. He said they had been ordered to look for 'possible messages for the Nazis written in invisible ink,' in case you were torpedoed." If I could be suspected of being a Nazi, I thought, what next? Suspicion seemed to create its own conspiracies.

Normandy was invaded while we were at sea. I hung about the radio operator's cabin, to his disapproval—everything was so "top secret." There were messages for undergrounds and resistance movements in French, Danish, Norwegian, Swedish, English: *Emma has the eggs. Buy bacon tomorrow.* By the time we landed in Egypt the Allied armies were well into France. Hulks of the French fleet lay rusting in the port of Alexandria; it was my first sight of war. I waited three days in Cairo, then got a seat in a military plane over Beirut and Damascus, to Teheran, and flew on, very airsick, via Baku to my destination. When I landed at Moscow airport, an Intourist car met me and I was asked, "What do you want to do?"

"Die," I said.

I had to learn the ropes of my job as foreign correspondent. I deposited my credentials at the Narcomindel (Foreign Office), got my first week's ration from the journalists' store, and a day later joined a trip to Botosani in Romania, just occupied by the Red Army. I rode in a jeep with Paul Winterton, a young British correspondent, and Dina Aldridge, the Egyptian wife of James Aldridge the novelist. Dina was beautiful, exotic, black-haired, and spoke with an enchanting accent. She had long Egyptian hands, narrow long feet out of Egyptian friezes, and had been married but a year or two to her young, blond, dashing husband. Jimmy Aldridge was a warm and shining personality; square-shouldered, muscular, intelligent, well informed—and Australian. He even talked with a slight Australian accent. We became fast friends.

The jeep trip was a warning introduction to wartime Russia. The country had suffered famine beyond imagining from the enemy and from her own scorched earth policy; children had died in thousands of hunger or disease, or were mutilated by the Nazis. There were three million orphans. In Botosani, I visited an orphanage of Jewish children rescued from a Nazi death camp in Southern Russia. One of the teachers said, "We tell them, Jews were born to suffer," to which defeatism I objected. When I left, fifty little hands stretched out after me, the children pleading: "Take us to America, take us away to America."

Once more, as in the thirties, I went everywhere: to hospitals and farms, libraries, churches, rehabilitation homes for the blind and mutilated, psychiatric clinics, orphanages, the ballet, the children's theater. I discovered that when the Nazis entered a village, they hanged librarians and schoolteachers first. We were taken on trips to Leningrad, Minsk, Tallin in Estonia, and the Volga-Don canal. I interviewed tank drivers, farmers, women fighter pilots and snipers—even the famous girl sniper Pavlichenko, who had shot sixty men. I talked to an eighteen-year-old red-cheeked peasant girl who had fled from a German prison and spent three terrified weeks on the road.

"And what are you going to do now you're back?" I asked

her. She lifted her weeping face, threw her head back, and in a sobbing voice cried, "I'm going back to my farm and I'm going to *double* my potato production!"

In a Leningrad orphanage I picked up a tiny three-year-old who had lost everyone—one of five thousand in that home. She put her arms tight around my neck. "Adopt me," she wailed, "please, please adopt me!"

One little boy told me he had "written Daddy again and again, and given the letter to a postman." It was addressed only by name, and when they asked where they'd find his father, the little boy said, "Oh, you'll know him easily enough from the hole in his shoe." And a child under drugs in a clinic, reliving the death by torture of his mother and a cherished uncle, cried out despairingly: "Grandmother, your heart can break with sorrow." The woman doctor found herself weeping as she wrote.

We saw fifty-seven thousand German prisoners marched silently through Moscow, with dulled, frightened eyes, their feet in rags, broken glasses lacking earpieces. People lining the route were silent. "Poor devils," one old woman said, "they couldn't help it, I don't suppose; they were forced into it like all the rest." When we interviewed the German prisoners and asked them why they had committed their outrages, they, one after the other, like mechanical toys, replied, *"Befehl ist Befehl"* ("Orders are orders").

Day after day in Russian cities or the rutted roads of villages I saw feats of endurance hard to conceive. In one village, where no men were left, the old women lived in holes underground, and smoke came out of the earth. I called on the mother of Zoya, the nineteen-year-old girl whom the Germans had tortured and hanged naked in the snow for her part in a partisan raid. The mother was in agony, but dared not give in. "If only my boy Shura lives!" she cried, "if only he be spared." He wasn't.

I went to a hospital where Doctor Frumkin, the surgeon who had cared for Lenin after he was shot, was constructing new sexual organs for mutilated soldiers. He told me about one young man so encouraged at the prospect of not being a eunuch that, under the guise of visiting a dying grandmother, he took a weekend off with his nurse "and tore my whole six-month surgical work to pieces." The doctor grinned. "But the young man didn't care, he was so jubilant that it had worked!" When I wrote this story, another correspondent, Dick Lauterbach, received a cable from

*Time* announcing my "scoop," requesting him to check and asking querulously, "What sex organs does she mean?"

A children's writer, Eugene Schwartz, told me graphic stories of the "Leningrad Hunger" and how people had survived it. "The worst were the long, cold, black nights in cellars," he said. "A girl asked me how one could get through them, with hunger gnawing, in the freezing dark. I told her to go over in her mind, page by page, long novels like *War and Peace,* paragraph by paragraph, picture by picture, each scene, visualize each character and its struggles. The girl said it worked."

William Averell Harriman was the American Ambassador to Moscow, and invited the correspondents in rotation to dine with him. He shared my friendship for Jo Davidson and told me of his excitement at the prospect of the presentation to Stalin of Jo's bust of F. D. R. Harriman had a deep, friendly respect for the President. "I don't think I could ever leave politics again," he confided to me.

We saw something of the "hidden" Russia, the tyranny of which no one spoke and which was not to be publicly acknowledged in the USSR for another decade. I would overhear writers talking contemptuously of *"his* works" coming out in several volumes, in an edition of many thousands, whereas their own would not be published at all or in small editions. At concerts the hall would be half empty during the exaggerated eulogy of the Leader, the audience coming later for the music. One could not escape the busts, statues, portraits, the laudatory articles, poems, posters and banners, the imprint on almost every official paper. Every hotel floor had its portrait or bust.

Ivy Litvinov would meet me only in the Kremlin Gardens; she asserted her servant girl was certainly a spy. I thought she exaggerated. She was writing a book about her girlhood in Maida Vale and wanted me to take the manuscript out, but she was afraid. Everywhere one felt hampered. I could not see my old acquaintances of 1931 in their homes; they would receive me only in the company of officials. Lozovsky and Litvinov, both Foreign Office officials, would answer questions only in the presence of a secretary taking careful notes.

A girl took me secretly to visit Dovchenko, the film director, who was under a cloud for making a war picture that gave too much credit to the Ukraine. (The film was finished by his widow many years later.) Dovchenko was a sad and broken man. Sergei Eisenstein let me watch the shooting of *Ivan the Terrible,* with its Aladdin *décor* of gold, brocades, and jewels, but he was tense with apprehension and was cutting now one scene, now another, in a panic of suspense and dread. Writers and artists and others were daunted and intimidated, but no one knew what was really happening, the full scope of the shocking truth.

I had been told to try and find some of the work of the constructivist painters—Malevich, Rodzenko, Lissitzky, Tatlin. Two had died; Tatlin was doing stage designs, and I would have gone to see him, but Ivy Litvinov told me not to. "He's old, seventy-two, he may get into trouble if a foreigner calls," she said. There was a pathological fear of foreigners. I asked the Artists' Union for the whereabouts of Lissitzky. They told me he had died, but his widow was still in Moscow, and one day I was summoned to VOKS and introduced to Mrs. Lissitzky, who had a portfolio full of her husband's work. To my surprise I was permitted to buy all she had, though under the disapproving eyes of two young officials. I was just a foreign formalist.

I visited the circus, theater, bookshops, puppet shows, exhibitions, and artists. I had long talks with Sergei Gerassimov, head of the Artists' Union, who strenuously opposed all modern "distortion," all abstract art. We had violent arguments. "Why should I waste valuable wall space," he asked when I suggested he show Picasso, "on work any three-year-old could do?" I said, "Why not let the audience judge?" He replied, "Looking at Picasso could ruin taste." "You mean it could ruin all the taste of all the people for all time?" Yes, he meant just that. I said I thought that this was counterrevolutionary and anti-Marxist, and Lenin would not approve, but it made no impression.

We were taken to Minsk two days after the Germans had evacuated, when, in fact, some Germans were still at large hiding in the woods. We were assigned a semidestroyed bunkhouse, without water or sanitation; and, as would happen, I had an attack of dysentery. As I tiptoed out in my pajamas in pitch-dark, I found myself deep in a bed of nettles, and at that moment was challenged by a Russian guard with bayonet. What could this suspicious rustling be but a German? He kept shouting something incomprehensible at me and threatening to shoot. What an ignominious end, I thought, shot by a Russian with nettles stinging my posterior. Well, you always wanted to be a foreign correspondent.

In Minsk we met the first victims of concentration camps we had seen—three out of twelve Jews saved from tens of thousands in Treblinka. We sat on a low escarpment on a sunny morning in the destroyed town and listened while a white-faced, wizened specter of a man dully intoned something about "the Nazi commandant of Treblinka, who invited me into his office to celebrate. 'Today I shot my ten-thousandth Jew,' the commandant said and held out his cigarette case to me and told me, 'Take a cigarette.'" As he talked, he kept pulling a shabby little bundle out of his pocket, till we asked what it was.

"My papers," he said, "my papers—all I have—a snapshot here of my young wife, who was killed. . . ." He kept folding and unfolding another bit of paper, and we saw it was a drawing of the sole of a shoe. "It's the sole of my little boy's shoe," he said, in the same toneless voice. "I carry it with me. He was five."

A Russian major strolled up in the same sunny piazza to tell us a very different story. A young girl had killed, singlehanded, the Gestapo commandant of this area by placing a bomb under his bed. We asked for details, any details. Where was the girl now, could we reach her; but the major, a former railwayman and partisan, would not say.

"I don't know," he told us. He was a Hero of the Soviet Union and he had modest, twinkling eyes, and we pressed him in vain. "I don't know," he said as tanks rattled and bumped across the cobbles on their way to the front. *"Ya ne znaiu"* (I don't know) and then he looked at us quietly. *"Ya znaiu"* (I know). He smiled quizzically and terminated that question. Then he related guerrilla exploits: how the partisans had dug up rails, derailed trains, placed explosives in tanks. "Our population learned that it could protect itself in German-occupied territory only by guerrilla warfare," he said, "and this cemented an extraordinary solidarity." He paused. "This was a place of terror," he ended abruptly.

With the other correspondents, I attended diplomatic gatherings and Kremlin parties in Moscow. Winston Churchill and Anthony Eden came after the Polish Lublin government had been set up. Churchill offended the Russians, sticklers for the proprieties, by wearing his zippered flying suit. When Charles de Gaulle was invited to a Kremlin banquet, he warned his entourage to be prepared to see their hosts eat peas with a knife. "They are, after all, still barbarians," he instructed.

Very occasionally we were granted individual press interviews at the Foreign Office. Litvinov talked to me passionately of Soviet fears of a Germany resuscitated by the Allies, "as after the First World War," a rebuilt Germany that would threaten the Soviet Union and possibly invade her yet a third time. "This is why we support the Morgenthau Plan," he insisted. "A purely agricultural Germany would not be as dangerous to us as a reindustrialized country."

It was particularly noticeable to us (because afterward it was so much denied) how warmly the Russian people loved and admired the United States, particularly the President, and how grateful they were for American help; everyone could see the trucks and half-tracks and jeeps (called *"Veelees"*), the cans of food, Lend-Lease generally. During the United States election in November the whole population eagerly supported Roosevelt, and the country was jubilant when he won. "Our children have never known any other 'ruler' of America," a schoolteacher said to me. "Your President Roosevelt has held power all their lives." The man the politicians feared was John Foster Dulles.

In December the New York *Post* changed to tabloid form and had to cut down on space. I had been away over six months and wanted to get back. But before I left, we were taken to a Nazi-constructed death camp in Tallin, Estonia.

What we first saw as we came into the camp was the funeral pyre. Layers of tree trunks were laid across one another in a giant square, and between each two layers of trees was a layer of corpses. They were dressed, some even in overcoats, men and women indiscriminately. These people had been laid face down one next the other, then the pyre had been set alight in the kerosene-soaked logs; as the human torches tried to get up and run, they had been shot in the back. The Nazis burned all they could to cover their traces, but the Red Army came too soon.

It didn't matter how much one had read, when you saw it for yourself, you could not believe it. Human beings had done this. One tiny figure lay in the rain with its mouth open and arms outstretched, as if waiting to be picked up. I said, "That's a doll," but it was a baby. Its mother lay beside it.

It rained, a flat drizzle. In the sodden field the corpses lay indiscriminately, screams frozen into commonplace faces, fingernails black with congealed blood, tin cups, rusted spoons, a shoe, a shirt scattered about. One corpse had no head. "That's Matthew," a girl walking alongside me said in a toneless voice. "He was my friend." Then I saw the head lying in the wet grass.

"No babies were allowed to be born, either in the ghetto or here," a girl said, "but three were born here. The officials didn't know what to do, so they wrote and asked Berlin. They threw one baby into a steamboiler, the second they banged against a brick wall. Another woman was attended by our gynecologist, Professor Gecow, but Untersturmfuehrer Willi Bahr waited for Gecow to deliver the baby, then threw it into the furnace." "I saw it," Abram Aronson, the bookkeeper, said, "I was tending the furnace. It was February."

The women jailers were the worst, the girls said. "Three women overseers especially—Frau Inge Weizmann, who spoke English, because she had been eight years in America; one called Marianne; and Aggie Gastren, the worst of all." Genia, a beautiful, brown-eyed girl who had been a nurse in Vilna, told me, "She always hit you with a stick"; another, named Marta, was saying, "Always on the head or the breast or in your eye or ear. She was not content until you became blind or deaf, or lost your mind."

I started to ask something, anything, but they went on inexorably: "She wanted your last blouse, your shoes, underwear, your last pennies, or if she found a bit of bread on you, or just for the lust of beating."

I had seen very disturbing developments in the USSR: the exaggerated power and worship of Stalin, the enervating bureaucracy and overcentralization, the conformity, fear, and lack of individual assertion among intellectuals. And a philistine attitude to art. Yet the Soviet people had suffered so tragically, with their people tortured, their millions of acres scorched and ruined, that I did not feel it my job to attack the regime now. The paramount job was to continue the fight against Nazism, and, whatever else, the Soviets uncompromisingly fought fascism. We discussed the subject among ourselves at the Hotel Metropole and again with friends after my return, but such were the factors that weighed when I reached home from Moscow.

And I still felt that a dictatorship with a plan for the welfare of people differed fundamentally from a fascist tyranny for the glory of one man or one race or one Reich, for national or military gain alone, from a regime based on the suppression of labor, on the maintenance of vast economic inequalities, on the oppression of whole peoples and races. I could not join with those who claimed, "a plague on both your houses," or opposed "dictatorship of the Right or the Left." To me there was a difference between socialism and fascism.

Shortly after my return to New York, I was invited to the White House to tell of my war experiences in the Soviet Union. My hostess came into my room and said, "I am having a Negro lady for tea and am telling you beforehand, as I tell all my guests, in case you prefer not to meet her." The lady was the wife of an official of the Urban League, a Negro organization, and she told the President's wife that her husband was very embittered that not more had been done for Negroes as a result of their war participation. "In fact, he is against all white people," she said. "I know that is wrong and he knows it is wrong, but that is the way he has been forced to feel." Mrs. Roosevelt was very perturbed and argued against this position. One felt her great desire to help all downtrodden and underprivileged people. Her concern, I thought, comforted her guest at least a little. After my brushes with dictatorships, the democratic give and take of the White House, the close touch that both the President and his wife tried to keep with ordinary people, were a comfort to me.

I had talked with Mrs. Roosevelt before my departure for the USSR, and she was anxious to hear what had befallen me. Later, all the guests, including Anna Roosevelt and her then husband, met in the President's study for cocktails. At first I did not recognize him sitting behind a huge glass-topped desk; his face was so gray and shrunken. I thought of Jo Davidson's description of Stef when he was so ill, "a piece of green cheese." But he was gay and hearty, welcomed me warmly, and insisted on mixing the cocktails himself: "I do it better than anyone else." He was so talkative, in such good spirits, that one forgot how his face looked. We discussed Laski's recent visit, and F. D. R. chuckled and whispered to me, "Harold is always quite sure he knows."

He then told an amusing story of Yalta. "The work of the conference was over and we were to drink toasts; the question was, to whom? Stalin suggested, 'Let us drink to fifty thousand dead Prussian officers.' We raised our glasses, but Churchill suddenly put his down. 'No, I won't drink to that toast; the Prussians may be our enemies and brutal, but their officers fought well and gallantly, and must be respected. I won't drink to dead Prussian officers.' Uncle Joe was nonplused," the President said gleefully. " 'But Mr. Prime Minister, *Prussian* officers—*Junkers, Prussians!*' 'I know, I know, but they were a gallant enemy, and I will not drink to their death.' "

"Things were getting pretty warm," the President went on in delight, "we'd had a good relationship I didn't want to spoil, so I said, 'I've got it, gentlemen, I have the solution. Let us drink to *forty-nine* thousand dead Prussian officers!' " and he laughed triumphantly. "Stalin raised his glass and Winnie raised his glass, the air cleared, and we all drank happily to that toast."

We went down to supper around a long table. Mrs. Roosevelt made scrambled eggs; the meal was simple and, to my relief, very informal.

"I'd like to know what will happen when Uncle Joe has his first free elections," President Roosevelt said to me as we sat down.

They asked about my experiences and I told them many stories. Mrs. Roosevelt's secretary, "Tommy" Thompson, asked about children, motherhood, birth clinics. When I told them childbirth was free with all the fixings, she would not believe it.

"But all in all it costs about two thousand dollars to have a baby here!" she exclaimed, "counting hospital and doctors and nurses and help. I should think everyone would have their babies in Russia."

Next morning, Mrs. Roosevelt came to my room to chat, telling me about her children, their divorced wives and husbands, and the stepchildren, and how she always had them all at the White House. "And there is never any trouble, I get on with all of them, the present wives and husbands and the former husbands and wives, and the new partners and stepchildren. Only the nurses give me trouble. Quarrels arise between the white and Negro nurses."

What she didn't tell me was how to get out of the White House, and I wandered about halls and passageways with no one about, quite lost. Finally I pushed open a door, and there sat the President behind his desk. He smiled and excused himself for not being able to ask me in. As he rang for a butler to show me the way,

I tried to imagine the Kremlin or the Wilhelmstrasse under similar circumstances.

At tea, just before I left, Mrs. Roosevelt had talked about how much she had resented the lies told her by young radicals and Communists she had invited to the White House a year or so before. "I didn't mind their being Communists, if they'd only told me," she said. "I minded being lied to, and finding out afterward from the FBI." The President's wife also told me of her distaste for Madame Chiang Kai-shek, who had made a great display of luxury in wartime Washington. "When she came to my New York apartment, she couldn't believe I had no butler." Mrs. Roosevelt laughed. " 'And where is your chauffeur?' she asked me, 'and all your servants?' She had expected the ménage of a reigning monarch, I think." The President's wife was gently amused and rather disapproving.

Now that I was back from the Soviet Union, and Don from Hollywood, we decided on Cambridge, Massachusetts, as a quiet place where I could work on my book about my Russian experiences and Don could begin his new play. Also, we could be near the boys, Duck at Exeter, Ames at South Kent, and Pete in training at Harvard for a commission in the Navy.

But the tragic April followed, when the man who had seemed so much a personal friend to so many millions suddenly died. The whole nation mourned F. D. R. One could not imagine any man able to follow him in the White House. With May came the end of the war in Europe. In Boston, as in London so many years before, the crowds came out, shouted and danced and jubilated. But I was struck by the difference from that other armistice day. Had that other war been worse, or had it been that it was the first? Or was I so much younger and more impressionable? People who went through both wars have commented on the much greater sense of relief felt that November 11, 1918. Perhaps we distrusted more now, knowing that this war might very well not be "the war to end war."

We had hardly returned from the rather joyless celebration when Ted Thackrey, of the New York *Post,* telephoned me and asked me to go to San Francisco to cover the founding of the United Nations. "I want you to report for the *Post* especially on the Russians. Follow Molotov around," he said. I was tremendously tempted to be in at the beginning of this new attempt at a world

order, to be at the "hub of the universe" again—for everybody
would be there. But I could not interrupt my book, and very regretfully I gave up this opportunity. Soon after, Thackrey asked me
to take another job, this time to represent the *Post* in Berlin, but
again I could not accept. I had been away from my family so long,
and Pete might go to war any time now. So, regretfully, I said
another farewell to my favored profession.

But there were compensations. In Cambridge we came to know
and dearly love "Mattie"—Professor F. O. Matthiessen, one of Pete's
teachers at Harvard. He visited us often with Ted Spencer, the
tall Shakespearean scholar. The boys loved Mattie and had exciting discussions with him; we talked much about the James family
he was writing about, and he took us to tea with some of them.
Mattie was very independent and very sensitive, and I felt like
mothering him. He had humor and warmth and a great love of art,
particularly of Klee, my favorite. His close friend, who had lived
with him for many years, Russell Cheney, had been a painter.
Since Cheney's death, Mattie had lived alone with two cats. He
entertained America's poets and writers who came to Harvard to
lecture, and we met at his house Tennessee Williams, Karl Shapiro,
Auden, the Irish actor Barry Fitzgerald. Mattie felt deeply about
politics and was in despair over the slow erosion of the pro-
gressivism of the F.D.R. years.

After the Bomb, things changed rapidly. This is not a history
of the changing world, or even of America during thirty years,
but in any personal story one must take into account overwhelm-
ingly changing patterns, if only to appreciate the increasingly altered role in it of any individual—especially one like myself, who
wanted to keep abreast of events and play as large a part in affairs
as a private citizen could. Our era had had its shocks, its new,
unheard-of happenings, but now had come one event that would
make a difference in all our lives, in our whole *condition humaine*
—a change not only in degree, but a basic difference in kind. The
problems were widening emphatically, the ability to encompass a
known universe (which we had developed only a short few hundred
years ago) was being shattered, and the task of organizing societies
for greater welfare was overshadowed, with this blast of the
mushroom cloud, by anxious doubt, by a questioning of all funda-

mentals. Little use to have a better society of human beings if all humanity could be blown to smithereens.

I have sometimes thought it would make a good parlor game, if not a television program, to make a survey of where people were, what they were doing and thinking, how it affected their immediate pursuits, when they heard of a decisive event in history. The reactions to the first shock of the Bomb could be an intriguing study. What does one do when something occurs that one cannot take in? You sit around, you look at familiar things, you get irritated at the cat, you call your friends. Can they shed light, say something to make you feel you are still sane, still live in a known and rational universe? Can they help you feel you are not quite alone? This was indeed dynamite—to the $n$th degree.

It triggered Don into writing his play *How I Wonder,* which involved the Bomb and also the problem of the nuclear scientist in this new atomic age; it was the first play to be produced on the subject. Professor Harlow Shapley, of the Harvard Astronomical Observatory, came to tell us about the heavens, about planets that break apart or are blown up and become stars; this is what happens in the play, and a girl comes from one such blown-up planet to warn us of our own possible fate. It was a play for our times.

# 23

# COLD COLD WAR

After my Soviet war book, *I Saw the Russian People*, came out, I hopefully began to lecture again. But Winston Churchill had spoken at Fulton, Missouri, the Cold War was on, and the enemy was the USSR. War alliances were being forgotten, Stalingrad, Lend-Lease; war enmities, too.

It hit my work. "Inquiries" were made to owners of halls where I lectured; one of my chairmen stammered, "You won't say anything untoward, will you?" I did still speak, even in towns in the deep South, where stations had toilets "For Negroes" and "For Whites," but lectures and even debates were beginning to be canceled. My agents said that threats included boycott of others of their speakers who had nothing to do with politics—readers of poetry, talks on the bird songs of the Rockies. So I turned to making a house.

With three growing boys we wanted a home in New York, and I found an old brownstone house on Tenth Street, in the heart of the Village we liked so much. It had large rooms, high ceilings, old chandeliers and fireplaces, and even a small back garden, and it was around the corner from Henry James's Washington Square. I had not heretofore made a house of our own—The Getaway was finished and furnished when we bought it—and my inexperience made me hesitant and unsure. At Don's suggestion, therefore, I called in a leading interior decorator. I went proudly over the old place, and when we had examined it in detail, I asked, "What would you do with a house like this?" "Sell it," the man said without hesitation. We did not, though, and we made a house, old and Victorian and full of our now considerable art collection, and it served us for a good many years.

At this juncture Don was offered another Spencer Tracy movie,

*Cass Timberlane,* and we found ourselves once more in Hollywood, with the problem of where to live. In the postwar housing shortage, dwellings were scarce, and hotels allowed five days' stay. When a rather ramshackle place fell vacant at the corner of Salka Viertel's Mabery Road, facing the Pacific, we sold The Getaway and bought that, and made of it a modern house, with glass-enclosed verandas, sun porches on the ocean, patio and garden and oleanders before the door. And an avocado tree. I gardened furiously in this Mediterranean climate, which seemed to be my happy fate, for I had now lived in almost all the Mediterranean climates—Melbourne, the Italian Riviera, California. Now I had my familiar trees and shrubs once more, from St. Kilda, San Remo, Alassio, Carmel, red and purple bougainvillaea, pepper, palm, and cypress, loquat and datura, that marvelously scented trumpet vine, and wattle (or mimosa), and, of course, eucalyptus. I planted one tree new to me— a red lotus in the patio. So with a farm in New York State and a house in New York City, I was now *châtelaine* of three domains— not exactly the fulfillment of a girlhood dream to absent myself from domesticity.

Sunday evenings we usually went to Katharine Hepburn's for supper with Tracy, usually just the four of us; sometimes Katie's old "dresser," Emily, would join us with "Murph," her "stand-in," who had married a Los Angeles research physician. Katharine and Emily would cook the supper. I cherished these Sundays. I loved Katie for the unhesitating way she attacked any problem, for her definiteness and her honesty. She prized her independence and had many stories of how she had bested studio heads, even "L. B." (Mayer), the redoubtable king of M-G-M. From the moment you put your coat on the nearest chair and Katie swept it up and into her bedroom—she could not abide untidiness, coats or hats lying about the living room—throughout the evening, to the good-by at the door, she never left you in doubt about what she felt, what she wanted, what she meant—by the rather simple expedient of saying it with forthright candor.

Once I asked Katharine what she had wanted to be as a girl. "You'll laugh," she replied. "But all my life I wanted to be—a movie queen."

By late 1947, with so many people going to Europe, to de-Nazify Germany or see what the war had done, I was again overwhelmed with a desire to go abroad. Don had found a producer to put on his play *How I Wonder*, and was immersed in discussion, rewriting, and rehearsing. I sold my publisher the idea of a book on postwar Europe, armed myself with newspaper assignments, including an interview with Tito, and flew off.

My first night in Berlin there was a news conference by a United States general and correspondents eager to find fault with the Russians. There was cynical awareness of the lack of serious de-Nazification, as also of the whole meaning of Nazism: in Wiesbaden the toilets at United States Headquarters differentiated between Allied and German personnel, like stations in our South between Negro and white.

I wandered about a Berlin in ruins, with rubble and broken structures where showy houses and arrogant *Siegesallee* statues had stood; in 1947 very little had been rebuilt. I looked up Renée Sintenis, the celebrated sculptor of small animals, who told me of the days immediately after the surrender, when "nothing worked, and we women had to bake bread for the Russians, and the Russian soldiers stole our wrist watches." She recounted an incident that amused her. "Two rough Soviet soldiers, their arms covered with stolen watches, demanded mine, too, but desisted when they learned I was an artist, and instead asked to see my work. It was all destroyed or lost, except three little figures I found by chance— a sleeping foal, a dromedary, and a horse. They looked at them and disapproved. 'Why do you make your statues so small?' they demanded. '*Gross, Frau, gross.*' And they stretched their arms to indicate what I suppose were the monster statues of Stalin they were used to." I asked if I might buy those three too-small animal figures, and when Sintenis asked for cigarettes in payment, we both felt we had made a bargain.

I spent unexpectedly gay hours, though the fun was rather of the gallows' humor variety, with Anna Seghers, the German novelist who had returned to her homeland from Mexico, where she had lived as a refugee throughout the war. She was paying for her two children, who were studying in Paris, and for her Hungarian economist husband, still in Mexico, from the book and film proceeds of her best-selling *Seventh Cross*. Anna was short, square-shouldered, white-haired, and she indulged in constant persiflage: she could see the farcical side of the things going on in Germany. Her brown eyes twinkled, and her husky voice was emitted through almost-closed teeth—lest she express too openly her real opinions,

I thought. We laughed together, perhaps too sardonically, at American and German pots calling German and American kettles Nazi or anti-Nazi, according to the degree of de-Nazification claimed but hardly carried out, since many American officials neither understood nor desired that process. Anna Seghers' glee at every fresh irony was a relief to me, who tended to see this second up-building of an unregenerate Germany with a good deal less than delight.

A *Time* reporter wanted to take the first jeep trip through the Soviet-occupied part of Germany, to Prague and Vienna. He spoke no German and, finding I did, asked me to accompany him. I had not known Dresden before, but I found the total destruction of that beautiful city appalling. People still spoke in unbelief of the sudden raid in which a hundred thousand people were struck by bomb blast or fire and burned alive, including the imprisoned, invalids, and orphans. The whole center of the city was gone—opera, theater, schools, hospitals, museums. Dresdeners could not grasp why only their city of beauty and art, "not a military target," should have been selected for an Allied bombing; they assumed it was "in revenge for Coventry," but that was not much comfort.

Our next stop was Prague, where we were entertained by our Ambassador, Laurence Steinhardt. An old friend, Howard K. Smith, had driven in from Yugoslavia. Steinhardt talked politics in his garden; among other things he told us how, when he was Ambassador to the USSR, he knew beforehand that the Germans were going to attack in 1941: the behavior of one of the German attachés had given it away. "This man, who was a homosexual with no family, had a beautiful dog he was attached to; one day I saw the dog sitting at the railroad station alone, with a ticket marked BERLIN hanging on his collar. His owner would not have parted with him except for a vital reason and at the very last moment. The Germans invaded Russia three days after." Many people had tried to warn Stalin and Molotov, he said, "but they wouldn't listen."

I explored the beautiful city, discovering my old friends Egon Erwin Kisch and Otto Katz. We had a strange reunion; Kisch, who had become mayor of his beloved home town, was as bubbling as ever. André Simon was more disillusioned. He said to me sadly, "There's not much left for me, an old and impotent Jew."

Then I spent two days at the Salzburg school organized to inform European students, mostly refugees, about American culture. Mattie was teaching there, in the old Schloss Leopoldskron that I had seen in its prime in 1926 under the aegis of Max Reinhardt. Now the gardens were neglected and rank with weeds, the stone statuary broken, the tapestries gone. Young people of a dozen nations, ex-concentration-camp inmates, ex-soldiers, friend and "enemy," were trying, as fellow students, to build a new life. I spent long hours talking with Mattie of the cherished Europe that he and I had known and which had vanished. One tragic little story seemed to sum it up for me. A Romanian Jewish girl, saved at the last moment from a gas chamber, was passionately eager to get to the United States; nothing would persuade her to go back to Romania; but she would not say why until I finally elicited the reason. She had deeply loved a young man, who, believing her long dead, had married her best friend and they had recently had a child. "He must never know I am still alive," the girl said, "the conflict would be unbearable for him, and how could I want him to leave his wife and child? No, no, I must never go home." I said, "Doesn't the truth also have its rights?" But Mattie sided sadly with the girl. "It shows she really loved him," he said a little wistfully.

Of Vienna I could say in parody, "Nothing became me so well as the leaving of it." My 1920 Vienna had disappeared. I did not want to stay in this forlorn and desolate city. Then I found that the Russian "Commissar" in charge was a certain Kisselev, who had been the consul in New York when I waited with such impatience for my USSR visa in 1944. He asked me with nostalgia about the Americans he had known: "What is Odets doing? And Mr. John Garfield, and Mr. Arthur Miller and Miss Lillian Hellman—all those men and women in the cultural front, in those friendly days when we were allies together?"

I wanted to leave Vienna by train, but the railroad passed through Soviet jurisdiction. One needed Soviet permission, and that was "impossible to obtain"; when I said I would try, my colleagues had laughed merrily. So it was more as a joke that I told Kisselev.

"Why not?" he said. "Just ask our consular representative," and he laughed off my reports that that official would never do it. When I showed up later before the American authorities for the counterstamp I needed, I was told, "But we have already explained, you need a Soviet permit and you cannot get that." I laid my document on the major's desk. "You cannot get that," he repeated, hardly looking at this slightly cracked, persistent woman—women correspondents really shouldn't be allowed. "That's right," he said patiently, "that's the document you can't get."

"But," I said, and then he really looked at me. The United States guard at the outer door gazed at me in the same way.

"Listen," he whispered, "do me a favor, will ya, an' tell me, how d'you get that?" "I'll tell you," I said. "You know how the Russians worship Charlie Chaplin? I told them I was Charlie's mistress, and they gave it to me right away."

I then spent three weeks in Yugoslavia. I toured the country in a jeep with some friendly Americans, followed the new railway being built by students from different countries, saw illiterate peasants sitting on the ground in a circle learning to spell, their first word being *Ti-to, Ti-to*. We asked questions of every passenger we picked up along the route; in one village I protested to a husband in a Turkish fez about the veiled wives.

"Why do you keep your young wife's pretty face hidden?"

"If I let her unveil, no one will greet me, I will be an outcast," he wailed. I argued with him, explained the new freedom of women, assured him people would accept, would not boycott him, I had seen it happen. I talked long and patiently, and my earnestness had an unlooked-for result. "Will you be my seventh wife?" the gentleman demanded, and described to me in glowing terms the delights that that honored position would provide. I was finding this quite a lovely country.

In Belgrade I met the head of the press bureau, a short, eager, enthusiastic Serb, who told eagerly of the hard years of turmoil and struggle. When I asked him how they had ever managed to have their revolution, he smiled happily.

"It was quite easy," he said. "When Tito said 'Rise up,' we rised up."

Just before flying back to New York I had one of the first interviews with Tito, for the North American Newspaper Alliance. I sat alone with him and his German shepherd dog for two hours; since he spoke German, the handsome Marshal said we needed no interpreter. I had spent several days preparing questions with David Leacock—the head of United Nations Relief and Rehabilitation Administration in Belgrade, who knew the country's problems—and was well primed. The discussion centered about Tito's interest in "a *small* country trying socialism for a change," its many problems, and his great pride in what he believed its considerable success despite overwhelming odds.

"They take our bauxite," he said, "all our raw materials, and our countrymen have to emigrate, a million and a half of them, because there's not enough left to make a livelihood here. We should keep our own raw materials and make it possible for our countrymen to live in their own homeland." He was a patriot, a broad, strong-featured, imposing man, and independent, who had fought valiantly for his country and whose courage was legendary. Whatever vicissitudes he had to undergo in the following years, he never ceased to care passionately for the welfare of Yugoslavia as he saw it.

After Don's play had opened, M-G-M asked him to see *Edward My Son* in London with a view to writing a script for Spencer Tracy. It was winter in London, cold and gray, and again I hardly recognized the city I had grown up in. I could not find old landmarks, so much had been bombed and wrecked. I did find Kitty Melville, now the mother of three grown girls, and with a successful lawyer husband about to be knighted. She was full of her difficulties with the Egg Marketing Board. Mollie had not married, she was in New Zealand, farming. Marion Phillips had died. I called on an old college friend who had married an M.P. and lived a political life, and, seeking some all-embracing question to cover so many aeons, I asked her, "What do you regret most in these many years?" Without much hesitation she replied, "The times I said no." You can't go home again.

In all these old countries of Europe I had felt the chasm of experience, suffering, agony, and endurance that separated them from a certain unawareness of the realities of invasion—war at your own door—that existed in our own untouched America. Could that gap in awareness, understanding, sympathy ever be bridged?

We flew on to Paris. On the plane I read of the appearance in Washington, before the Un-American Activities Committee, of our old friend Bertolt Brecht. When Hollywood directors and writers were called to Washington to testify before the committee, Brecht was also summoned, and had appeared on the preceding day. He apparently had been nervous, and had asked for a translator to give him more time to think of answers; the translator, it seemed, spoke somewhat worse English than Brecht, and the hearing had become quite comical, somewhat to Brecht's advantage. When, finally, the chief investigator had asked, "Have many of your writings been based upon the philosophy of Lenin and Marx?," Brecht had replied, "No. I don't think that is quite correct. Of course I studied; I had to study as a playwright who wrote historical plays. Of course I had to study Marx's ideas about history. I do not think intelligent plays today can be written without such study. Also history, as written now, is vitally influenced by the studies of Marx about history."

After a grueling questioning, the committee, seeing it was getting nowhere, had dismissed the hearing and even thanked Brecht for being "such a helpful witness."

When Don and I arrived early in Paris, we found the air terminal at Les Invalides deserted except for a small figure thumbing over the books at the literature kiosk. I looked absent-mindedly at the shabbily dressed little man, unshaven, with rumpled suit, chewing a short cigar. He seemed somehow familiar, and I ambled over to the kiosk, pretending to be interested in the papers. A worn felt hat slouched over the face, hiding it, but my curiosity overcame manners and I peered beneath. It was Brecht, owl-eyed behind his glasses, cigar and all.

"But you're testifying before the committee in Washington!" I exclaimed.

"When people accuse me of stealing the Empire State Building, I know it's time to go" was the pure Brechtian reply. He had booked seats under different names on every plane flying out of Washington for two weeks, and the moment his hearing was over, he hightailed it to the airport. That was his last moment on United States soil.

Years later I saw the Brechts in Berlin when they had organized their great theater, the Berliner Ensemble, with over two hundred actors, directors, scene designers, musicians, assistants of every kind, and Brecht was being translated and produced all over Europe. He was always the same Brecht, untouched by acclaim, sardonic, mocking, ironic, uncompromising, in the same flannel shirt and workman's cap, always chewing the same short, evil-smelling little cigar.

In Paris we also saw Richard Wright, the Negro author, who had come to France to escape the atmosphere in which a Negro,

Wright said, "could not walk down the street without being afraid, every day and every night." Wright had been welcomed in Paris and published by Jean-Paul Sartre in his magazine *Temps Modernes*. He liked French writers and French freedom, and the fact that he was accepted as a writer and not "merely" a Negro writer. He was a handsome, passionate, willful man.

When Sartre, his friend and patron, turned further left and adopted a Communist-sympathizer position, it was a blow to bitter, ex-Communist Dick; it was an equal blow when the State Department, asking him to lecture under its auspices, requested "Please do not attack American treatment of Negroes." Wright refused that assignment. I sympathized with his predicament, as an artist seeking to tell his truths, as he had done so magnificently in *Native Son* and *Black Boy,* and as a human being caught in conflicting loyalties and ideologies. He had to be Antigone in a world in which even the shrewdest Creon might find it difficult.

# 24

## SOME KIND OF A BIRD REFUGE

At a party at the Polish Embassy the Polish consul asked me what
I thought of the idea of a great conference for peace to be attended
by the writers of the world. What American writers did I think
might come?

"How many?" I asked, a little bowled over.

"All that will come," he said, "five hundred, a thousand—any
writer who wants peace."

This was how we happened to take a train from Prague to
Wroclaw to the first Writers' Peace Congress. It was a large and, to
me, harmless congress, with the usual number of dull papers. The
evenings, however, were fun. Picasso played his guitar, usually
with his shirt open to his belly button, and Jo Davidson reminisced
about old times. The Hungarian critic George Lukácz and the
playwright Julius Hay talked about modern literature, while white-
haired old Zaslavsky ranted in his raucous voice, "And where is
Howard Fast?" (The Russians were under the false impression he
was then in jail.)

Afterward we went to Warsaw, another city in ruins, and walked
over the muddy, deserted fields that had once been the Warsaw
Ghetto. I picked up a forlorn, broken teacup that seemed to me a
symbol of the hearths and families that had been wiped off the
earth in those two years. The Poles were trying to rebuild their
country out of the rubble practically with their bare hands, for
they could not get machinery. We writers dug some shovelfuls of
earth for what was to be "The House of the Word," a Polish publishing house. One still hoped words might help prevent, for all
time, such events.

The need to have done with wars had created a powerful peace movement in Europe, and when we got back to Paris, plans were being made for a world peace gathering. Peace didn't seem "subversive" in these countries. But first the French had a women's meeting at their prize-fight and racing stadium, the Vélodrome d'Hiver, known affectionately as the Vel d'Hiv, where, a generation before, Hemingway had followed the six-day bicycle races. Women from many countries were to speak, but they lacked an American representative; would I, they asked, represent my country?

I prepared my speech carefully, in French, but on the platform I found an intimidating row of what the French call *personalités:* Jorge Amado from Brazil; Anna Seghers; Louis Aragon and Elsa Triolet; Pablo Neruda, the Chilean poet; the editor Claude Bourdet; and Madame Cotton, the venerable French women's leader. I took an empty seat on the platform next to a rotund, melancholy-eyed abbé in a long cassock, who, I found out later, was the Abbé Boulier, a French Jesuit who devoted himself to peace. He greeted me courteously in a low, musical voice. The hall was packed, and as I gazed upon those thousands of upturned, expectant faces, I quailed. The first two speakers spoke too earnestly and too long, and I saw I must cut my speech. As I slashed more and more paragraphs, the abbé looked over my shoulder. *"Mais, c'est tout un massacre,"* he murmured sympathetically, which somehow gave me heart as I rose to speak.

In France women speakers are not usually humorous, particularly not on a serious subject, and they certainly do not indulge in risqué jokes, but I had cut out so much, I couldn't cut my jokes.

"It is always said that important things originate in Moscow," I said, "Moscow gold, Moscow propaganda, Moscow-inspired peace schemes; and one is told to 'go back where you came from.' Now, I have something intimate to confess that must not go beyond these walls." I dropped my voice, and twenty thousand ears pricked up. "My secret is that part of my interest in peace stems from the fact that I have a son whom I love—but what I must tell you is that his birth took place without the assistance of Moscow or Monsieur Vishinsky."

There was a stupefied silence, then a few tentative giggles, a few more, till the hall was chuckling, then cheering, and I heard to my astonishment shouts of *"'Ip 'Ip Veenterre, 'Ip 'Ip Veenterre."* The abbé was extravagantly complimentary, and my neighbors on the platform laughed. I felt I had made it, and though some of our officials might not happily support the purposes of this gathering, I did not think they could have anything to reproach me with.

Next day at the official Soviet reception for November 7, to which Mrs. Roosevelt came, Monsieur Andrei Vishinsky, the Foreign Minister, was host. When I told him how I had misused his name, he listened carefully. *"Mais, madame, je serais enchanté"* was his beaming response.

After this the First World Peace Congress was held, again with artists, writers, and scientists from all over the world, West, East, and underdeveloped. I was to report it as an observer—no more speeches. I ran into Picasso at the Salle Pleyel the day his daughter was born; he was hopping with ecstasy. "I shall call her Paloma —*la colombe.* Do you not think that is fitting, born during this great conference whose symbol is the dove?" Picasso sat through it all, his brown eyes snapping and burning. Later he took me to his studio on the Quai des Grands Augustins and showed me rooms stacked with paintings, statues, paint pots, easels, frames, in grand confusion, while outside strutted his white doves, the models for his world peace symbol.

A monster demonstration topped the conference, again people from all over France and Europe, a third of a million of them, who marched by in national costumes—dancers, actors, peasants, miners, teachers, steelworkers. It has become fashionable to jeer at "peace," to call those who cared about it "naïve." Could such a demonstration not mean what it seemed to? We believed in it, and the people who came had faith in it.

But dark days followed. Our friend Houdek, a Czech delegate to the United Nations, spent New Year's Eve with us in Paris, desperately troubled. He had been home to Prague and seen the bloody hand of Stalin in action in the satellite countries. "The most terrifying thing," Houdek said, "is that one cannot trace where it comes from, one does not see the source."

A short time after, in New York, when the Czech Foreign Minister Clementis was recalled from the United Nations, Houdek, his friend and protégé, was summoned to accompany him. He called on us in a frenzy of distress. "I don't know what to do," he exclaimed, almost sobbing. "Our leading Czechs have fled from there with their files, there's nothing left to protect. I know if I go back I will never return alive." He had a wife and child in New York.

When Yugoslavia and the Soviet Union broke off relations, a knowledgeable European scholar and political analyst told me that he felt the socialist countries were having to work out new inter-relationships: until the war there had been no other socialist countries for the USSR to have relations with. They would go through evil days and make many bad mistakes, he believed, before these new relationships were established. The countries were at different levels of development and had different histories, needs, and economic and social problems. This had made sense to me; but something else was obviously happening now, something secret and unacknowledged and fearful. Must it accompany the birth pangs of socialism, be a concomitant of revolution? Must revolutions turn to terror as the French and other revolutions had? One had much to think about, but not enough facts for final judgment. Clementis went home—and was executed. Houdek "defected"— and lived.

In New York we received the chilling news that Mattie had killed himself. He had written me just before, saying he expected to teach again at Salzburg that summer and asking, "Will Pete still be in Europe?" I had not even answered yet. Mattie had been despondent about many developments—the change in Czechoslovakia, the threat of yet another Harry Bridges "hearing," the inroads of the witch hunt that was decimating his Teachers' Union. For a sensitive person, and one so politically involved, the blows were discouraging, and Mattie suffered, despite what one might consider compensations. He enjoyed teaching, his students considered him one of the most stimulating and sympathetic tutors; he had many warm friends, both in the college and outside; and he enjoyed the work he was doing—on the James family and Theodore Dreiser. But he was a lonely man, and he suffered from severe depressions. Quiet, in many ways timid, Mattie turned his end into a symbolically aggressive act. He arranged it as methodically as he lived his life, renting a room in a Boston hotel in the afternoon and returning to Cambridge for dinner with a colleague, after which he went home, made his will, wrote farewell notes, and fed his two tortoise-shell cats. Then he went to that Boston hotel, to the twelfth floor, removed his glasses and watch, and jumped. His death left a big gap in all our lives.

The political atmosphere grew bleaker, the Cold War more threatening. The Wallace campaign had failed, there were spy scares, subpoenas were being handed out indiscriminately. The M-G-M studio wanted Don to "answer questions"—a request that always led to a demand for names, so he refused. That was the end of Hollywood for us. Don's last assignment had been *Huckleberry Finn*—now Huck Finn would never float down the Mississippi on his great adventure, at least not from Don's pen.

*The Kidders,* Don's latest play, was to go on in New York in September. It had had an exciting tryout in Cambridge's Brattle Theatre, and we were full of expectations. Don felt he had said everything in it he had wanted to say about the bafflements, frustrations, neuroses, and fears that our competitive, acquisitive civilization bred. There were casting difficulties, and the producer suggested waiting until the fall season; so we decided to spend the summer in Europe. In the course of a month or so, in Paris, we got word that the production was off. It was a bitter disappointment. With stage and films seemingly closed to Don, and my lecturing and writing to me, there was little reason to return. Pete was at Oxford, the other two boys finishing college, so with hopes for an English production of the play, we decided to go to London.

While hauling some heavy cases of books down five flights of our Paris hotel when I could not find the concierge, I dislocated a spinal disc, and in London had to stay in hospital many weeks, till an operation removed the pain.

Don was working on a movie for Ingrid Bergman in Rome; when the director, Rossellini, was in London, he came on a visit to my nursing home with the beautiful young monk who had played St. Francis in his film *Saint Francis of Assisi,* and I found my eyes more on him than on the film director. But the visitor who created most stir at my clinic was Katharine Hepburn. She stalked in one afternoon unannounced, past staring nurses and orderlies, holding before her, as the Speaker holds the mace at the opening of Parliament, a solitary, purple thistle.

"Ella," she stated in that unambiguous, challenging tone of hers, "I bet no one has brought you a flower like this"—and they hadn't. She had been lunching on the grass in Regents Park, reading Shakespeare aloud, and had found the thistle in the grass. That was her entire, and my most appreciated, bouquet during my illness.

We had to find a new home, and an agent mentioned a "dilapidated old house in Hampstead, in such bad condition that I advise you against it." It was Ramsay MacDonald's old house; the family had moved out on his death eighteen years before and it had not had regular tenants since. Window panes were cracked, the roof leaked, the walls had woodworm and dry rot, the garden was a neglected, overgrown meadow. But I liked the high, beautifully proportioned rooms, the old fireplaces and old-fashioned door handles, and, in this synthetic age, the real wood and honest brass. The Georgian house stood in its own grounds in an almost hidden corner of old Hampstead. But as I quailed before the work it needed, Miss Hepburn again came to my rescue, our *dea ex machina*. She loved gardening and came to work in the garden; dug, hacked, weeded, pruned, and scythed the onetime lawn. She brought a packed hotel lunch every day, which we ate off a rickety old table, sitting on broken chairs. One day she said, "Are you going to take the house or aren't you?" "I don't know," I hesitated. "If you don't, I'll come and pour creosote over it," she said, confident, convinced, commanding. I felt a great weight lifted. "Okay," I said, "I'll take it."

We sent for our furniture and art collection. We worked on that decaying old house from roof to cellar. We remade the garden. Our friends came in numbers, from Europe, from America; the spare room was always occupied. Gradually, we acquired a small zoo—a monkey named Peter, a toucan and a bush baby, budgereegahs, a tortoise and tropical fish, besides a poodle family, cats and rabbits. The boys came for vacations, for "a year in Europe," which for Duck extended to almost five years and the writing of his first novel. Pete had studied in Italy, France, Central Europe, and Oxford, and was now a working journalist in London.

It was Duck who reassured me when I grew dismayed at my increasing domestic involvement. "It isn't just a house," he argued, "it has a function the way our other homes have had," and he grinned. "It's still some kind of a bird refuge." I thought of The Getaway, an escape hatch for underdogs. And looking back at the variety of people who streamed through on our Sunday afternoons, from so many countries—from Don's theater and movie world, Ingrid Bergman, the "Hollywood Ten," Christopher Isherwood, or Salka Viertel; from New York and Carmel, Doctor Kocher and the Flavins and even Robin Jeffers after his Una's death, with Donnan, now married, and his children; or those who had sailed through storms in the McCarthy times and now were making new lives—it seemed to me that even providing tea and muffins can have its merits.

And so, almost nostalgically, we became a little oasis for our kind of America overseas. The big studio room was filled to greet Paul Robeson when his passport was finally returned and he could travel and sing once again for his friends, Welsh miners, French workers, the Russians; for the old Negro scholar W. E. B. Dubois, now in his nineties, when he came by with his wife, the writer Shirley Graham, on their way to Ghana or China or the Soviet Union to garner honors that, despite their many books and scholarly studies, had never been theirs before. Professor Barrows Dunham came with his artist wife, he the gifted philosopher, teacher, and writer whose *Man Against Myth* had helped a generation understand its social pressures, yet who, though exonerated, was never reinstated in his university position. There were Angus Cameron, courageous, honest—and out of major publishing for almost a decade; the writer Ira Wolfert, and his poet wife, Helen, witty, curious, and ironic about all our faiths so battered and hammered in these years. In New York Ira had gone with Don to all the baseball and football games, and the whole family had spent a riotous Christmas at Frazzle Top Farm, during which period Don and Ira fashioned a hilarious comedy together.

We had parties for the Berliner Ensemble on their first London visit—sadly, three weeks after Brecht's death—and the people from the Moscow Arts Theatre, who had come with Chekhov plays in Russian. Peggy Ashcroft greeted her "three sisters," while British visitors to Moscow—Paul Scofield, who had taken them *Hamlet,* Diana Wynyard, and Vivien Leigh—mixed with their Soviet stage colleagues.

I had not meant to stay away from America; I had had no intention of returning to England. But it had happened. Why? Many times I and others asked this question. I had not changed either my fundamental views or interests, except as these were modified by events, but our avenues of expression had closed. Don's plays were produced in England and in Europe, even in South Africa, but, except for *How I Wonder,* not in the United States.

One might have lived a "private life," enjoyed travel, plays, books, friends—the life many people, women especially, do live. One might have attended even an occasional protest meeting. But we had so many good friends in the United States who had suffered, who had lost jobs in teaching, publishing, medicine; attorneys unable to practice, doctors to operate, reporters fired from newspapers, and movie writers able to sell scripts only "under the counter." Students had to be "careful," or else endanger their chances of postgraduation jobs. Even dancers and musicians could not appear on television programs if they had been too active fighting fascism. It was all an indication of the climate of thought and opinion; America in one phase was no longer free.

We discussed endlessly with old friends from the United States, and new English or French ones, where our world was going, what one could do: the Cold War, relations between two worlds, the nuclear universe, the changed socialism. We were all up a tree. Paraphrasing our old saying, "We were brought up to grace the drawing room and they've taken the drawing room away," we could have said, "We've been brought up to care about issues and the issues are now beyond us"—too stark and terrible, too far removed from the possibility of any individual's influence. Perhaps all we could do was add some small push to the idea of one world, of coexistence, of peace and international understanding—or even plain good will and common sense. We were held together by the common fight we had fought, and our visitors helped give us a sense of continuity.

One afternoon Arthur Miller talked about the effects of automation with Ira Wolfert, who, for *The Reader's Digest,* had crisscrossed the United States examining industry and the postwar American *Epidemic of Genius*—as his later, exhaustive book on the subject was titled. He was impressed by the genius of a United States that could invent, create, construct. "But where is the country going?" he asked. "Where are any of us going?" Miller countered, and drawled the story of his uncle's zipper factory in Brazil, which faced the situation of a world saturated with zippers. "When there are no more people to buy zippers, what do you do then?" the uncle was asked, to which he had replied despairingly, "The factory could convert, but there aren't many other products that haven't also reached consumer saturation." Miller described the slowness he found in England; "Almost like death," he said. "My country may have developed new evils, but it has a vitality that could lead it anywhere. That must be our hope."

When Graham Greene, who was an occasional visitor, came, with his ravaged face and the haunting agony in his blue eyes that always startled one afresh, he seemed to say the opposite. To my remark that he did seem to be always on the go, he responded direfully, "One must keep the ice from melting." I asked Greene if he minded the Hollywood film of *The Quiet American,* falsifying, as it did, the ending and implications of his novel. "It doesn't matter to me," he shrugged. "I wrote the novel, and my literary responsibility ends there."

Simone Signoret, who was shooting *Room at the Top,* told us about the Soviet travels and political adventures she and Yves Montand had experienced on his phenomenal Soviet tour. We loved Signoret. She had Katie Hepburn's forthrightness, and a bare honesty and intelligence. She would take over the kitchen, cook mounds of spaghetti, make a French salad, and insist that we eat in the kitchen. She talked about life, the stage, marriage, her marriage, in a Frenchwoman's realistic way.

"He's Italian, Yves, he likes his woman at home, so I don't do a play or movie more than once in two years." And she more or less kept to that program. Equality was still some distance away for women.

Whenever she made movies in England, Ingrid Bergman came to see us, and when we were in Rome, and later in Paris, we spent time together. It always astonished me how simple, unspoiled, and unpretentious this actress remained despite her world renown and certainly her world publicity. For years she could not move in public without a crowd of photographers, chiefly on account of her unconventional relationships. In the country near Paris, in the house she and Lars Schmidt bought and kept adding to, she would walk or queue up with the villagers to shop, run her errands and her dogs like any country girl, enjoying herself and her friends, her children and the puppies. Despite her stormy marital relationships and legal tangles, no one could have been more joyous, happy, freehearted than this woman, young and beautiful in her forties as in her twenties, laughing in the winter sunshine as she ran with dogs and a small, frisky Sicilian donkey across the fields of her farm. I see her always laughing. In view of her much-publicized personal life, I could not prevent the ironic reflection on my mother's *"Nur mit dem Ring am Finger,"* those dire prophecies of the effects of irregular behavior, which Ingrid Bergman so signally disproved. She was another from whom I learned the lesson that it was needless to give in.

We had great pleasure from our art collection and some fun with Russians about its modernity. Like all Russians, Michael had been brought up seeing no abstract art, and here in our house he was surrounded by Klee, Mondrian, Picasso, Schwitters. He worried about even slight distortion, but saw our pictures often enough to get used to them, and finally, one day, he challenged me on our Marino Marini "Horse and Rider" garden bronze. "But why does the horse's head have to turn that way? Why is the whole figure twisted?" And his wife summed up their bewilderment when she looked carefully at a bronze "Cow" by Ewald Mataré, and then burst out: "But why has it no tail and no udder?" I maintained this would be an instructive opening to a film on modern art.

England was so near the Continent that we could go easily to events that interested us. I went to Germany to cover the theater festivals and see the Berliner Ensemble plays, and once took Annie Ross, the jazz singer, to do a story for an English magazine on night life in both Berlins. On this occasion I attended, with Helene Weigel, the first performance in West Berlin of *The Diary of Anne Frank,* which had a tremendous effect. There was no applause; the audience left the theater in silence, heads bowed, as if now, at last, they felt some sense of guilt.

It was again thirteen years since I had been to the Soviet Union. In 1957 I went to the Moscow Youth Festival to see the changes in the USSR since Stalin's death. I asked many people how they felt about Stalin, and we had frank discussions; most had been overwhelmed to learn the extent of the crimes.

"We accepted that there must have been gross errors," one said. "We assumed there must have been spies, and they certainly corrupted individuals, with the Central Intelligence Agency spending a hundred million dollars here. But we did not know of this organized terror." One girl, though, a student and our guide in Tiflis, gave me a different reply. Our last evening, at a farewell banquet, I asked her, "Tell me, what do you really think about Stalin?" There was a pause. "Who?" she said.

We often visited our fellow exiles the Chaplins, in their Swiss *manoir* above Vevey on Lake Geneva, a spot hallowed by Rousseau, Byron, Henry James—and now by ex-royalty from the thrones of Europe. The place stretched through forty acres of parkland, lawns, and woods, and in summer was kept ablaze with flowers and bushes and even a Japanese ginkgo tree. I saw it in winter covered with snow, in spring and summer in blossom. The large kitchen garden yielded, to Charlie's delight, all the fruits and vegetables that could be cultivated here. The growing family of charming children would play or swim or bicycle around the paths, and in the evenings act out something from Peking Opera, or strum a guitar or play the piano. Or merely run a new projection machine, possibly with an old "Little Tramp" movie, which Charlie laughed at as much as the delighted children. Once we all went to *The Gold Rush* at Vevey. It was the first time some of the children had seen it, and the little boy on my knee asked, as that house in the film teetered precariously on the precipice, "Daddy isn't in that, is he?" Charlie loved his new serenity, and spent many hours on his veranda gazing at the snow peaks.

I was particularly fond of Oona, who managed an extraordinary variety of duties with what seemed like absolute serenity. She was housekeeper, cook (always cooking the meal on the cook's day off), companion and adviser to her husband in all his affairs; she entertained myriads of visitors from all over the world, watched over her children's education, read and reread Charlie's scripts (or listened to him read them aloud), and his autobiography. She went with him on travels—to Hong Kong, Java, the animal reserves of Kenya and Tanganyika, Bangkok, Morocco—sometimes with children, sometimes without; or to some spot where all vacationed together—the south of France, or Waterville, County Kerry. I never heard Oona complain about difficulties, or the chores of keeping her vast household going, or take refuge in that universal woman's excuse, "No time." She seemed to have time for everyone and everything, every child's new interest or friend, time to watch their ballet lessons and listen to the newest song. And she read enormously. The best modern books were stacked in her bedroom or study, or in the anteroom, where the latest baby had its crib. She seemed to do it all without effort—and in the middle would suddenly take a course in cooking at the Cordon Bleu, learn to prune roses, wash and comb the Siamese or Abyssinian. (I even inveigled her into joining the Rose Society of England and the Abyssinian Cat Club to confuse the next Un-American Activities Committee hearings.) Charlie loved, appreciated, and depended on Oona as he never had on any woman, or indeed on anyone in his life.

I watched the shooting of *King in New York* at the Shepparton Studios in England, where Oona's calm rescued Charlie from many an outburst. He was hot-tempered and sudden in anger, and here the uncompromising perfectionist was up against the practical difficulties of shooting a picture in a new country in unfamiliar conditions; so Oona would pacify many an outraged sensibility. The children came and went during these sojourns abroad, riding, swimming, boating on the Thames, watching the shooting. Always Oona was aware, without fuss or bother, of all that went on.

One evening Charlie spent imitating the early theatrical days, in which he had played a part as a boy actor, giving us excerpts from the dramas and melodramas—but in admiration, not mockery. "They were the days of real theater," he said, "Martin Harvey, Beerbohm Tree, Henry Irving. . . ." And he peopled the stage in that living room, hour after hour, with the exact words of the speeches—Trilby, Mark Antony, Conan Doyle's Miss Faulkner. And Fagin. How he gave us Fagin, shrewd, mean, cunning, egging on big dumb Bill Sykes to his hate and murder; enticing Nancy—wily, shifty, smart, so that Nancy, terrified, could still impossibly believe she might save herself, only the next moment to be hammered to death with that strangling cry. And then Fagin slinking out, smiling his crafty, satisfied smile. And the poor tortured Miss Faulkner coming down at last from upstairs, in the Sherlock Holmes classic, into the presence of the calculating, almost too sure, murderers. Charlie made your flesh creep more than a Hitchcock movie could, as, after sixty years, he remembered hours of exact dialogue, as hot off the stage as it was then when he was twelve years old.

I thought he had never been so contented, so at peace, as looking across the lawn to the lake and mountains in these latter years of his life, in another country.

# 25

## MARCO POLO, 1958

They were all going to the new China—playwrights, novelists, artists, scientists; Joris Ivens, Sartre, Simone de Beauvoir, Claude Roy, Henri Cartier-Bresson—so many people, and they kept coming back with their tremendous stories. I had by now seen several socialist countries and revolutions—I must see this one.

I could get the Russian royalties from Stef's *Autobiography* to finance myself, my passport was British, and finally, after six months, the Chinese National Women's Federation suggested I spend two months inside the country to write a book. And so I flew to Moscow, by jet this time, and on to Peking. There the women submitted an itinerary that arranged for me to travel the length and breadth of the country, to Shanghai and Chungking, Hangkow and Hang-chow, Yunnan province in the farthest southwest, Inner Mongolia in the far north and its capital, Huhehot, whose name I had never heard. As a writer I was an "engineer of the soul," they said, and must see everything—all the workings of the new order. I would go to old sites, the Cave of a Thousand Buddhas in Datung, pagodas, temples, and mosques, to the excavation site of the first Ming emperor; and to the new co-operative farms and factories, a fish hatchery, clinics and cotton fields and dams in construction, new houses replacing "old lanes," a silk factory, a steel mill, a tea collective. I would study old Chinese and new Western medicine, the work of artists and artisans, weavers and cloisonné workers. And the ethics and attitudes of today. Could I think of anything else? A prison, I said, a divorce court, and a plant nursery.

Stef had always wanted to go to China, to try out his political experiences on "a people who have no conception of American life," on the theory that "they will ask the questions that will drive me back to my fundamentals." He had never realized this dream, and now here was I, perhaps with a similar hope. But what a different China from any he had envisaged! It was my second big "revolutionary" country, to compare and contrast, and I spent two incredible months, seeing an age-old civilization, a feudal country, trying to meet the twenty-first century. And achieving some miracles in speed and change. I was rather distressed to see so much of the old and "picturesque" disappear—the old architecture with glazed tiles, the narrow lanes, painted wooden shop fronts, even the pedicabs—vanishing to make way for automobiles; large, standardized, uniform, rectangular brick buildings with one-room apartments; wide boulevards; buses. Yet one must have progress, and it was not I who had to live in a fly-infested hovel in a muddy impoverished "colorful" lane, or work in a cold, dark, dank shop, though it be painted, quaint, and unusual.

But they hated to show you "the old." I got into trouble trying to photograph it. The girl interpreter in Shanghai whizzed by the ancient, turreted "Amusement World," which I had read about in Western novels. "In the past this was a hangout of thieves, prostitutes, gamblers—not good, eh?" she crowed. And in the narrow, muddy, back lanes of Shanghai they now had primitive steel furnaces. The peasant women of Pearl Buck's *The Good Earth* were bringing their old pots and pans from all over the country to melt down and make steel—themselves.

Here, as in Russia, there was a heavy emphasis on freeing women, as there was on the importance of children, their education, their learning early the required sense of participation, of ability to achieve, of co-operation, in everything. They were watched over, favored, indulged, both in families and nursery schools. In these new nursery schools they were taught not only to dance and sing, to put away their toys and make their beds, but to plant trees and water them with their tiny buckets, and to blow their noses in handkerchiefs pinned on with safety pins. This was turned into a social duty: "A clean, healthy little Chinese is a better, more valuable builder of socialism." The children were given power, too: fly swatters to help in the campaign to eradicate the four pests, orders to try and abolish the universal Chinese habit of spitting. They went about in keen-eyed search, and ringed around any blob of expectoration with chalk and the admonition SHAME.

The women took to their new freedoms with earnest application. I met an Outstanding Housewife, who had grown from a selfish lipstick user and mah-jongg player, given to interminable quarreling with her sister-in-law, into a social-minded, disciplined local leader. She had organized the neighborhood women, who had never worked outside the house before, into thirteen workshops—carpentering, engineering, plumbing, bicycle repairing—and putting into daily practice the five domestic "Do It Wells." To my more self-indulgent taste, she was a little priggish, but she had won her medal and she ruled her women with iron determination—and no longer engaged in malicous neighborhood gossip against the sister-in-law.

And some of the older women, who had hobbled on "little golden lotus feet"—the euphemism for feet bent and broken to provide the beauty husbands were supposed to admire—hobbled now to useful work like tending a back-yard furnace.

The women approved the new ways that were changing their lives so completely. Instead of having families so large that they must kill superfluous daughters, or sell them into prostitution or slavery, they could now control the family's size. There had been for several years great campaigns of enlightenment, including posters showing in vivid pictorial detail the processes leading to conception and parturition. When I cross-examined one woman about the actuality of their new knowledge, she exclaimed at my lack of perception. "But see, my youngest child is four!" Enough time to have had three more in the old China.

In Hangchow I caught up with a divorce case. There were so few now, it was hard to find one, they said. My women guides were fascinated by the drama of two individuals after so much collective psychology. A young girl of eighteen had irritated her older husband by wanting to dance with the farm lads and have a good time; he wanted her to stay home and have his family, like a proper Confucius-fearing wife. The girl feared the "disgrace" of a divorce, but the husband insisted that they were incompatible. They should try once more, the judge decided. The young wife, her hair in two long braids tied with magenta ribbon, and a clean shirt and shorts for the occasion, greeted the decision with a triumphant skip and jump. On this occasion China was certainly for the stability of the family.

The year was 1958, the year of the "Great Leap Forward," and one soon caught the infection, the enthusiasm and excitement. People were constructing, digging, planting, learning, discovering, building "their own." Everyone experimented, or taught, or studied to become literate. I had seen the Russians do the same, and the Poles and the Yugoslavs: their countries belonged to them, their own hands were building them into modern nations, and, in the process, they were developing a pride they had never felt. The enthusiasm could not have been "manufactured." No people would work under duress as these Chinese worked, irrigating, uprooting, building bridges, making the "mother machines" that would make machine tools and a cyclotron.

The old towns and buildings, the temples and glazed roofs and snorting dragons captivated me, as did the flowers, trees, and gardens, and the plants in pots placed on the pavements outside almost every house or store—they were never stolen. Jacaranda and tiger lilies, wistaria, passion vine and oleanders, corn and scarlet-runner beans flourished in patios or on barn walls. And as for trees— everyone in China planted saplings, for shade, for beauty, as windbreaks, or to reforest, or to hold back desert sands so that a railroad could be built. Trees by the millions spruced up dusty boulevards or the bare hillsides of the Chinese Wall. It seemed as though every boy and girl, every housewife and office worker, every butcher and candlestick maker planted and watered trees somewhere in China.

Daily life was a fascination. From a high-up hotel window in Hangkow, I watched the awakening of a busy Chinese city. Children were out at 5:30 A.M., shouting and calling; a peddler cried his wares, ice, sherbet, the morning newspapers. The persistent high staccato of an auto horn—cars were too new for Chinese pedestrians to make way—mingled with truck klaxons, pedicab and peditruck horns that rasped and screeched, and trilling bicycle bells. A rhythmic jingle like sleigh bells puzzled me, but I could not identify its source—until I discovered the local locksmith carrying a pole with boxes of keys on each end.

Enlightenment, urging, propaganda took place everywhere, all the time. Public loudspeakers on every square issued commands for physical exercise, or blared forth news, comment, slogans, exhortation, mingled with the shrill, high singsong of Peking Opera. Gong, drums, and cymbals beat as labor details marched to work, announcing some new target achieved. A brilliant red fire engine whizzed by, with girls in long plaits perched among the men, wearing neither uniform nor helmets. Passers-by walked around a

woman asleep on a bed in the street; kindergartens filled with
babies left by working fathers and mothers, chirruping at their
little wicker gate. Sewing machines whirred as women sewed
bright-red shirts in a tailoring co-operative.

Streams of traffic rolled by: trucks and pedicabs laden with
lumber, sacks of flour or tobacco, furniture, scrap iron and old
bottles—either loose or bound in bales, bundles, boxes, baskets;
nothing was wasted in the new China. Cyclists carried packs like
mules. Laughing girls, arms about one another, their long black
braids tied with lime-green or pink ribbons, gossiped as they walked
to work, and small workshops whirred, tempered, hammered,
mended, as brassworker, watchmaker, bamboo weaver, jewelry
maker patiently bent over bench or table.

I found that patience was a Chinese characteristic; patience to
expound, to explain, elucidate, help. If only one "explained"
enough, it would sink in. The blue-capped warden of the Peking
jail, an ex-teacher, said it; all the women I met maintained it.
One may call it "brainwashing," or education, or persuasion,
or indoctrination, but there was sincere belief that once you saw
the logic of something, comprehended it, you must surely embrace
what it stood for.

The women took me to Neighborhood Committees, consisting of
housewives who ran the Street Government, which was the unit
of administration. Children were led by these committees to the
clinics to be vaccinated or inoculated, and epidemics were almost
gone. The local committee assisted everybody; saw to it that children did not play truant, that the plumber called, that another
butcher shop was opened if too long a queue formed outside the
only one. They doled out cloth to make shoes, insisted that quarreling neighbors make up, that pregnant women ("forthcoming
mothers") be taken to clinics. "If she does not know where to go,
you must show her." Instead of not knowing where to turn, every
person seemed to have somebody to go to—a miracle of organizing.

New houses were being built; hygiene, sanitation, and cleanliness
taught—the war on flies, watersnails, mosquitoes, cockroaches, rats
never halted. Illiteracy was "attacked" by every method: the "word
for the day" was scrawled on a barn, or the side of a cow, or the back
of the man in front as you marched to work (the method used in the
Liberation Army). Words were writ large in small books for illiter-

ates, or pinned up on factory walls. And, as I had seen in Russia almost thirty years before, as soon as children had learned their lessons they became teachers, and gathered adults, including their parents, into their classes. Everyone was learning and everyone was teaching, trying to make up for centuries of miserable ignorance and backwardness.

That they felt the land was theirs, that they were achieving results —in increased production, industrialization, irrigation, construction —by their own efforts, one could not disbelieve. At Wuhan, a young ex-soldier was in charge of the first bridge built over the Yangtze, the river that had never been tamed, and described to me with fervor and passion that major work; now railroad and truck, bus and pedestrian crossed that bridge in no time at all. The young ex-soldier displayed not only overweening pride in this achievement but also a feeling of triumphant superiority over "all those great and powerful nations to whom we had to submit for so long, who did not accomplish this bridge in all the years of colonial rule." He gave me messages for "the industrialists of America."

There was Girl Shopkeeper Number 27482, who had earned her medal of Outstanding Shop Assistant and who believed that by "making contented shoppers I serve my country, because everyone is a shopper, and if I serve them well, they will like this regime." She was carrying out the "Consumer's Seven Satisfactions," to hers and apparently theirs. She illustrated the new attention to the smallest detail. "We tell the waiting customer, 'We'll be right with you, please to look around,' so they will not grow impatient."

And there was the little ex-concubine with short black hair, on a distant farm near Kunming, Yunnan province, who told me her story in a hot whitewashed barn, with portraits of Marx, Lenin, Stalin, and Mao Tse-tung staring from the walls. Other young girl farmers listened open-mouthed to a recital of events they knew so well from their own lives—but which now were happily over for them forever.

The girl had been a slave from the age of seven, married off for a sack of rice to a landlord, from whom she ran away, and then at twelve given as concubine to a rich peasant, who, she said, "beat and starved me and made me work till I dropped, grinding corn like a blind bullock." Six years later she joined the Liberation Army and afterward returned to this farm as vice president of fifteen thousand families, forty-five thousand souls. The ex-concubine told of the indignities of her former life with tears of resentment, indignation, and remembered despair; at the end, after a silence, I remarked, "I suppose you don't know what became of your ex-master?"

"Oh yes," she replied unconcernedly, "he's on this farm." "On this farm?" I stammered. "What does he do—do you ever see him?" She did. "Do you talk to him?" That too, but she did not seem to find it strange.

"Well," persisted the Westerner, "what do you . . . er . . . talk about?" And as she rose to show me over her new agricultural domain, she answered matter-of-factly, "Production."

Achievement sometimes took comical forms. In Yunnan province I met the Champion Ratcatcher, an old Tao woman, who had personally killed 10,500 rats, and written a brochure telling how to discover their habitat and routine. She had first become interested when the Japanese made villagers bring them rats and then released them, injected with plague. Now the old lady, her skin wrinkled, in native dress, had been rewarded with household china and painted towels and a promise to meet Mao, and was on the faculty of Yunnan University as Professor of Ratcatching.

A Shanghai "capitalist" further clarified the new order for me. He had a handsomely furnished twenty-room house, plenty of money, a well-groomed wife, could enjoy long holidays, travel where he wished, and his children went to school in a pedicab. He was paid a good salary as manager of his factory and received interest on his money; he enjoyed his privileges, he said, but he felt somehow "out of it." He wistfully took courses "to try and understand Marxism"—not very successfully. His children wanted to walk to school "like the other children," wanted him "to wash in a shallow enamel basin like other fathers," not in his deep marble one. They asked, "Daddy, why aren't you a worker?" His wife taught poorer women in the neighborhood, in order, she said, "to be more like other women." They were torn, and a little melancholy; they wanted to help their country—had not the leaders asked private businessmen to help?—but did not want to give up too much. I understood and was sorry for them. "Keeping up with the Joneses" is an instinct to be recognized the world over, even when reversed.

What struck me most forcibly everywhere was the coexistence of the very ancient with the very latest. Transport trucks pulled by girls with reins over their shoulders, the shoulder pole, the bullock and oxcart existed alongside Skoda buses, Zis cars, trains, airplanes. The very variety of goods carried in pole baskets and pedicabs confronted one with a thousand years of history.

In the hospitals they were mingling age-old Chinese medical wisdom—herbs, acupuncture, and old wives' remedies—with modern medical knowledge. A steelworker had been so badly burned in Shanghai that they thought he must die. But with incredible effort and by unbelievable perseverance they pulled him through. When I asked the doctors what they had learned from this experience, they were quite definite. "That we can do it ourselves, that we no longer have to feel so dependent on foreign physicians, and that when all pull together you can do the impossible."

People in the West spoke of the hundreds of thousands of workers on every construction project as "ants." Well, ants; if there was no machinery yet, it must be done by hand. We saw Poland rebuilt by hand when they could not import one excavator. Here I witnessed a dam being constructed with one tractor; the Ming Tombs Reservoir was built by the volunteer labor of almost half a million "ants"—in three months. It had become "the done thing" to give your free time—from classroom, lecture hall, stage, studio, shop, radio station, and, of course, office, factory and rice field—to do your stint there. Thus, everyone was given that sense of participation, felt they had a hand in it, knew it as theirs.

Even in the farthest reaches of Inner Mongolia, which provided the greatest contrast with my own world, I found this to be true. Camels wandered about the streets; and I went on a jeep ride, which used to take four days on horseback, to a nomad farm where men and women in long silk gowns herded sheep and goats—wandering Bedouins now organizing modern co-operatives. I had my tea sitting cross-legged on a k'ang—a bed heated by bricks—and was presented ceremonially by an old bearded shepherd with the guest's conventional silken scarf. A Mongolian skin tent housed the family, and we investigated collective pigs, goats, and fleet Mongolian ponies. In Huhehot, after a banquet of rinsed fish stomach and marrow of goats' horns, I spent an evening listening to an ancient Mongolian singer recite in a hoarse singsong many songs about bandits and brigands carrying off beautiful maidens, chased by brave lovers and troubadours. When I asked if the old man could get someone to write down the music of one of the haunting songs, he replied, "In Shanghai you can buy my records."

The year I saw China, the last good year before the natural disasters of 1959-61, it did "leap": too far and too fast perhaps, with too little consideration for some, too harsh a regime of conformity for those intellectuals who could not go along; a regime of effort and hard work. But there was a realizable vision: the poor were better in almost every respect, their hovels now a room with running water and toilet, their children not dying of disease or undernourishment. Everyone contrasted Before and After. Grave mistakes were made—could it be otherwise? When drought, floods, bad harvests overtook the country, many policies must be modified. Yet few died of hunger, though rations were short; in 1929-31 some twenty millions had starved. There was shoddy work and inefficiency, bureaucracy, laziness; there were grotesque claims and exaggerations; statistics were falsified; and one frequently met arrogance and stubbornness, or the same evangelical righteousness I had seen in the USSR. There was little awareness of how far removed the population was from the outer world, either in knowledge or understanding, and often they did not want to hear.

But that the population was overcoming a hopeless poverty and wretchedness, that by pulling together they were conquering a feudal servitude, there could be no doubt. The humiliation and ill treatment by foreigners, or by their own "upper" class and landlords, was over, and they were trusting their leaders and their government virtually for the first time. So far they had not been let down—and they were not being fobbed off with pie in the sky.

Opportunities were being created to develop innate possibilities for millions in art, science, technical work; and they were studying, learning, developing their gifts with an enthusiasm and eagerness one could look far to find anywhere. To become "expert" was a prize as coveted as being a leading baseball player is to us. Some of the defects and blunders, faults and flaws were to be deplored, no doubt, but sometimes they were the defects of their virtues. The puritanism could grow prim and pedantic—and grim. The triumphal achievements could lead (and often did) to boasting and arrogance. The regime was aware of some of these dangers, as it showed by putting out, in one of those series of numerical maxims the foreigner found so comical, the five warnings against "Giving Oneself Airs." And I was amused at the university students, warned of this, haughtily explaining to me how they were now giving up being haughty, or staying up all night debating heatedly how best to get eight hours' sleep.

Many writers on China have borne witness to the overwhelming changes. "They [the millworkers] were so hopeless," Pearl Buck writes of the past, in *My Several Worlds*. " 'No one can help us,' they wept. 'Who wants us? No one, anywhere. Who cares whether we live or die, or has ever cared? . . . What can we do? Nothing—and we know it.' " Han Suyin, in *A Many-Splendored Thing*, tells how the peasants came to drain their fields with eager enthusiasm after their revolution, to dredge their rivers, build their dams, plant trees on the hard, bare slopes, and how they came to feel that all this was theirs. "That public spirit did not spring out of centuries of apathy," she comments, and describes the early days of her country's liberation, which she witnessed:

Hour after hour, day after day, week after week, young leaders would go up and down the countryside explaining, patiently, talking at the shut, sullen, resentful faces, the peasants intent on giving away as little as possible, intent on hoarding rice and defaulting at every turn; suspicious of anything from the outside, too often betrayed not to disbelieve.

I saw the same effects of the patient explaining, the insistence still, eight years later, on the need for little and big leaders to "live with, eat with, work with." Han Suyin describes how she saw "the slow unfolding, the faces come alive, the mouths open and speak that had remained obstinately silent, and the whole man flower, conscious of his dignity as a man upon the earth." When I asked the woman editor in Huhehot what her most striking experience had been, she answered, after reflection, "That the peasants send me in poems by the pound." In Cotton Textile Complex Number Two in Peking, a woman of forty told me, "I started in the Shanghai textile mills at eight years of age. I learned all I know from being beaten." Now she was a forewoman in charge of two hundred girls weaving at modern Chinese-made looms. And she added, "Before, I had no status." No wonder a woman writer commented, "The people say things poets can't."

Would China have to go through all the same agonies as other revolutionary countries in birth? That was a question I could not answer. Whatever the drawbacks, one must concede that no such experiment had been made in history, no undertaking in social engineering attempted on so vast a scale. China's population was six hundred and fifty million—a quarter of the people on earth.

They had in ten years covered centuries of development. What I had seen was millions caught up in a program that needed their cooperation, and made them feel it, that gave them incentive, opportunity, and a purpose for living beyond their personal concerns. Creative possibilities had been unleashed on a scale unheard of. Now they had a future—and I was willing to settle for that.

# 26

## BRIEF AND YET ENDLESS

My story ends with my journey to modern China, which for me embodied one more attempt at a rediscovery of the dream and the vision by which I lived. Experimentation belongs to our age with its "impossibilities unlimited": what we need is more social experimentation. It becomes an exciting adventure to follow man's repeated attempts to control his universe, and his ingenuity in the physical world grows with giant strides. But if welfare for all is within our grasp, as it is, why is our era still the age of anxiety, why must we live under the threat of mankind tooling for its own destruction? It seems to me that to understand, control, and direct into new and fruitful channels the race between the creative inventiveness of man and his ancient fears, taboos, and outworn attitudes, even his dislike of change, could be a challenging and inspiring goal. Can we not replace the ingenuity that invents ever more effective engines of death by a genius for life? Is it beyond our powers to work out a more decent world order: wiser, more tolerant, just, and generous, more cultivated in its widest sense? To bring greater perception, awareness, ability of man to face himself?

Poised in my jet above the earth as I flew from Peking, I tried to look back over those last months, and found my thoughts gradually merging into a reflection over my whole life. What had it meant to me, what had I learned, what had I really wanted from it? "Choose well: your choice is brief and yet endless." That motto of my school years kept coming back to me. Had it been a guiding principle for me? Did I choose consciously?

I had sometimes been asked why I kept going to these countries of popular revolutions, why they seemed so important to me, and I had wondered myself. Perhaps I sought in some unconscious way to renew myself by seeing societies renew themselves. This visit to China, as my other journeys to worlds that had uprooted the old and tried to form new attitudes, seemed part of the design of my life. What was I seeking?

It was certainly a deep satisfaction to witness the replacement, for so many millions, of wretchedness, deprivation, and humiliation by a greater share in the world's goods, an unfolding of possibilities, an end to subjection. The waiter feeling he could share with me my cigarettes had been a relief to my class-bound soul. "Everyone is Somebody" had reached into profound depths of my "social conscience." "I am my brother's keeper," they seemed to say, and there were a lot of brothers. It relieved me of a weight I felt personally. It might be the opposite of the Western picture, but I must believe my own eyes. "One seeing is worth a hundred hearings," the Chinese preached in one of their "old Chinese sayings"—which I saw them blend with such apparent ease with Confucian ethics, modern economic ideals, and Christian precepts, not to mention my Melbourne copybook's proverbs and maxims. I could not disentangle them. "A hundred years in a day." "To make the mountains bow before you, and the rivers give way." "Jesus was a good man, he loved the poor." The insistence that "You can do it, all together" perhaps impressed me most; was it very different from "Faith can move mountains"?

Perhaps there was nothing very new in all that. They sometimes seemed childish, those moral precepts set out in numbered array— The Five Loves of Children, The Six Satisfactions, The Five Airs You May Not Give Yourself, The Three Exacts—campaigns to capture the imagination, "targets to be aimed at," "fortresses to be stormed," as one might arrange for children. But for the Russian and the Chinese peasant, the simplest person, they had worked; and what was that other saying, "Except ye become as little children"?

As my mind roamed, I kept coming up against the question: What was really new for me, and what was not, in all this? The early promise of human betterment of those new societies I had seen had not borne all their expected fruits, in fact the negation of some of their promises had been startling, discouraging, sometimes shattering. Should I give them up because the results had been different than expected, because the stream of history had gone off in other directions? What had I started with?

My mind went back to that starlit "Seine-light night," when Steffy had been so fascinated with "a new world a-borning," had coined his phrase, "I have seen the future and it works." Had it been my aim in some way to forward that goal of the future? In my Fabian days I had determined to "reform the world," in Paris to participate in plans that would "end war forever." How utopian those hopes sounded now, with the individual so far removed from power. Yet it is true that "we are all members one of another," that "the bell tolls for thee." Certainly in many lands the peasant, the tribesman, the simple man was being taught this. It did add up.

At any rate, I could not subscribe to despair. I do not believe that humans count for nothing in a decaying, helpless world. I do not forget the tyrannies and terrors, as I believe no one ever should. Loneliness, frustration, depression and weariness, fear, a sense of not belonging had been my feelings at different times, as they are perhaps of the majority of people today, since they are the subject of much Western writing. But in my journeyings I had seen the fresh hope, the power and faith, the sense of participation, the belief in ability despite centuries of degradation, and I could not deny what I had seen. One must trust one's inner experience.

But was not greater welfare, more opportunity, a fuller life for all what everyone wanted, in both our worlds? Tolerance, concern for one's fellows, freedoms of many kinds were absolute goods to me: limitations on some of them were growing, as was the pressure toward greater conformity and persecutions for political ends, which restricted the free atmosphere. I did not wish to bury my truths in silence. And so I arrived once more at a platitude: we are one world, we must live together. I could not see it as a crime when a society tried to raise itself fast, by its own efforts, by "revolution," rather than more slowly, with aid from outside, by what we chose to call "evolution." "Gradualness" might be inevitable; but in the long run, was revolution much more than one fast kick forward in the long process called evolution? We condemned the "cost" of revolution; but was it higher than the cost over centuries in backward, underdeveloped communities, which still covered two-thirds of the earth and which still could not guarantee their populations daily bread?

I must trust what I had seen, I must believe my own senses, I must "experience my experiences." We need to know more about the science of human behavior, the laws of social change. Freud and Marx introduced ideas that were to become two great trends of my day, shedding great light, unlocking many doors. I had learned from some of their discoveries. But we needed to know more. I wanted more tools of understanding, tools I had always sought.

In my own life I consider myself to have been lucky. Personal fulfillment I have had, friends and love, family and creative activity, interests and satisfactions of many kinds—and fun. I do regret that I shall not see all the future of mankind. I wish I could be sure there will be a news service in heaven. Yet, even if I do not see the fruits, the struggle has been worthwhile. If my life has taught me anything, it is that one must fight.

Fasten your seatbelts.

*London, 1963*

# INDEX